Empowered Voices

Empowered Voices

Scandinavian Women in Early Pentecostalism

EDITED BY
RAKEL YSTEBØ ALEGRE,
JAN-ÅKE ALVARSSON,
NIKOLAJ CHRISTENSEN,
AND TOMMY H. DAVIDSSON

With Foreword by Cecil M. Robeck Jr.

☙PICKWICK *Publications* · Eugene, Oregon

EMPOWERED VOICES
Scandinavian Women in Early Pentecostalism

Copyright © 2024 Wipf and Stock Publishers. All rights reserved. Except for brief quotations in critical publications or reviews, no part of this book may be reproduced in any manner without prior written permission from the publisher. Write: Permissions, Wipf and Stock Publishers, 199 W. 8th Ave., Suite 3, Eugene, OR 97401.

Pickwick Publications
An Imprint of Wipf and Stock Publishers
199 W. 8th Ave., Suite 3
Eugene, OR 97401

www.wipfandstock.com

PAPERBACK ISBN: 979-8-3852-1853-0
HARDCOVER ISBN: 979-8-3852-1854-7
EBOOK ISBN: 979-8-3852-1855-4

Cataloguing-in-Publication data:

Names: Alegre, Rakel Ystebø [editor]. | Alvarsson, Jan-Åke [editor]. | Christensen, Nikolaj [editor]. | Davidsson, Tommy [editor]. | Robeck, Cecil M. Jr. [foreword writer].

Title: Empowered voices : Scandinavian women in early Pentecostalism / edited by Rakel Ystebø Alegre, Jan-Åke Alvarsson, Nikolaj Christensen, and Tommy Davidsson.

Description: Eugene, OR: Pickwick Publications, 2024 | Includes bibliographical references.

Identifiers: ISBN 979-8-3852-1853-0 (paperback) | ISBN 979-8-3852-1854-7 (hardcover) | ISBN 979-8-3852-1855-4 (ebook)

Subjects: LCSH: Pentecostalism. | Pentecostalism—History. | Women in church work—Pentecostal churches. | Pentecostal women. | Scandanavia—Church history.

Classification: BV2565 Y78 2024 (paperback) | BV2565 (ebook)

12/03/24

Cover: Norwegian Pentecostal Women from Sunndalen around 1930. Alma Halse—striped dress, holding a Bible. Used by permission of the family of Alma Halse.

Contents

List of Illustrations | vii

Foreword | ix
    Cecil M. Robeck Jr.

Acknowledgments | xi

List of Contributors | xiii

List of Abbreviations | xv

1   Pioneer Women in Early Scandinavian Pentecostalism | 1
    Jan-Åke Alvarsson

2   Laura Barratt: "Mother" of the Norwegian Pentecostal Movement | 27
    Rakel Ystebø Alegre

3   Dagmar Gregersen Engstrøm and Agnes Thelle Beckdahl: Pioneer Evangelists and Missionaries | 59
    Rakel Ystebø Alegre and Glenn Gohr

4   Anna Larssen Bjørner: A Drama of Institutionalization and Independence | 93
    Nikolaj Christensen

5   Anna Lewini: From a Radical Conversion to a Hidden Ministry | 115
    Malene Kjær Eriksen and Nikolaj Christensen

6   Gerda Åström: Apostle and "Standing Witness" in Northern Sweden | 127
    Tommy H. Davidsson

7   Frida Vingren: Hitting the Glass Ceiling | 153
    Jan-Åke Alvarsson

8   Hilda Backlund and Linnea Halldorf: Early Pentecostal
    Missionaries to Congo and Burundi | 189
    Gunilla Nyberg Oskarsson

9   Ingrid Løkken Chawner: "The Missionary on the
    Steel Horse" | 213
    Liv Toril Rinding Skjeggestad and Rakel Ystebø Alegre

10 Alma Halse: Pentecostal Pioneer in Northern Norway | 243
    Kristina Undheim

List of Illustrations

Image #1   Lovisa Johansdotter. Courtesy of Alf-Göran Göransson.

Image #2   Scandinavian Pentecostal leaders gathered in Stockholm around 1920. Lewi Pethrus, Laura Barratt, T. B. Barratt, Anna Larssen Bjørner, Sigurd Bjørner. Used by permission of Pingst—Arkiv och Forskning.

Image #3   Laura Barratt. Used by permission of Norsk Pinsehistorisk Arkiv.

Image #4   Dagmar Gregersen Engstrøm and Agnes Thelle Beckdahl. Public domain.

Image #5   Anna Larssen Bjørner. Public domain.

Image #6   Anna Lewini. Public domain.

Image #7   Gerda Åström. Used by permission of Pingst—Arkiv och Forskning.

Image #8   Frida Vingren. Used by permission of Pingst—Arkiv och Forskning.

Image #9   Hilda Backlund. Used by permission of Pingst—Arkiv och Forskning.

Image #10   Linnea Halldorf. Used by permission of Pingst—Arkiv och Forskning.

Image #11   Ingrid and Austin Chawner. Public domain.

Image #12   Alma Halse. Used by permission of Norsk Pinsehistorisk Arkiv.

Foreword

Cecil M. Robeck Jr.

It is difficult to imagine what the Church would look like without women. In most churches regardless of denomination, women form the largest percentage of membership. This is the case in the Pentecostal Movement as much as it is elsewhere. In fact, from the beginning, women have played a monumental role in carrying the Pentecostal message to the world.

I come from a family in which women have played such roles. When my paternal grandmother died in 1958, my Norwegian grandfather married a Swedish woman, Emmy Pearson, who had served from around 1928, as a single, Pentecostal evangelist, holding meetings and planting a number of churches in the tiny lumber towns among the redwoods of Northern California. Before my mother married, she began to go door to door in the San Francisco area. She collected some children, asked a young man to drive a bus to pick them up, and planted an Assemblies of God Sunday School, which soon became a thriving church on the Bay. She went on to play many important roles alongside my father for over fifty years. She helped to plant another church as an equal partner with my father, preached, coordinated Sunday Schools, taught, led Vacation Bible Schools, led in music and led women's missionary meetings. She also became widely known for her creative work among children.

Women have always played a significant role in the spread of the Pentecostal message. Scandinavian women are among some of the first and foremost Pentecostal evangelists and missionaries, although most Pentecostals in North America are ignorant of this. While we celebrate William J. Seymour as the pastor of the famous Azusa Street Mission, and rightfully so, his wife, Jennie Evans Moore Seymour is often forgotten. Buried in the same grave as her husband, the stone marking their grave bore only his name for over six decades. She was essentially forgotten, even though she served in the role of minister of music at the Mission, oversaw the work among children, became a worthy assistant to Pastor Seymour, was the only woman elected to the Mission's Board of Trustees, and succeeded him as the Pastor of the Azusa Street Mission for a decade, following his death. So, it is with far too many Pentecostal women, whose only recognition ultimately comes when they meet Jesus face to face. They deserve much more.

This volume is a welcome addition to a small but growing number of biographical accounts of women who have contributed substantially to the Pentecostal Movement around the world. Often, the hard work in towns where men refused to go, or with groups where men were unable to work for cultural reasons, women went. Many of them were single women that, men quickly replaced, only after these women had done the hard work to establish a viable church or mission.

The stories of Scandinavian Pentecostal women are no exception to the failure of churches and historians to recognize them and their enormous and costly contributions. Pentecostal women have spread the Gospel in ways seldom recognized. It is time for their stories to receive a broad hearing! It is time for Pentecostals to recognize the gifts that these women were to the Movement. It is time for us to recognize the gifts that they used, often creatively, to spread the Pentecostal message around the world.

It is with deep gratitude that I want to thank the authors and editors of this volume for retrieving the stories published here. May their work on these Scandinavian women encourage others to follow suit and write more accounts of Pentecostal pioneering women who have made substantial contributions to the Kingdom of God.

Acknowledgments

The authors listed in the table of contents of this book have each given of their valuable time and effort in order to unearth the fascinating stories of ten forgotten pioneers of the Scandinavian and global Pentecostal movement. We are deeply grateful to them, and also to Cecil M. Robeck for his generous foreword.

There are many more people to thank, however. We would like to thank all who attended the online symposia at which these chapters were first presented for feedback, and especially the invited respondents: Ingunn Breistein, David Bundy, Helje Kringlebotn Sødal, Ulrik Josefsson, Åse-Miriam Smidsrød, Jakob Egeris Thorsen, and Magnus Wahlström.

We would also like to thank all archivists and others who have helped with sources, including but not limited to: David M. Gustafson at Trinity Evangelical Divinity School, Geir Lie at the Norwegian Pentecostal Historical Archive, James Craig at the Pentecostal Assemblies of Canada Archives, and Darrin Rodgers and Alice Harris at the Flower Pentecostal Heritage Center. It is also worth mentioning that this type of research has been made much easier through the growing availability of digitized periodicals and other works from places like the Institute for Pentecostal Studies in Sweden, Pingst—Arkiv och Forskning, the National Library of Norway, and the Consortium of Pentecostal Archives in the United States.

It is now widely understood that projects tend to take longer and have a lower chance of ever coming to fruition than those initiating it would have estimated. This book is no exception. It has been underway since 2018, and had it not been for the addition of Tommy Davidsson as editor in the last year of the project, it might never have seen the light of day. Tommy has taken the lead in both organizing the symposia and editing the final manuscript, and his fellow editors are deeply grateful to him for his hard and meticulous work.

THE EDITORS, JUNE 2024

List of Contributors

Jan-Åke Alvarsson (PhD), professor emeritus of cultural anthropology at Uppsala University, Sweden.

Rakel Ystebø Alegre (PhD), associate professor at The Norwegian School of Leadership and Theology, Oslo, Norway, and dean at la Universidad Evangélica in Buenos Aires, Argentina.

Nikolaj Christensen (PhD), priest and tutor, Diocese of Oxford, Church of England.

Tommy H. Davidsson (PhD), associate professor at The Norwegian School of Leadership and Theology, Oslo, Norway.

Malene Kjær Eriksen (BA), Mariager Bible College.

Glenn W. Gohr (MDiv), reference archivist, Flower Pentecostal Heritage Center.

Gunilla Nyberg Oskarsson (ThD), former lecturer at the Pentecostal Theological Seminary, Uppsala, Sweden.

Liv Toril Rinding Skjeggestad (ThM), missionary and teacher, Norwegian Pentecostal Movement.

Kristina Undheim (ThM), assistant professor, Department of Culture, Religion, and Social Studies at the University of South-Eastern Norway.

List of Abbreviations

ca.	circa
1 Cor	First Letter to the Corinthians
ed.	edition, editor
EFS	*Evangeliska Fosterlandsstiftelsen*
EH	*Evangelii Härold*, published in Stockholm, 1915–1993.
Eph	Letter to the Ephesians
Exo	Book of Exodus
Gal	Letter to the Galatians
Heb	Letter to the Hebrews
Isa	Book of Isaiah
1 John	First Letter of John
KS	*Korsets Seir* (later spelled: *Korsets Seier*), published in Oslo, 1910–.
Matt	Gospel according to Matthew
ms.	manuscript
NFEH	*Norges Frie Evangeliske Hedningemisjon*
no.	number
NT	*Nordisk Tidende*, published in New York, USA, 1891–1983.
PAOC	Pentecostal Assemblies of Canada
1 Pet	First Letter of Peter

Ps	Psalm	
PT	*The Pentecostal Testimony*, Pentecostal Assemblies of Canada, published in Mississauga, Ontario, 1920–.	
Rev	Book of Revelation	
rev.	revised	
Rom	Letter to the Romans	
RSV	Revised Standard Version of the Bible	
SFM	Swedish Free Mission	
SV	*Sanningens Vittne*, published in Minneapolis, USA, 1911–1939.	
1 Thess	First Letter to the Thessalonians	
1 Tim	First Letter to Timothy	
UK	United Kingdom	
US, USA	United States of America	
YMCA	Young Men's Christian Association	

Image #1. Lovisa Johansdotter.

Pioneer Women in Early Scandinavian Pentecostalism[1]

Jan-Åke Alvarsson

INTRODUCTION: LOVISA—THE APOSTLE

In 1887, a young Swedish woman, Lovisa Johansdotter, left her home country in an effort to get a better life in the United States. The situation in Sweden was tough. It was one of the poorest countries in Europe, and just 18 years earlier Swedes had suffered the second starvation period in just two years. A million Swedes did just like Lovisa: they emigrated to the United States.

From the few records we have of Lovisa's emigration, we believe that she was part of a program that paid the trip for young Swedish women if they worked as housemaids in the state of New York for at least two years. Swedish housemaids had the best reputation of all at the time. They were considered hard-working, orderly, and adaptive.

Something happened, however, after the plans were made. She met Victor, a young man from the same region as she was, the northern part of the province of Småland, and they fell in love. Lovisa had signed the contract, so she had to go, but she promised to come back. And so, she did, in 1895—after eight long years—and Lovisa and Victor finally got married and bought a farm.

---

1. This chapter is to some extent based on my manuscript for: "The Annual Hollenweger Lecture" at the University of Birmingham on June 12, 2018. All translations in this chapter are the author's own.

Lovisa was not entirely the same person, however. She was eight years older and more mature, but she had also gotten into contact with what we would today call a pre-Pentecostal movement in the United States. There were several such movements in many places in the late nineteenth century, but this one was special because it had its roots in Pietism and the Scandinavian free church movement. Critics called them the "Free-Free," because they sprang from the Evangelical Free Church of America—a free church that in turn sprang from the Pietist movement within the Swedish Lutheran church. The "Free-Free" spread among immigrants of Nordic origin in the states of North Dakota, South Dakota, Minnesota, and most probably in the city of Chicago. We know about them from the research done by Darrin J. Rodgers.[2] We also know that they successively merged with the later classical Pentecostal movement in the twentieth century.

The heritage that Lovisa brought from the United States was identical to what the "Free-Free" movement in the Midwest stood for in terms of spirituality, ecclesiology, and theology. We know that from her activity when she returned to Sweden and Adelöv. Soon after returning to the village of Adelöv, she started a prayer group, and in 1901, 23 members of this prayer group founded a "Free congregation," explicitly *not* associated with any of the churches in Sweden at the time. The brother of Lovisa became the first secretary.[3]

The group of around twenty people that gathered around Lovisa soon started to celebrate services in the so-called "Mission Hall of Ryd," a chapel of the Swedish Covenant Church that was always open. But as this dissident group was so "loud," the people of the Covenant Church locked the chapel and hid the key, and thus excluded the pre-Pentecostal group from meeting there. Instead, they started meeting at a nearby farm where they, in 1902, also built the Betania church that stands there still today.

The spirituality of the Adelöv congregation was from the start marked by Lovisa's experiences in the United States: a combination of radical congregationalism, openness for lay preachers, women leaders, loud prayer, speaking in tongues, divine healing, and open communion. This was also corroborated by the rapid acceptance of the Azusa Street revival that reached Sweden in November 1906 through Andrew G. Johnson. The Adelöv congregation was the first one to collectively join

---

2. Rodgers, *Northern Harvest*.

3. Information from the early documents in the Adelöv archives and interviews with members and relatives of Lovisa Johansdotter.

the incipient Pentecostal Movement in 1907 and, despite its limited size, exerted a disproportional influence on the growing movement.[4]

What I have just told is an example of the wide-ranging effects of a Pentecostal woman that—up to date—is unknown to the public. The urge to tell the stories of these women, and what they accomplished, gave rise to this book!

There are so many life stories of Scandinavian Pentecostal women, little known or totally unknown to church history, that need to be told. The women we have chosen to present in this volume represent three countries: Denmark, Norway, and Sweden. They represent a variety of professions and activities. They worked within the national borders and overseas. They preached, wrote, edited, administered communion, baptized, led meetings, founded congregations, built churches, clinics, orphanages, and much more. Regrettably, they have one thing in common: They have been largely overlooked in historical accounts! We aim to remedy this somewhat—even if we only manage to tell a fraction of these stories.[5]

THE BACKGROUND IN SCANDINAVIA

Today, the Scandinavian countries are known worldwide for having "feminist governments," female CEOs, women priests, and female university professors. This was not the case, however, when our protagonists were born in the late 1800s.[6]

At that time, Scandinavian women suffered from the transition from an agrarian to an industrial society. In Sweden, Norway and Denmark, the legal system had been forged so that unmarried and married women were classified as underage, with a husband or nearest male relative as guardian, but became of age as widows. If the widow married, however, she again became a minor.

Here, we can note an interesting difference between the three countries studied. In Norway, the legal age for women was twenty-one in 1869. The two other countries lagged way behind. Not until 1911 did Denmark, and ten years later, in 1921, did the Swedish parliament decide

---

4. Alvarsson, *Varför reste Lewi Pethrus just till Chicago?* 18–21.

5. For another overview of the impact of Scandinavia Pentecostal women, see Alegre.

6. Our protagonists were all born in between 1866 and 1899, except Alma Halse who was born in 1907.

that women became of legal age at twenty-one, the same age as men. Could this discrepancy be attributed to lesser class differences in Norway? Or could it be related to the stronger grip of the Lutheran churches in Denmark and Sweden?[7]

The right to vote underwent a similar pattern. Suffrage for women was introduced in Norway in 1913, in Denmark in 1915 and not until 1919 in Sweden. If we look at women's right to preach or become priests, however, the pattern is somewhat reversed. The Danish *Folkekirke* [State church] ordained its first female priest in 1948, while the Swedish Lutheran Church got its first female priests only in 1960 and the equivalent in Norway in 1961.

The universities were in practice also closed to women for a long time. For example, the first female Doctor of Theology at Uppsala University did not receive her honors until April 1965. And—who was that woman taking the opportunity? It was Berta Millrot, a former Pentecostal Missionary to Tanzania![8]

THE FORERUNNERS

How could the Pentecostal women, our protagonists, have such liberty to preach, lead congregations, and start spiritual and mundane enterprises when the surrounding world in practice was closed to most of those activities? One answer is found in the forerunners in the other free churches.

Church historian Mats Larsson has provided us with a study of one such early example: the Maiden Society in the Baptist Congregation of Asker, close to the city of Örebro. It was founded in 1865 and their women were able to hold regular society meetings, with a democratic vote, lead meetings—*and* discuss theology, something entirely reserved for men at the time.[9]

This tradition was even more palpable in the Holiness movement and the Salvation Army. The first Swede in the nineteenth century to

---

7. The fact that Norway was way ahead of the other two countries may be attributed to several factors, among them the fact that women often had to take responsibility from running the household or even the farm when men were away on sea or migration. Another reason might be the strong grip that the two state churches in Denmark and Sweden had on the population, while the Lutheran movement in Norway was more diverse.

8. Berta Johansson-Millrot (1914–1976), missionary to Tanzania. Alvarsson, forthcoming work on Swedish Pentecostal missionaries.

9. Larsson, *Vi kristna unga qvinnor*.

promote women preachers was Holiness preacher Fredrik Franson, a disciple of Dwight L. Moody in Chicago. Heavily influenced by, among others, Catherine Booth, co-founder of the Salvation Army and the author of the book *Woman's Right to Preach the Gospel*, published in 1885, Franson himself wrote a book called *Prophesying Daughters*.

He published it first in German because he did not want to be "caught in any polemics." Later, in 1890, it was published in Norwegian, *Eders døtre skulle profetere*, and in 1896, finally also in Swedish, *Profeterande döttrar*—but then published in St. Paul, Minnesota—not in Sweden! As the title indicates, Franson's biblical point of departure is Joel 2:28–29 and Acts 2:15–18: "The spirit fell on men and women alike."

Franson was pragmatic. People had to be converted. Since "almost two-thirds of all the converted people in the world are women," Franson concluded that "the issue of the participation of the woman in evangelistic work is of utmost importance."[10]

He knew that women were barred from almost all preaching. Nevertheless, he concluded, "if there is no prohibition against the woman's public activity, we are facing the fact that the devil has succeeded in excluding almost two-thirds of the believers."[11]

After having stated this, he proceeded to "discuss the portions of the Scriptures that relate to the position of women."[12] He brought up women as leaders, commanders, prophets, apostles, etc., basing his argument on quotations from the Bible. In so doing, he questioned the contemporary, Eurocentric interpretation of especially the New Testament. He even quoted Martin Luther to strengthen his argument, concluding that "each one of God's children, women included, has the right to minister the Word, baptism, and the Holy Communion."[13]

The discussion that follows in his book, seems very "modern" without becoming "liberal." He discusses terminology, like "brethren,"[14] as well as cultural contextualization in the interpretation of prescriptions for women.[15] Franson also provides a somewhat contradictory piece of advice, however, stating that "One thing that all missionizing sisters ought to avoid in their home countries is—especially in public—to

---

10. Franson, *Profeterande döttrar*, 4.
11. Franson, *Profeterande döttrar*, 4.
12. Franson, *Profeterande döttrar*, 5.
13. Franson, *Profeterande döttrar*, 19.
14. Franson, *Profeterande döttrar*, 15.
15. Franson, *Profeterande döttrar*, 22, 23.

defend women's right to preach. As soon as they do that, they appear as *teachers* in a matter of dispute, and thus enter an area where their appearance is, to say the least, dubious."[16]

A few years later another Swedish-American, John Ongman, trained as a minister in the US, but now back as a Baptist preacher in Örebro, Sweden, wrote a sequel to Franson's pamphlet. It is a booklet called "Women's Right to Preach the Gospel," published in Swedish in the year 1900. The influence of Catherine Booth and Fredrik Franson is clearly visible and therefore I will not repeat the main arguments. A few things are noteworthy though.

Ongman calls this "a burning issue" and states that "in our days" this issue has "often been partially presented."[17] In the account, he provides a [proto-]feminist argument, that in the contemporary debate has been called "*global male supremacy*": "Since the day of the fall the woman has been more or less oppressed and disdained by the man."[18] Then he gives a history of humanity and repression of women that echoes that of nineteenth-century social Darwinism.

Then he provides a most idealized image of his own circumstances: "It is true Christianity that has restored women's lost rights; a fact that no one would dare to deny."[19] And the living ideal state of Ongman actually has a geographical localization: "There we find a people who has experienced full freedom of religion for over one hundred and twenty years; the people of the United States of North America, and it is impossible to deny that the woman there generally holds a higher position, intellectually, religiously and morally than among other peoples."[20]

Ongman's theological argument for equality is that woman was created, not from Adam's head, nor his feet, but from his "side."[21] This indicates "equality with man."[22]

16. Franson, *Profeterande döttrar*, 31.
17. Ongman, "Kvinnans rätt att förkunna evangelium," 33.
18. Ongman, "Kvinnans rätt att förkunna evangelium," 35.
19. Ongman, "Kvinnans rätt att förkunna evangelium," 35.
20. Ongman, "Kvinnans rätt att förkunna evangelium," 35–36.
21. Gen 2:22.
22. Ongman, "Kvinnans rätt att förkunna evangelium," 36. After the rise of the Pentecostal Movement, T. B. Barratt in Norway followed this theological position. In 1933, he wrote the pamphlet *Kvinnens Stilling i Menigheten* [Women's Position in the Church]. Barratt wholeheartedly believed that in Christ there is no difference between man and woman. Barratt even elected female leaders in his congregation, and he taught that there were female apostles in New Testament days.

What perhaps was even more important, however, was that both Franson and Ongman put their ideas into practice. Franson organized a large group of young missionaries to go to China in the 1880s and the 1890s, a majority of them women.[23]

From 1885 and onwards, Ongman organized short Bible courses for "evangelists" in Örebro, for men and women alike. When Pentecostalism hit Sweden in 1906 and 1907, this resulted in petitions from a number of female students to start a theological seminary open for men as well as women! This led to the foundation of the "The Örebro Mission School" in 1908, a three-year theological seminary that from the start was open to women.

The women evangelists trained in Örebro were especially noted as they deviated from the established norm of the time.[24] Because of the radical standpoint of the organizer, Ongman, these women evangelists were most often called "Ongman sisters."

They became known for their sacrificial efforts, moral character, endurance, and faithfulness. They were obvious models for the early Pentecostal women evangelists and missionaries. In fact, many of the "Ongman sisters" later became Pentecostal evangelists, so it is hard to distinguish clearly between the two categories.

When Pentecostalism, of the Azusa Street brand, fused with Örebro Baptism and the Holiness movement, nothing much happened to the role of the woman in church work. Both traditions essentially held the same position. Women could preach, administer the Holy Communion, baptize converts, and, in practice, found new congregations—even though male pastors often presided at the formal inauguration.

THE AZUSA STREET MOVEMENT AND WOMEN

Some works have been written on the position of women in classical Pentecostalism, for instance, the Azusa Street movement in Los Angeles,[25]

---

23. Lundström et al., *Svensk Mission*, 468.

24. With the possible exception of the women of the Holiness Movement (*Helgeseförbundet*), led by extraordinary women like Nelly Hall (see Gunner 2003). The Ongman sisters (*Ongmansystrar*) and the women evangelists from the Holiness Movement (trained at Götabro Bible School in Närke) were almost indistinguishable. Both categories were important for the growth of the Pentecostal movement in Sweden (and initially in Finland).

25. See, e.g., Alexander, *Women of Azusa Street*.

but, as I see it, not enough. One of the most important devices of the Azusa Street Mission was *"No instrument that God can use is rejected on account of color or dress or lack of education"*[26]—in today's English we would probably write it: *"No person that God can use is rejected on account of race, sex, or social status."* Some researchers, like Walter Hollenweger, have emphasized the African American roots of classical Pentecostalism. Others have pointed out that the African American family, at the time of abolition, probably was the most equal of all family constellations. Thus, equality between men and women came naturally to the Azusa Street protagonists.

It is true that "equality between the sexes" did not mean exactly what it means today, but according to how people conceived of it at the time, it was there! Out of the eight functionaries mentioned in the Azusa Street letterhead, four were men—and four were women! In the Credentials Committee, there were more women than men. The Azusa leaders lived as they taught.

In retrospect, influenced by Eurocentrism, revisionism, and male bias, William J. Seymour has been given a leading role. In my research, I have indicated that one may interpret things differently. The mentor and advisor of Seymour—a woman—Lucy F. Farrow, may be just as important or perhaps even *more* important than Seymour for the birth and configuration of Pentecostalism.

Lucy Farrow took on Seymour in Houston and introduced him to congregational work. She mentored him and showed him confidence. When she was away preaching, she left her congregation to him. That was how he was "discovered" by people from Los Angeles—and what brought him there.

Up until the arrival of Lucy Farrow, there was no outpouring of the Spirit in Los Angeles. Seymour preached it, but it did not happen. Thus, they sent for Lucy Farrow—and it happened! She was obviously crucial to the spiritual breakthrough.

In the reports from Azusa Street, Lucy Farrow is the one most clearly associated with healing, xenolalia, and intercession for the reception of the Holy Spirit—more than Seymour, and more than anyone else of that time. During this limited period in Los Angeles, Farrow in practice laid the foundation of what was to be known as Pentecostalism! She created the configuration of spirituality that is now "Pentecostalism"!

---

26. *The Apostolic Faith* 1 (1906) 2.

The disregard for the sex of a person, replaced by a respect for the "instrument" that "God used," was an attitude that the Scandinavians brought back from the Azusa Street revival. When Pentecostal pioneer Andrew G. Johnson wrote: "One brother and one sister have left for the field and God accompanies them in their work,"[27] this was no lip service. He had been trained at Azusa Street, he believed this, and he was reinforced in his faith by the Swedish tradition of women evangelists.

Image #2. Scandinavian Pentecostal leaders gathered in Stockholm around 1920. Lewi Pethrus, Laura Barratt, T. B. Barratt, Anna Larssen Bjørner, Sigurd Bjørner.

SCANDINAVIAN PENTECOSTALISM AND WOMEN

When Pentecostalism was transferred from the US to Scandinavia, the position of women in church work became more complicated than at Azusa Street. This was because the "New Movement," as it was often called at the beginning in Sweden, recruited people from the Methodist church, the Salvation Army, the Covenant church, the Holiness movement, and the Baptists; both from Örebro and Stockholm Baptists. The rising, and later the most prominent Swedish Pentecostal leader, Lewi Pethrus, was trained at the "men-only" Bethel Seminary of the Stockholm Baptists and his equivalent in Norway, T. B. Barratt, was trained as a conventional Methodist.

So, when the relationship of European Pentecostalism to other traditions later was to be discussed, we can note more of an uncertainty

27. *Svenska Tribunen* (October 9, 1907).

regarding the position of women. This is visible in for example *Principles of the Pentecostal Revival* based on drafts from a Pentecostal conference in Germany in 1917. This booklet has a special section entitled "The Ministry of the Sisters in the Congregation:"[28]

> Here we just want to express our conviction that in the edification of the congregation there is a special task left for the women, within the lines drawn for their sex in the Scripture. The false development intruding on Christianity is becoming apparent here in different ways. On the one hand, one has circumscribed the role of the woman in the congregation, as if her task were solely within the *family*. And as the one extreme causes the other, on the other hand, there have been attempts to place the task of the sisters on par with that of the brothers. Both are unnatural and unscriptural. May therefore the Holy Spirit give us the fine guidelines, determined for the particular character of the female sex, and at the same time let their multifaceted talent for the service of the Gospel, "the work in the Lord," fully and entirely prove of use to the Body of Christ. Under all circumstances we would not want to lose the blessed assistant service that our holy sisters, precisely in our time, carry out in our work circles.—--May we read with contemplation the following Bible portions: Luke 8:1–3; Mark 15:41; 16:7–11, John 26:17, 18 (*sic!*); Acts 1:14; 9:36–41; 18:26; 21:8, 9; 1 Cor 11:1ff; 14:34, 35; Rom 16:1–4, 6, 12; 1 Tim 2:8ff; 5:3 ff; Tit 2:3–5; Exo 15:20, 21; Judges 4 and 5. Considering these portions, one will find how great a task also our sisters have in the edification of God's congregation on earth. How this sisterly service each time is to take place will become apparent through the respect for all of the guidelines once and for all provided by the Holy Spirit, this the Lord will demonstrate to his Church through the anointment and the given conditions.[29]

The first impression of these guidelines is that they condemn the position of the Evangelical churches in general at the time that "the woman's place is in the home." Here, it is made clear that *the woman is needed, even necessary, in the edification and formation of the congregation*. There are many keywords, "special," "false," "great," and so on, that emphasize the important role of women in Pentecostalism.

28. This pamphlet was translated into Swedish as *Pingstväckelsens riktlinjer* and printed by the Pentecostal publishing house *Förlaget Filadelfia* in 1917. It was reprinted in 2008.

29. *Pingstväckelsens riktlinjer*, 72–73.

Studying this section somewhat closer, however, it becomes obvious that the writer is walking a tightrope, probably slightly uneasy about an unfamiliar situation, not yet entirely defined. In comparison with many other sections of this booklet, there are few clear statements. Here we see several allusions to the expected guidance of the Holy Spirit, or that "the Lord will demonstrate."

At a second reading, we also find a series of restrictions, *not* present in the declaration of the Azusa Street Mission that I presented above. Among the restrictions, we find a supposed, even an expected, difference in the "guidelines" for each sex. It is also noteworthy that Paul's revolutionary statement, also the most important foundation for the Azusa Street declaration, Gal 3:28—"there is neither male nor female" (RSV), is entirely missing from the list.

This close reading unveils the struggle that the Azusa Street Pentecostalism met with when it reached Europe—just like in the encounter with other churches within the U.S.

Norway had a parallel situation to that in Sweden. Pentecostal pioneer Thomas Ball Barratt, who, together with his wife Laura, became one of the strongest early advocates for women's right to preach, teach, and administer in the Pentecostal church, did not even succeed in implanting this view in his own congregation in Oslo. According to Ski, Barratt was successful in almost everything, except "this that women should be able to become first pastors [bishops] and elders."[30] After Barratt's death, his successor quickly declared that he did not believe in this type of equality before God.

In Denmark, the situation was quite different, partly because the movement did not gather momentum until later, and because the most prominent leader was a woman. Through Barratt's visits to Copenhagen, his openness to women's contributions to Pentecostal spirituality, and his social competence, the well-known actress in Denmark, Anna Larssen (later Bjørner), was converted to Pentecostalism in the early twentieth century. At that time, her conversion was very much questioned because of her status in Danish cultural life. Anna Larssen was, for example, held in isolation at a mental hospital for examination for six weeks before she was declared sane. She later married Sigurd Bjørner and the couple became the natural leaders of the movement in Denmark for years to come.[31]

---

30. Quoted in Lindberg, *Förkunnarna och deras utbildning*, 215.
31. See Frodsham, *With Signs Following*.

Returning to Sweden, it is necessary to acknowledge that John Ongman, and his followers among the "Örebro Baptists," were *exceptions* within the Baptist Movement of Sweden during this period as the "Stockholm Baptists," and their Bethel Seminary, were advocates of a men-only ministry. In *Wecko-Posten* we can follow the debate within the Baptist movement, especially during the Annual Conferences, year after year. In 1891, the conclusion was just "Most [speakers] were definitely against women preaching and everyone considered it to be against the Word of God and what was considered proper."[32]

It was probably this strong fundamentalist view of women in Biblical light, that slowly but surely quenched almost all public female participation in Pentecostal circles for decades to come. It is generally believed that the Stockholm Filadelfia church was the first "genuine" Pentecostal congregation, but regarding church government, it was one of the most Baptist one can imagine. Before Lewi Pethrus, the upcoming leader of the Swedish Pentecostal Movement, entered the scene, two women formed part of the leadership: Anna Carlsson was one of those signing the letter calling Lewi Pethrus to Stockholm and Selma Engzell was the treasurer.[33] After Pethrus had become established, however, women were never again heard of as official leaders.

It is natural that the congregation, which started as a *Baptist* congregation in 1910, would cling to some of its heritage for some time. But in the 1970s, when most other Pentecostal congregations had a system of "elders" and "deacons," and in many places allowed women to become deacons, Stockholm Filadelfia still had an all-male system of elders. The fact that the Pentecostal church Filadelfia in Jönköping, for many years led by pastor Georg Gustafsson, as late as in 1968 (after Gustafsson's retirement) rewrites its statutes, now stating that "only men" can be on the board, seems to corroborate the hypothesis of Norwegian church historian Bloch-Hoell, that Lewi Pethrus did not get a full grasp of the Swedish movement until the 1950s.

The organizational development of the Swedish Pentecostal movement that followed in the 1970s and onwards is outside the scope of this chapter. Here it suffices to state that most congregations within the classical Pentecostal movements of Scandinavia, at the beginning of the

---

32. See Rakel Ystebø Alegre's chapter in this volume.
33. Blomqvist, *Den svenska pingstväckelsen femtio år*, 14.

twenty-first century, are back where they started a century earlier. Again, Pentecostal women are allowed to preach, teach, and administer.

WOMEN IN SCANDINAVIAN PENTECOSTALISM

Now, *how* did women act and exert influence in twentieth-century Pentecostalism in Scandinavia? To give an example, I will quote Swedish social anthropologist, Göran Johansson. He grew up in a Pentecostal congregation, called Betania, in southern Sweden in the 1950s, and he left the movement in the 1970s—but he never really stopped coming back to his Pentecostal upbringing. In a book with an autobiographical touch, from 2005, he states the following:

> In my memory of Betania, women dominated. They dominated in spiritual intensity, in sanctification, in prayer and in participation in general. Men could at times appear somewhat foreign, a bit wondering and reserved. But not the women. When I think about it, Betania has probably formed my image of women and their role in society. To me it has always been natural that women have dominated most things. This may be the reason why I have had a hard time comprehending the intense debate about the ruling patriarchal order in our country during the last few decades. I simply cannot identify myself with the picture. Thus raised in a spiritual, female movement I have usually felt left behind.[34]

During my *own* Pentecostally-dominated childhood in the 1950s, I was surrounded by "sisters" and "brothers." Just like Göran Johansson, I grew up in something that had great similarities to an extended community—a small, tight-woven Pentecostal congregation. There were old and young, men and women. Just as for Johansson, however, the middle-aged and older women dominate in my memories. They were everywhere, except in the chairs on the platform.

There were a few unmarried men, but the number of unmarried women was much higher. Women constituted the majority—and marriage outside the movement was frowned upon. Therefore, the spinsters never found anyone to marry. But the congregation was their family—and being the son of the minister, I was somehow a collective child, someone they all could care for.

34. Johansson, *Särlaregnets tid*, 99.

My parents were ill-paid. The servant of the Lord was supposed to live by faith. The economy was one of the fields where you were particularly expected to trust God. (I am happy that my father never learned about the salaries paid to the pastors of the Filadelfia church in Stockholm, the leading church of the Swedish Pentecostal Movement at that time). Nevertheless, when I needed something as a child—whether I verbalized it or not—there were always a few spinsters around, arranging for me to get what I wanted. They were great second mothers, and I loved them.

As I grew up, I saw that they had their fingers in more than one pie. They organized the social activities of the congregation, visits from other places, annual meetings, and activities in between campaign meetings. And all this meant sandwiches and coffee, and sometimes cookies. My whole childhood somehow smelled of newly made coffee and sandwiches.

Also from a global perspective, the majority of the Pentecostals are women. The ratio of women versus men varies, but up until the present, I have never encountered a Pentecostal movement that has consisted of as many men as women. When Bloch-Hoell in 1956 presented one of the first global surveys of Pentecostalism, his statistics were nevertheless very surprising. In U.S. Pentecostalism of the 1950s, there were 34 percent men and 66 percent women in general. The extreme case was *Apostolic Overcoming Holy Church of God*, where 22 percent were men and 78 percent were women.[35]

Sweden did not lag very far behind, however. In an analysis of the Filadelfia church in Stockholm in 1915, it was found that 762 members were women and just 238 men. This represents a ratio of 23 percent men and 77 percent women, just slightly lower than the most extreme North American church. We also learn from amateur historian Eriksson that the average member was "a relatively young woman with a 'simple' profession"[36]—probably a shop assistant, a housemaid, or a nurse's assistant.

Even if other Swedish Pentecostal congregations were not as extreme as the one in Stockholm, we can clearly distinguish a pattern. While there is a clear connection between high activity in a church and being a woman—Christian church goers in general consist of 56 percent

---

35. Bloch-Hoell, *Pinsebevegelsen*.
36. Eriksson, "De första tusen," 1.

women—the relationship in the Pentecostal movements is even more conspicuous. In Bloch-Hoell's overall statistics, women make up 66 percent of all Pentecostals in the world.

Today, the Scandinavian Pentecostal movements have been settled and "domesticated" so that the ratio has most certainly come closer to 50 percent, but in the parts of the world where Pentecostalism is growing fast, we probably have the same figures as for the Stockholm Filadelfia church in 1915 and the *Apostolic Overcoming Holy Church of God* in the 1950s.

In the beginning, this female predominance was also reflected in the ratio of Pentecostal ministers. When the first Bible school in Stockholm Filadelfia had ended in January 1916, twenty-one evangelists were sent out unto "fields." From the addresses published in *Evangelii Härold* we can see that, out of these twenty-one, twelve were women (that is 57 percent) and nine were men (that is 42 percent).

Two years later, in 1917, we have the names and photographs of those attending the same Bible school. This shows that out of 145 registered students, eighty-six were women (59 percent) and fifty-nine were men (41 percent). The following year, in 1918, the attendance had risen to 176 students. Out of these, ninety-eight were women (56 percent) and seventy-eight were men (44 percent).

There are two conclusions to be drawn from these figures. First, we can see that women dominated the numbers of evangelists, both attending the Bible School and in actual work in the field. Secondly, we may note that the figure of women is diminishing slightly, and if we had added statistics up to the 1950s, we would have seen how the number shrank gradually until women constituted a small minority—destined as it were, for the still unworked and fairly barren fields in predominantly rural areas in Scandinavia or tough conditions on the mission field.

Pentecostal women were the ones starting up work in all types of locations. They preached, they taught, and they administered. People were saved, baptized, and experienced Spirit baptism. But there was a notable trend regarding the ratio between the sexes. When any of the congregations started to grow and were big enough to support a family, a man took over. He officially declared the group a "congregation" and organized the paperwork involved. Thus, after the phenomenal spread of new Pentecostal congregations in Sweden—from a handful in 1915 to 125 in 1920, 272 in 1925, and over five hundred congregations in 1934—the work of women as leaders of independent groups was reduced to the most inaccessible and barren fields of Sweden.

PROMINENT PENTECOSTAL WOMEN

The African American culture that bred classical Pentecostalism has a tradition of strong independent women. This ethos has somehow fused with dormant views of strong women in the Bible (and Gal 3:28), and thereafter accompanied Pentecostalism as an integral part of its soul when it has spread over the globe. The fact that there has been a theological struggle, as well as exclusivism in terms of organizational opportunities, has never stopped women from exerting a strong influence in their respective congregations.

This Pentecostal ethos has given birth to, and nourished, more outstanding women personalities than in perhaps any other church tradition. It is tempting to provide ample proof from the impressive list of notable Pentecostal women, but I will limit myself to just a few names that I find representative.

I have already mentioned Lucy F. Farrow, "God's anointed handmaid." If there is a "founder," or rather a forger or maker of Pentecostalism, it is her. Because of that, I have many times called her "The Mother of Pentecostalism."

Among the other African American leaders, we may mention Jenny Evans Moore, later Mrs. Seymour, and from 1922 the Bishop of Azusa Street, and Emma Cotton, an early participant at Bonnie Brae and the only woman who left us a written testimony about her experiences. She was later the "manager" of the 30th anniversary celebration of the Azusa Street revival at Angelus Temple in Los Angeles. Among other prominent North American Pentecostals, we may also mention the following well-known, and very influential preachers: Maria B. Woodworth-Etter, Aimee Semple McPherson, and Kathryn Kuhlman.

Among the international personalities, we may include Pandita Rambai, called *"the first feminist of India,"* Laura Barratt from Norway,[37] and Anna Larssen-Bjørner, Denmark—all three important Pentecostal leaders in their home countries; two of them presented in more detail in the following chapters.

---

37. See Rakel Ystebø Alegre's chapter in this volume.

In Scandinavia, many of the early women preachers and teachers are still unknown to the scholarly world. Because of an obvious male bias among the reporters, and subsequently among historians, they are often referred to merely as "sisters." That is the fate of, for example, the "two young sisters" who lit a Pentecostal fire in the city of Tranås in Sweden as early as March 20, 1907. They are merely described as "two young sisters from Ongman's Bible school, filled by God's Holy Spirit and its gifts"[38]—but we do not even know their names![39]

Because of this obvious bias, the following list of notable, but almost unknown Pentecostal women in Scandinavia that appear in this volume, should not be viewed as an exhaustive one, but as a homage to this category as such.

OUR PROTAGONISTS

In this volume, we present eleven of the many outstanding women leaders in Scandinavian Pentecostalism.

Laura Barratt was an important Pentecostal actor in Norway, together with her husband, Thomas Ball Barratt. She supported her husband's ministry, but she was also independent, visionary, strategic, and a pioneer of several ministries. Her work in Pentecostal publishing, her promotion of foreign missions, her role as a spiritual mother, and her advocacy for female ministers had a strong impact. She often led meetings in Christiania in Thomas's absence, and she preached with great fervor and effect.

Dagmar Gregersen and *Agnes Thelle* worked together for many years. They became known as the "Norwegian sisters" when they were instrumental in initiating the Pentecostal revival in both Germany and Switzerland. One of the surprising features of their ministry was that they practiced xenolalia under the influence of the Holy Spirit. Thus, they both spoke German in public, totally ignorant of that language. In 1910, they became the first missionaries to be sent out by the Pentecostals in Norway. Most of their lives were dedicated to their missionary work in India.

Anna Larssen Bjørner was a well-known theater actress in Denmark. But after an encounter with the spirituality of Pentecostalism, she left the

---

38. Söderholm, *Den svenska pingstväckelsens historia*, 381.

39. Cf. Grant Wacker's claim that the role of women in Pentecostal history frequently has been downplayed. He has described this as a "persistent gender bias." Wacker, "Are the Golden Oldies Still Worth Playing?" 95.

stage and became a traveling evangelist, preacher, and healer in Denmark and across Scandinavia. In 1919 she formed a rapidly growing congregation in Copenhagen together with her husband Sigurd. For a long time, she was the foremost representative of Pentecostalism in Denmark.

Anna Lewini was another Danish actress who converted to Pentecostalism and became an evangelist. She traveled to several countries, among them Sweden, to preach the Gospel. Eventually, she became the first foreign Pentecostal missionary to be permanently based in Ceylon, today's Sri Lanka. There she adopted the lifestyle of the locals. Barratt said that her testimony was simple but "spot on."

Gerda Åström has been called "A Standing Witness" and "The Apostle of Västerbotten" (the northern part of Sweden). She had a divine encounter that she described as "nimble waves of light and fire" to appear and "walk around her bed." She decided early to become an evangelist, first in Örebro Mission and later within Pentecostalism. Her main geographical focus was in Ånäset between Umeå and Skellefteå in northern Sweden. There she purchased an old cinema, dismantled it—and rebuilt it as a chapel, "Elim." When a congregation was established, a man was elected senior pastor, but Gerda continued to exercise indirect leadership. The church leadership sought her "advice and council" and it was she who wrote the reports of the work to the Pentecostal journal *Evangelii Härold*. Gerda also wrote a pamphlet on Pentecostal theology.

Frida Vingren was a Swedish preacher, writer, social worker, and poet who became a missionary to Brazil. In Rio, together with her husband, she built one of the largest Pentecostal congregations in the world at the time. She edited two national journals, wrote a score of articles, and authored and translated numerous hymns. She became a role model and a promoter for many young Brazilians. Unfortunately, she lost a daughter and her husband and was forced away from successful work in just about two years. Because of her standing as a missionary and being a strong woman who went against the establishment, she was excluded from her sending church and finally admitted to a mental hospital.

Hilda Backlund, called *Mama Mpenda* by the locals (loving mother), was an unusual Swedish missionary to Congo—she had a three-year theological education and an extraordinary linguistic ability. During six months at Nia Magira, she learned to speak Swahili so well that she could use that language during the services. After moving to Machumbi, she studied the local language, Kihunde. During her first period, she translated a hundred songs and the Gospel of Mark. During the second period, she finished the translation of the Gospel of Luke. She employed a "walking ministry," walking from village to village, always ready to preach.

Linnea Halldorf was a professional schoolteacher from Sweden and taught at the primary school in Lemera, Congo. She formed schools in the villages, together with teachers whom she had taught how to read and write. Linnea was the first Swedish missionary to learn Kirundi, the main language of Burundi. Just like Hilda, she employed a "walking ministry." All her tough walks earned her the name *Kanyabuyange*, which is a hardy African mountainous herb.

Ingrid Løkken Chawner, a Norwegian woman nicknamed "The Missionary on the Steel Horse," became the first Pentecostal missionary to Mozambique. Before this, she worked in Swaziland and was there called *Nkosazana*, which means "a king's daughter." Ingrid was a "talented writer" and wrote something intended to be an ethnography of the Thonga people. She worked as an amateur nurse and an amateur teacher. A tangible result of Ingrid's labor was fourteen assemblies with ten certified workers and twenty assistants.

Alma Halse was a traveling evangelist who settled down in Finnmark in northernmost Norway. She was a social entrepreneur. She started a nursing home, an orphanage, a private elementary school, a brick manufacturing facility, and a seafood factory. But she was also a Pentecostal evangelist and a spiritual leader, recognized by many Pentecostals in Norway. She was awarded the Norwegian Golden Medal for Outstanding Civic Service.

These portraits serve as a token of the efforts that many more Scandinavian Pentecostal women accomplished at home and overseas. Hopefully, they will also serve as incentives for future research.

THEORETICAL AND METHODOLOGICAL CONCERNS

The texts in this volume have been inspired by research in both women's history and gender studies. Historical research on women has often engaged in writing women into a history that ignored them. Unfortunately, much of this research reveals the problem of obtaining relevant source material. Gunilla Gunner's dissertation on the female preacher Nelly Hall from 2003 clearly demonstrated precisely that difficulty. Men have traditionally collected more material about themselves and archives have also been more inclined to receive and care for their material. Unfortunately for the researcher, many women have not considered their work or their material as important.

If research in women's history has put women at the center, then gender studies have above all problematized the relationship between the sexes to be able to ask questions about power and influence. Male supremacy and female subordination are a theme throughout our Western history, where the visible power has been attributed to men.

This volume shows, on the one hand, alternative power, which has often been associated with periphery or low status, but on the other hand, shows the mutability of the gender concept. What is "feminine" is clearly relativized in the comparisons between the outside world's view of "female spheres" and the Pentecostal contexts described in the life stories.

Even within Pentecostalism, however, there are discrepancies in the perception of male and female spheres. When the Danish missionary Anna Lewini had gathered a large group of followers through her preaching activities in Ceylon, she still asked a man to come and perform the water baptism that these converts required. In many other contexts, especially the more peripheral ones, Pentecostal women baptized the converts without a problem.

The intra-Pentecostal conflict between women being able to do "everything" and the patriarchal order in traditional Christian circles are also hinted at, for example, in the chapter on Gerda Åström, in which a man is called to become the president of the congregation while Gerda still functions as the leader. In this way, female leaders are related to structural issues of gender and power.

In this volume, no opposition is made between women's history and gender studies. Instead, they must complement each other. The women are seen as actors in relation to the contemporary discussions about theology, church planting, and evangelization methods. They are also presented—in contrast to how women were seen in their time—as independent, creative, and active agents. They exercise agency in relation to the surrounding structure. This naturally includes theological reflection and analysis of the world around us.

THE PENTECOSTAL WOMAN ISSUE—SOME CONCLUDING REMARKS

Finally, why were women so important in the establishment of the Scandinavian Pentecostal movement? There is no single or simple answer to that question, as I believe many different factors have combined to make them indispensable. In the following section, I will discuss some of these.

1) *The "Status Argument"*: The "status argument" claims that any task of "high status" will attract more men than women and that a "low-status position" will be occupied by women, rather than men, simply because in general prestige means more to men than it means to women. This argument may help us explain why women took on the difficult task of being evangelists in the backwoods of Scandinavia or started up work in any "difficult" area—while men showed up when the congregation they had planted was large enough to support them. In Townsend-Gilkes's words: "[women] *are indeed indispensable*" as they do what men would not do.[40]

2) *The "Character Argument"*: Many scholars have claimed that Pentecostalism is an "experience-oriented" or an "emotional" religion. The latter statement has often been used on the female sex by psychologists and others. In 1956, Bloch-Hoell used this argument to explain the high ratio of women in Pentecostalism. Even though it sounds rather outdated in these post-essentialist times, it is not possible to leave it out. The persistence of female predominance is too obvious not to require a gender-based explanation.

3) *The "Discourse Argument"*: As we have seen, the diffusion of Pentecostalism was mainly done by women. One of the reasons for this should be found in the character of the religion, possibly the so-called "ethos" of Pentecostalism, a factor that somehow includes the emotionalism as well as the non-verbal part of religion. Such qualities are *not* best diffused through text or oratory skills but through practice. So, if men have the upper hand in dogmatic, literalist, Evangelical circles, women would be in that position when it comes to the spreading of an emotional religion like Pentecostalism.

Consciously or unconsciously, Harvard theologian Harvey Cox connects this dimension to music and the use of music within Pentecostalism:

> [T]here are two crucial factors. One is the extraordinary part that *women* have played in the spread of the movement. The

---

40. Townsend Gilkes, *If It Wasn't for the Women*, 69.

other is the remarkable centrality of *music*, not just as an embellishment but as the wavelength on which the message is carried. Pentecostalism is unthinkable without women.——women have continued to play a disproportionately prominent place in the pentecostal movement.——the salience of women in this movement has resulted in a dramatically different conception of who God is, and the quiet subversion of centuries of patriarchal theology.[41]

This connection between music and the "ethos" of Pentecostalism is further underlined by Cox's statement that "historically, pentecostals have felt more at home singing their theology."

4) *The "Culture Argument"*: I have mentioned the lingering influence of African American culture over early Pentecostalism. When Du Bois interpreted tendencies within the African American population, he pointed to the historic role of their women as "the intellectual leadership of the race." Strong women, women in leadership positions, etc. may have been new to the European and the White North American culture, but it was nothing new to those who gave birth to Pentecostalism, and who have developed it in African American Pentecostalism—like the *Church Mothers* of the American Church of God in Christ.[42]

5) *The "Space Argument"*: As we have seen above, women were welcomed to the Bible Schools—and from 1917, "space permitting." And space was actually permitted, most of the time. In comparison with the Methodists and the Baptists, women enjoyed relatively much more space among early Pentecostals. Elaine Lawless has given the following characteristics for a North American Pentecostal movement: "[. . .] it was the women who led the singing, prayed, testified, and spoke in tongues; the men preached and healed the women."[43] Townsend Gilkes draws the following conclusions: "[Holiness and Pentecostal women] were somewhat more successful than Baptist and Methodist women in gaining access to the pulpit or lectern——In some cases, Baptist and Methodist women defected to the Sanctified Church in order to exercise their gifts." She even adds that "the most powerful Women's Department of any black denomination arose within the Church of God in Christ."[44]

---

41. Cox, *Fire from Heaven*, 121.
42. See Butler, *Women in the Church of God in Christ*.
43. Lawless, *Handmaidens of the Lord*, 8.
44. Townsend Gilkes, "If It Wasn't for the Women. . .," 46.

6) *The "Pragmatic Argument"*: In difficult social situations, as in Scandinavia in the early twentieth century, Pentecostalism may be "used by women to domesticate men." As David Martin and Elisabeth Brusco have put it, Pentecostal fervor "literally restores the breadwinner to the home and restores the primacy of bread in the home."[45] The ideals of *not* drinking alcohol, *not* philandering, and *not* fooling around have helped Pentecostal women all over the world attain more safety in their lives.

7) *The "Theology Argument"*: Even though many women would have fought harsh battles over women's issues in many Pentecostal congregations, they would have a hard time admitting it. Pentecostal theology is *relatively* progressive regarding women's possibilities to "preach, teach and administer." Townsend Gilkes's claim that "*Women may teach*"—even though it has seldom, if ever, been without restrictions—has attracted many a devout woman, anxious to serve the Lord and her fellow human beings. It may very well be that the theology argument is not sophisticated at all. Maybe it is as simple as Lewi Pethrus once put it "The Spirit is for all, for women as well as for men!"

It is even possible, if not probable, that the "complementary issue," that of "men *and* women," surpasses theology in Pentecostalism. Right from the start a woman and a man, Farrow and Seymour, stood side by side. While Farrow organized and prayed through Pentecostals-to-be, she left the theology and most of the teaching to Seymour. And while *she* was experience-oriented, social, and outgoing, *he* was doctrine-oriented, quiet, and reflective. In this division, maybe *she* created the strongest role model, a role model integrated into the Pentecostal ethos and diffused all over the world.

As an epitaph of this introduction, I cannot help but quote Harvey Cox again, this time on the importance of women for the success of Pentecostalism:

> Yet either because of, or despite their pentecostal faith, women continued to lead. Barred from the pulpit, they preached in the streets. Refused ordination, they became missionaries and went to places where men were afraid to go. They became healers and teachers, writers and editors. Without them, pentecostalism would probably have died out long ago.[46]

---

45. See Brusco, *Reformation of Machismo*; Martin, *Pentecostalism*; and Cox, *Fire from Heaven*.

46. Cox, *Fire from Heaven*, 138.

BIBLIOGRAPHY

Alegre, Rakel Ystebø. "Women in Pentecostalism in Europe." In *Global Renewal Christianity: Spirit-Empowered Movements Past, Present and Future*, edited by Vinson Synan and Amos Yong, 4:259–73. Lake Mary, FL: Charisma, 2017.

Alexander, Estrelda. *The Women of Azusa Street*. Cleveland, Ohio: Pilgrim, 2005.

Alvarsson, Jan-Åke. *Om Pingströrelsen: Essäer, översikter och analyser*. Skellefteå: Artos, 2014.

———. *Svenskt Frikyrkolexikon*. Edited by Jan-Åke Alvarsson. Stockholm: Atlantis, 2014.

———, ed. *Varför reste Lewi Pethrus just till Chicago? Relationer mellan Sverige och USA inom ramen för pentekostalismen*. Studia Pentecostalia Upsaliensia 4. Skellefteå: Artos, 2019.

Barratt, Thomas Ball. *Kvinnens Stilling i Menigheten*. Oslo: Filadelfiaforlaget, 1933.

Bloch-Hoell, Nils. *Pinsebevegelsen: en undersøkelse av pinsebevegelsens tilblivelse, utvikling og særpreg med særlig henblikk på bevegelsens utforming i Norge*. Oslo: Universitetsforlaget, 1956.

Blomqvist, Axel, ed. *Den svenska pingstväckelsen femtio år: En krönika i ord och bild*. Stockholm: Filadelfia, 1957.

Brusco, Elizabeth. *The Reformation of Machismo: Evangelical Conversion and Gender in Colombia*. Austin: University of Texas Press, 1995.

Butler, Anthea D. *Women in the Church of God in Christ: Making a Sanctified World*. Chapel Hill, NC: The University of North Carolina Press, 2007.

Cox, Harvey. *Fire from Heaven: The Rise of Pentecostal Spirituality and the Reshaping of Religion in the Twenty-first Century*. Reading, MA: Addison-Wesley, 1996.

Eriksson, Olle. "De första tusen." Internal document. Stockholm Filadelfia Church, 1995.

Franson, Fredrik. *Profeterande döttrar*. 2nd ed. "Kvinnan som förkunnare—Vad lär Bibeln?" Stockholm: Normans, 1961 (1896).

Frodsham, Stanley H. *With Signs Following: The Story of the Pentecostal Revival in the Twentieth Century*. Rev. 3rd ed. Springfield, MO: Gospel Publishing, 1942.

Gunner, Gunilla. *Nelly Hall, uppburen och ifrågasatt: predikant och missionär i Europa och USA 1882–1901*. Uppsala: Svenska institutet för missionsforskning, 2003.

Johansson, Göran. *Särlaregnets tid: Fragment och bilder från Betania—Pingstförsamling i och ur tiden*. Stockholm: Sköndalsinstitutets skriftserie Nr 25, 2005.

Larsson, Mats. "'Vi kristna unga qvinnor': Askers Jungfruförening 1865–1903—identitet och intersektionalitet*. Uppsala universitet: Teologiska institutionen, Kyrko- och missionsstudier, 2015.

Lawless, Elaine J. *Handmaidens of the Lord: Pentecostal Women Preachers and Traditional Religion*. Philadelphia: University of Pennsylvania Press, 1988.

Lindberg, Alf. *Förkunnarna och deras utbildning. Utbildningsfrågan inom Pingströrelsen, Lewi Pethrus ideologiska roll och de kvinnliga förkunnarnas situation*. Bibliotheca Historico-Ecclesiastica Lundensis No 27. Lund: Lund University Press, 1991.

Lundström, Klas et al., eds. *Svensk Mission och kyrkorna som växt fram*. Skellefteå: Artos, 2021.

Martin, David. *Pentecostalism: The World Their Parish*. Oxford: Blackwell, 2003.

Ongman, John. "Kvinnans rätt att förkunna evangelium." In *John Ongmans samlade skrifter*. Part 1, 3–68. Örebro: Örebro Missionsförenings Förlag, 1900.

Pingstväckelsens riktlinjer, Utgiven av en pingstkonferens i Berlin. Repr. Stockholm: Skrifter utgivna av Insamlingsstiftelsen för Pingstforskning, 2008.

Rodgers, Darrin. *Northern Harvest: Pentecostalism in North Dakota*. Bismarck, ND: North Dakota District Council of the Assemblies of God, 2003.

Söderholm, Gustaf Emil. *Den svenska pingstväckelsens historia 1907–1927, Del I*. 2nd ed. Stockholm: Filadelfia, 1929 (1927).

Townsend Gilkes, Cheryl. *"If It Wasn't for the Women . . .": Black Women's Experience and Womanist Culture in Church and Community*. New York: Orbis, 2001.

Wacker, Grant. "Are the Golden Oldies Still Worth Playing? Reflections on History Writing among Early Pentecostals." *Pneuma* 8 (1986) 81–100.

Image #3. Laura Barratt

2

Laura Barratt
"Mother" of the Norwegian Pentecostal Movement[1]

Rakel Ystebø Alegre

INTRODUCTION

Laura Barratt stands out as one of the most significant leaders of the early Pentecostal movement in Norway, alongside her famous husband T. B. Barratt, the "apostle of Pentecostalism to Europe."[2] Laura was a strong support for her husband's ministry,[3] but she was also independent, visionary, strategic, and a pioneer of several ministries. Her work in Pentecostal publishing, for foreign missions, as a spiritual mother, and as an advocate for female ministers had a strong impact. The Barratts functioned as a pioneer pastor couple, like some other early Pentecostal couples in ministry.[4] However, Laura's important role in the leadership of

---

1. All translations in this chapter are the author's own.

2. Bloch-Hoell, *Pinsebevegelsen,* 267; Ski et al., *Fram til Urkristendommen,* 128; Orlien, "Fru Barratt hjemme hos Gud," *KS,* January 20, 1951, 26–27.

3. To avoid repetition and confusion with her husband I will primarily refer to Laura by her first name in this chapter.

4. Alegre, "Women in Pentecostalism in Europe," 259–66; Chapman, "Role of Women in Early Pentecosatlism 1907–1914," 131–44. Some other Pentecostal pioneer couples were Alexander and Mary Boddy (England), Mary Jane and Smith Wigglesworth (England), Gerrit and Wilhelmine Polman (Netherlands).

the early Norwegian Pentecostal movement has often been neglected. As Grant Wacker has pointed out, when the story of Pentecostal pioneers is told, the role of women is frequently downplayed. He describes this as a "persistent gender bias" in Pentecostal history, and in the case of couples in ministry, this may cause the memory of the wife's contributions to fade or be left out of the story.[5] During the last years of Laura's ministry, many Pentecostals recognized the key role she had in the movement, but today her contributions seem to have been largely forgotten.

In this chapter, I set out to map and analyze Laura Barratt's leadership role and influence on the Norwegian Pentecostal movement. I will first describe her childhood, youth, and ministry as a Methodist pastor's wife, and then her ministry as a Pentecostal leader in partnership with her husband T. B. Barratt. Thereafter I will analyze in what areas Laura had a significant and lasting impact, how the Barratts' views on women in ministry affected the early Norwegian Pentecostal movement, and how Laura and T. B. Barratt worked together as partners in ministry. By doing this I wish to demonstrate that Laura's leadership was of great importance and that she could be considered a "mother" of the Norwegian Pentecostal movement.

LAURA BARRATT'S EARLY LIFE AND MARRIAGE TO T. B. BARRATT

Laura Jakobsen was born in Bergen on November 30, 1866, as the third of four sisters. Her father, Erik Jakobsen, was a shoemaker, and her mother Louise had worked as a housekeeper in a mansion.[6] Her parents were central in the Lammers free church in the city, a small community that came out of a revival led by Gustav Adolph Lammers.[7] Lammers was a state church Lutheran priest, but in 1856 he left his position and organized a free church in Skien. This was the first dissenter church in Norway and several such churches were soon established in different cities and towns in Norway.[8] Many congregations that emerged from the Lammers move-

---

5. Wacker, "Are the Golden Oldies Still Worth Playing?" 95; Alegre, "Women in Pentecostalism in Europe," 260.

6. Barratt, *Minner*, 10.

7. Barratt, *Minner*, 11–16; Diesen, *Veiryddere*, 114–19. The Lammers congregation was founded in Bergen in 1858. Laura Barratt's grandfather, Tolleif Andersen, was one of the congregations first members.

8. Diesen, *Veiryddere*, 23, 37–61; Sødal, *Norsk Kristendomshistorie 1800-2020*,

ment were characterized by revivalism, pursuit of holiness, emphasis on foreign missions, and opposition against infant baptism. The ministry of Gustav Adolph Lammers and later the Swedish-American preacher Fredrik Franson led to the establishment of *Misjonsforbundet* (The Mission Covenant Church of Norway).[9] Laura Barratt's upbringing in the Lammers community meant that she and her sisters were not baptized as infants or confirmed. This was considered quite radical at the time since the great majority belonged to the Lutheran state church and the girls were sometimes teased about this by the neighboring children and their classmates.[10]

The Lammers church was on the same street as the Jakobsen's house, *Skostredet* in Bergen. The parents never required their daughters to attend religious meetings, but Laura became deeply concerned with evangelism, holiness, foreign missions, and reading Christian literature from an early age.[11] These were priorities that also influenced her later ministry and would become key characteristics of the early Pentecostal years. As a young woman, she participated in several revivals in Bergen, and one of the ministers that had a strong impact on her was Fredrik Franson. He visited the Lammers community in Bergen for the first time in 1883 when Laura was twelve years old.[12] In her autobiography Laura says that Franson stayed in their house when he came to preach in Bergen, and that his revival meetings and his presence in their home strengthened her spiritual life.[13] Franson was also a leader who mobilized Scandinavians and Scandinavian-Americans for foreign missions.[14] A visit from the Danish missionary to Congo, Peter Frederickson, also made a strong impression on Laura. Frederickson was a missionary with the Livingston Inland Mission in Congo, and he started his work there in 1881.[15] For

---

45–46. The Lammers church was called *Den frie apostolisk-christelige menighed*. Lammers ended up leaving the church he founded and returning to the Lutheran state church.

9. Diesen, *Veiryddere*, 62–118, 184–210.

10. Barratt, *Minner*, 12.

11. Barratt, *Minner*, 11–33.

12. Diesen, *Veiryddere*, 118.

13. Barratt, *Minner*, 15, 27–29. She was a young girl but he challenged her to seek and worship God several times a day. Laura visited Franson's grave in Chicago many years later (in 1928).

14. Palmqvist, *Fredrik Franson*, 67–151.

15 "American Baptist Foreign Mission Society 1930," 70–72. In Norwegian and Danish, Peter Frederickson's name is often recorded as Peder Fredriksen.

Laura, he became a demonstration of the sacrifices made on the mission field as well as of the possibilities of great revivals on other continents. Frederickson had spoken to Laura and her sister Jenny about the great need for missionaries to Congo, and Laura seems to have considered taking this path. In her autobiography, she concludes that since both she and Jenny became preacher's wives their work was at home in Norway.[16] However, she would play an important role in the Norwegian Pentecostal missions work a few decades later. Her strong concern for foreign missions was likely highly influenced by her upbringing.

Laura enjoyed reading when she was young and she primarily read Christian literature.[17] She carried this interest with her into adulthood and eventually spent much time producing Christian periodicals and promoting and selling edifying literature. She inherited her parents' conviction that one should only have Christian literature in the home, and as an adult, her personal hobby became reading the biographies of "holy men and women."[18] During her childhood years Laura also heard much teaching about the temperance cause. A preacher who affected her regarding this cause was a Norwegian-American pastor named Johnsen. He told of his experiences of "war" between the Methodist preachers and the liquor salesmen in the Dakotas. As she remembered the story the liquor salesmen came to camp meetings and started fights while the people were praying, preaching, and singing.[19] Already as a teenager Laura became involved in the temperance movement in Norway and her commitment to this cause would also become lifelong.

The Lammers community was quite small in Bergen and Laura seems to have had friends from various dissenter churches in the city. When Laura was thirteen the Methodists started arranging meetings in Bergen, and a young preacher by the name of Lars Petersen caused quite a stir in the city when he arrived in 1879.[20] Both newspapers and Lu-

16. Barratt, *Minner*, 32–33. Laura says that Gunnerius Tollefsen visited the Fredericksons. Peter Frederickson held meetings in the Lammers church in Skostredet in Bergen in 1880. This is likely the occasion Laura is referring to. She would have been thirteen years old at the time. *Bergens Tidende* (April 13, 1880) 1.

17. Barratt, *Minner*, 16–17. In their house they were not allowed to read novels, but they had some books by Krumaker, Rosenius and Brorson.

18. Barratt, *Minner*, 16–17.

19. Barratt, *Minner*, 41–42. The chronology is a bit unclear here. She may have heard him before or after she joined the Methodist church. Johnson was a Methodist preacher in America and Norway.

20. Barratt, *Minner*, 17–18; Lange, *T. B. Barratt*, 43–44; *Centralkirkens Menighet Bergen*, 4. Petersen is sometimes written Pettersen.

theran priests warned against the newly arrived Methodists saying that they were dangerous. Laura's father, however, let his daughters attend the Methodist meetings. He thought it would be good for them since there were more young people there than in their own church and since it was a revivalist community with inspiring preachers. Petersen's preaching made a strong impression on Laura and many others in the city.[21] One of the new converts was one of Bergen's well-known actresses, Fredrikke Nilsen. She left the theatre and became a Sunday school teacher in the Methodist church, impressing the young girls with her eloquence and dress. Nilsen became a close family friend of the Barratt family, and later she travelled as an evangelist in Scandinavia and America.[22] Witnessing Nilsen's ministry may have contributed to Laura and T. B. Barratt encouraging the Danish Pentecostal actresses Anna Larssen Bjørner and Anna Lewini to become preachers.[23]

The young Methodist preacher, Lars Petersen, soon became T. B. Barratt's best friend and in 1881 he also became Laura's brother-in-law when he married her eldest sister, Hanna.[24] The newlywed Petersens moved to Fredrikstad and then to Halden to pastor a church there. One winter Laura visited them and experienced a revival that was taking place in the Methodist church in Halden. In her autobiography, Laura reflected on how experiences of revivals in her childhood prepared her for the Pentecostal revival: "Many phenomena that people have disapproved of within the Pentecostal arrival, never made me uneasy, because I had seen how the Holy Spirit worked in very different and unexpected ways."[25] In Halden Laura had a Methodist baptism, but she was dissatisfied with it since it was only a "sprinkling of water" and not a full immersion.[26] In Bergen she joined the Sunday school work, went to prayer meetings, and sang in the choir in the Methodist church.[27] It was through the Jacobsen

---

21. Barratt, *Minner*, 16–17; Lange, *T. B. Barratt*, 51–52.

22. Barratt, *Minner*, 24–26; Lange, *T. B. Barratt*, 50. Fredrikke Nilsen became a close family friend of Mary and Alexander Barratt.

23. See Nikolaj Christensen's chapters on Anna Larssen Bjørner and Anna Lewini.

24. Lange, *T. B. Barratt*, 62–63.

25. Barratt, *Minner*, 18.

26. Barratt, *Minner*, 18–19. In her autobiography Laura said that she repeatedly told her husband that if he ever decided to be baptized by full immersion, she would join him.

27. Barratt, *Minner*, 30–31, 34–36; Barratt, "75 År," *KS*, November 15, 1941, 52–53. Three of the Jacobsen sisters eventually married Methodist pastors and became preachers' wives, which they viewed as an important ministerial role.

family's connection to the free church communities in and around Bergen that Laura became acquainted with Thomas Ball Barratt.[28]

Laura's future husband, T. B. Barratt, was born in Cornwall, England, in 1862, to devout Wesleyan Methodist parents. When he was five years old, he moved to Varaldsøy in Hardanger, because his father, Alexander, had become the manager of a sulphur mine on the island. The island was close to Bergen, and the family frequently visited the city where they befriended other free church Christians.[29] Barratt attended a Wesleyan boarding school in England from eleven to sixteen, and when he finished school, he moved permanently back to Norway. There he soon started preaching and became involved in the temperance movement.[30] Eventually Barratt felt called to full-time ministry as a Methodist preacher and later pastor.[31]

Laura and T. B. Barratt met through their families and the Methodist church in Bergen.[32] T. B. Barratt was nineteen and Laura fourteen when he asked her to marry him, and she said yes. However, when Barratt's parents found out, they asked them to call off the engagement because they were too young to make such a decision. They complied, but their affection lasted. They were married in May of 1887. Laura was then twenty and T. B. Barratt was twenty-four years old.[33] The years between their first engagement and their marriage T. B. Barratt took on more work as a Methodist minister in the region, in Bergen, and then in Christiania (now Oslo).[34] In January 1887 he was sent to Voss to start a Methodist

---

28. Laura was almost eighty when her memories from her childhood were recorded in the autobiographical work *Minner*, which is a key source of information on her early life. The memories that she selected, her emphasis, and the interpretation of her experiences would have been influenced by the rest of her life experiences and should be understood in this light. Reading her account does, however, give the impression that she from a young age was dedicated to revivalism, holiness, Christian literature, foreign missions, and the temperance cause. These were all things that aligned with her husband's values and work and became important in her future roles in Methodist and Pentecostal ministry.

29. Barratt, *When the Fire Fell*, 10–21, 28–38.

30. Barratt, *When the Fire Fell*, 22–35.

31. Barratt, *When the Fire Fell*, 37–49; Lange, *T. B. Barratt*, 88–97.

32. Lange, *T. B. Barratt*, 60–61. "Hun var en mor i Israel," *KS*, November 26, 1966, 5. Laura and her sister became close friends with T. B. Barratt's two sisters Louisa and Polly (Mary).

33. Barratt, *When the Fire Fell*, 55; Lange, *T. B. Barratt*, 60–62, 97, 102–3.

34. Barratt, *When the Fire Fell*, 37–53; Bundy, *Visions of Apostolic Mission*, 141–43.

church, and Laura joined him after their wedding in May. She thus became a pastor's wife and his partner in ministry at the age of twenty.[35]

MINISTRY AS A METHODIST MINISTER'S WIFE

T. B. Barratt encountered much opposition at Voss since he was trying to establish a Methodist church in a largely Lutheran community.[36] It was very difficult to find someone who would rent him a meeting hall, so he soon started building a chapel in the town. When Laura joined her husband in May 1887, she immediately became a great help to him in the ministry.[37] She was strongly committed to both supporting him and sharing the ministry work, and she considered being a preacher's wife an important responsibility. T. B. Barratt wrote that Laura "often led the meetings in my absence" and that she "preached with great fervor and effect at our farewell meetings."[38] Laura also seemed as determined as her husband to keep working in the face of opposition and rejection from people they thought were their friends. A Methodist community was gradually established and their chapel, *Zion*, was inaugurated in July 1887.[39] In 1888 the couple had their first child, Mary.[40]

After two years at Voss the Methodist Episcopal Conference appointed T. B. Barratt as pastor of the third Methodist church in Christiania (now Oslo). Thus, the family of three moved to the capital in 1889. There Laura continued her role as pastor's wife being actively involved in the church and in different organizations that her husband started, such as the Methodist Youth organization "the Epworth League."[41] When T. B. Barratt travelled, Laura managed both their home and many ministerial activities in his absence, though with help from Christian brothers and sisters and a maid. Laura would also regularly speak at events, especially when her husband was away, for instance on his eight-month fundraising trip to England in 1890.[42] Their family grew steadily and in the years

35. Barratt, *Minner*, 48–51; Lange, *T. B. Barratt*, 103–7.
36. Barratt, *Erindringer*, 53–58; Lange, *T. B. Barratt*, 98–102.
37. Lange, *T. B. Barratt*, 104, 114.
38. Barratt, *Erindringer*, 60.
39. Barratt, *Erindringer*, 56.
40. Barratt, *Erindringer*, 58. Mary inherited her father's musical talent and eventually became a famous pianist in Norway.
41. Lange, *T. B. Barratt*, 116–24; Barratt, *Minner*, 52–58.
42. Lange, *T. B. Barratt*, 123–27.

1888–1904 Laura had eight children.[43] In 1892, when Laura was twenty-five years old, T. B. Barratt became presiding elder of the Christiania district in the Methodist church. In this position, he essentially functioned as a superintendent or bishop for the Methodists in Norway.[44] The six years he held this position were very active years for the young couple, and they were involved in a variety of ministerial activities as well as continuing their engagement in the temperance cause. They seem to have been primarily concerned with evangelistic and diaconal work during these years, and among other things they started the Methodist diaconal work, *Betanien*, together with three nurses in 1896.[45]

During their early years in Christiania, Laura and T. B. Barratt became part of a community of revivalist dissenters from different denominations and organizations and they made many new friendships. Laura befriended several important pioneer women and her views on the role of women in ministry seem to have further developed during this time. Two of her close friends were Marie Bagger, a nurse who did much for the poor in the city, and Olafia Johannisdotter who was important in the women's temperance movement and in helping destitute women in the city. Laura supported both women in their work.[46] The women of the Salvation Army in Christiania also impressed Laura, and maybe especially Commander Hanna Ouchterlony from Sweden. Ouchterlony led the Salvation Army in Norway from 1894 to 1900 and was a pioneer for women as preachers and leaders in Scandinavia.[47] Laura describes how "her heart glowed" when Ouchterlony lent her the two volumes of the *Life of Mrs. Booth* (1900).[48]

In addition to the Methodist ministry, Laura was part of the Woman's Christian Temperance Union known in Norway as "*Det hvite band*"

---

43. The Barratt's eight children were: Mary Louise (1888–1969), Esther Alexandra (1890–1966), Susanna "Sussie" Wesley (1892–1904), Laura Jacobea (1893–1894), Solveig (1896–1968), Frances Gullbjørg (1899–1925), Thomas "Tom" Eivind (1902–1926), and Alexander "Alek" (1904–1960).

44. Hassing, *Religion and Power*, 93, 100–101.

45. Barratt, *Erindringer*, 74; Ski, *T. B. Barratt*, 57. Barratt emphasized that this was something he and his wife did together. One of the nurses was her friend Marie Bagger. This work eventually became very large within the Methodist church leading to several hospitals.

46. Barratt, *Minner*, 54–60. Marie Bagger was one of the first nurses at Betanien and later became a Pentecostal. Olafia Johannisdotter was from Iceland and was important in The Women's Christian Temperance Union (The White Ribbon). She was a devout Christian and joined a Baptist church in the Christiania.

47. Petri, *Hanna Cordelia Ouchterlony*, 248–91.

48. "Møtet som ble kringkastet gledet mange," *Krigsropet* 53 (1940) 6.

(The White Ribbon). During the 1890s she held lectures and helped organize events.[49] In 1900 Laura was one of the Norwegian delegates, together with her friend Olafia Johannisdotter, at the organization's world conference in Edinburgh, Scotland.[50] At one of the meetings she met Hannah Whitall Smith and told her that her book *The Christian's Secrets of a Happy Life* (1875) had had a great impact on her life.[51] Laura later reflected that maybe it was at this conference she "gained the understanding of women's importance in society." She further commented: "There were women there who every man here in Norway would have benefitted greatly to listen to."[52]

Laura's new friendships and experiences with female ministers in Christiania in the 1890s strengthened her convictions of the importance that women were actively involved in public ministry and society. It may also have strengthened her own confidence in preaching, speaking, and other public ministerial activities. Her experiences during her childhood and teenage years laid the groundwork for her views on this topic. Laura's mother encouraged her daughters to not think themselves inferior to boys in any way and to actively partake in evangelism and ministry. Laura had also witnessed the preaching ministry of the actress Fredrikke Nilsen and the spiritual leadership of Mary Barratt, T. B. Barratt's mother.

Shortly after Laura arrived in Christiania, the Swedish preacher Fredrik Franson published a book in Christiania on women in ministry. The book was called *Eders døtre skulle profetere* (Your Daughters shall Prophesy) (1890) and it was published by "Bible women" in the city.[53] Franson's ministry had been important in the Lammers community that Laura grew up in and it is highly likely that his views on women in ministry influenced her.[54] In his book, Franson argued that it was

49. Ski, *T. B. Barratt*, 58; L. Barratt, *Minner*, 54–58; L. Barratt, "75 År," *KS*, November 15, 1941, 552–53.

50. Barratt, *Minner*, 60–62. Olafia Johannisdotter was one of the main speakers at the congress. There were about 3,000–4,000 delegates. When Barratt was gone for long periods, Laura would sometimes ask her maid to watch the kids if she was tired and then go to Olafia's small house in Smalgangen. There she "got spiritual air and a view of God's work in the world" and they would talk and laugh together. Barratt, *Minner*, 64–65.

51. Barratt, *Minner*, 62; Barratt, "75 År," *KS*, November 15, 1941, 552–53. Laura had spread hundreds of copies of this book in Norway and after fifty years still encouraged all Christians to read it.

52. Barratt, *Minner*, 60–61.

53. Franson, *Eders døtre skulle profetere*, 1.

54. These views may have been transmitted to her when Franson stayed in their

evident in both the Old and New Testament that women were to preach prophesy, teach, and lead. He believed that the efforts to limit women's ministry were evidence of the devil's work to hinder the work of God in the world.[55] According to Franson there was ample evidence in the Bible that women were to have public ministry and that it was an error to establish doctrines based on just one passage.[56] The verses had to be interpreted correctly and understood in context, and all of Scripture had to be taken into account.[57] Franson further argued that women could be apostles (missionaries), prophets, evangelists, and shepherds, and that it was very important to mobilize women for foreign missions. To Franson's great joy, there had been a change in attitudes in America towards sending single female missionaries and now there were more women on the mission field than men.[58]

Laura seems to have become increasingly confident with ministering publicly in the 1890s in Christiania. She was influenced by new female friends and role models and the view on women in ministry that the Salvation Army and Franson represented. When she became a Pentecostal leader, it was evident that Laura also shared Franson's emphasis on mobilizing and sending female evangelists and missionaries.

In 1898, T. B. Barratt was assigned to be pastor of the First Methodist Episcopal Church in Christiania. Laura's role also changed somewhat as she went from being the presiding elder's wife to a pastor's wife of the church. However, her husband had for many years dreamt of starting a City Mission modelled on the Central Hall in London and he soon started planning for this new ministry. The goal was to be able to evangelize and do diaconal work among the poor and people who did not usually attend church.[59] In 1902 Barratt convinced the Methodist conference of his plan, and they elected him "city missionary." However, they decided it would be a position without salary or other expenses covered.[60] They took up a special offering for him and his family to get started, but the family lost

---

home, but when the book came out it also made an impact in the dissenter circles that she moved in.

55. Franson, *Eders døtre skulle profetere*, 23–24.

56. Franson, *Eders døtre skulle profetere*, 22–23. He refers to 1 Tim 2:12–13 and 1 Corinthians 14:34 and says it is an error to give these verses so much emphasis.

57. Franson, *Eders døtre skulle profetere*, 22–24.

58. Franson, *Eders døtre skulle profetere*, 31–32.

59. Barratt, *When the Fire Fell*, 75–79, 86–87.

60. Barratt, *Erindringer*, 81–82; Bundy, *Visions of Apostolic Mission*, 159–64.

a regular and secure income. This made Laura very worried, especially since they had six young children to provide for at the time. She sent a telegram to him after hearing the news that simply said "Impossible."[61] However, after some doubts and hesitation she eventually supported her husband's decision to "go in faith" that God would provide the means.[62]

In 1902 the Barratts established the Christiania City Mission (*Bymisjonen*). They rented different popular venues to have evangelistic meetings and lectures. They engaged in social relief work, started activities for children and youth, and published more literature. Laura likely played an important role in the emphasis on spreading edifying literature and the practical tasks related to this. In 1904 the couple started the periodical *Byposten* to further spread their message and obtain support for their work.[63] This periodical was a joint effort between them and several of their older children who also helped them with the administrative work.[64] Even though T. B. Barratt was the official editor and wrote many of the texts in the paper, Laura did most of the practical work. She was the publisher, treasurer, and translator. She selected several of the texts in the paper and managed the distribution and sales.[65] Laura also ran the periodical when her husband was travelling and was abroad for long periods. The Barratts published several small tracts or pamphlets from 1904 and established a small publishing company in their home.[66]

As their ministry with the City Mission expanded T. B. Barratt wished to build a headquarters for them in Christiania. In 1905 he embarked on a fundraising tour to the US.[67] Barratt spent more than a year in the US, but his fundraising was unsuccessful. Their daughter Solveig Barratt Lange points out that T. B. Barratt left his wife Laura with much responsibility when he went to America.[68] She had to manage affairs at home with their six children, edit, publish, send out the paper

61. Lange, "Hjemme hos oss i vekkelsens første tid," *KS* (December 8, 1956) 753; Lange, *T. B. Barratt*, 154–55.

62. Barratt, *Erindringer,* 82; Lange, *T. B. Barratt*, 154–55.

63. Lange, *T. B. Barratt,* 167; Barratt, *When the Fire Fell,* 89.

64. Ski et al., *Fram til Urkristendommen*, 1:10.

65. Barratt, "Om Laura Barratt," 3; "Laura Barratt: som redaksjonsmedhjelp og ekspeditør," *KS* (December 3, 1949) 596.

66. The publishing company was named *Byposten Forlag* and the work came in addition to their work with the periodical.

67. Barratt, *When the Fire Fell,* 95, 98. The building was to be named *Haakonsborgen* in honor of the new king of Norway.

68. Lange, "Hjemme hos oss i vekkelsens første tid," *KS* (December 8, 1956) 753.

Byposten, and manage many of the activities at the City Mission. Even though she had helpers, Lange says she carried the burden of the overall responsibility.[69]

LAURA BARRATT AND THE START OF THE PENTECOSTAL REVIVAL

During the Fall of 1906, T. B. Barratt was in New York and in his disappointment of having raised little funds and few open doors to preach, he decided to primarily focus on his spiritual life. It was at this time he read about the Pentecostal revival in Azusa Street. After having read *The Apostolic Faith*, studied the issue of Spirit Baptism and tongues in the Bible, and talked to people who had been at Azusa Street, Barratt sought the experience. On November 15 he was baptized in the Spirit in a small meeting in New York and started speaking in tongues.[70] This experience was transformational and gave him a new purpose: to spread the Pentecostal revival. Barratt wrote long accounts of his experience and sent them to several Norwegian and American periodicals, and Laura read his public and private letters with wonder.[71]

Laura had also had a difficult year in her husband's absence, and since his fundraising efforts were so unsuccessful, he sent little money home to the family. The rent was unpaid, the children had few winter clothes, and one of the children was hospitalized with diphtheria.[72] Reading about T. B. Barratt's spiritual search inspired her to also seek spiritual renewal. Laura wrote that she was tired of all the events such as bazaars, parties, and musical shows, and she decided to start attending the revival meetings of Erik Andersen Nordquelle in Torvgaten 7.[73] Initially she was hesitant to go to these meetings because she thought Nordquelle was too

---

69. Lange, "Hjemme hos oss i vekkelsens første tid," *KS* (December 8, 1956) 753; Lange, *T. B. Barratt*, 183–84; Ski et al., *Fram til Urkristendommen*, 1:10, 136. Dagmar Engstrøm, "Opplevelser og minner fra 1906–1907," *KS* (December 8, 1956) 752. Her main coworker in managing the tasks at the City Mission while her husband was gone was M. H. Sæther, but several others also helped her, for instance, Dagmar Gregersen (later Engstrøm).

70. Barratt, *When the Fire Fell*, 102–32.

71. Barratt, *When the Fire Fell*, 133; Barratt, "Da jeg fik min Pintsedaab," *Byposten* (November 3) 190, 93–95; Barratt, "Baptized in New York," *The Apostolic Faith* (December 1906) 3; Barratt, *Minner*, 74–75.

72. Barratt, *Minner*, 75.

73. Barratt, *Minner*, 75.

critical or harsh when he spoke of other Christians, and because several of the coworkers in the City Mission and the Methodist church did not approve of him. A Methodist pastor said it "would hurt her husband's reputation" if she went to the meetings, but she decided she had to go to seek God and spiritual renewal.[74] At Nordquelle's meetings Laura experienced strong "meetings with Jesus," which gave her peace of mind.[75] She developed a good relationship with the "friends" and Erik Andersen Nordquelle, and this may have contributed to the warm welcome her husband received in this community when he came home from the US.[76]

Laura's experience of spiritual renewal during the fall of 1906 prepared her for her husband's return and his dedication to spreading the Pentecostal revival. The letters he sent about baptism in the Spirit also gave her some time to think about his experience and new teachings.[77] Though she did not understand everything that was happening to her husband, she decided to trust him and was prepared to support him in his new endeavors.[78]

T. B. Barratt arrived home right before Christmas in 1906 after more than a year in the US. His homecoming was met with great expectancy among the "friends" of the City Mission, and a Pentecostal revival started during the last weeks of December. By New Year about twenty people had been baptized in the Spirit and spoken in tongues. News soon started to spread about the revival in Christian and secular newspapers.[79] By January 1907 crowds started to come to the meetings as well as ministers and journalists from countries such as Sweden, Denmark, England, and

---

74. Barratt, *Minner*, 74–75.
75. Barratt, *Minner*, 75–76.
76. Bloch-Hoell, *Pinsebevegelsen*, 117, 140–44; Barratt, *Minner*, 73–76.
77. Lange, *T. B. Barratt*, 183–85; Lange, "Hjemme hos oss i vekkelsens første tid," *KS* (December 8, 1956) 754. Laura was initially concerned when she started to receive letters about Barratt's search for and later experience of Spirit Baptism with tongues. She was hesitant to publish them in *Byposten*. She worried that people would think her husband was acting strangely. She went to Barratt's spiritual mentor, the Methodist pastor Ole Olsen, for advice, and after he read the letters, he recommended she publish them.
78. Lange, "Hjemme hos oss i vekkelsens første tid," *KS* (December 8, 1956) 754; Lange, *T. B. Barratt*, 185.
79. Bloch-Hoell, *Pinsebevegelsen*, 139–42; Barratt, *When the Fire Fell*, 140–45. They started with meetings in *Bymisjonen's* rented hall in *Citypassasjen* but had to leave when office workers complained about the noise. They moved their meetings to Erik Nordquelle's hall since he was willing to co-host the meetings. They cooperated from 1907 to 1909.

Germany.[80] The pastors and preachers that arrived spent much of their time at the Barratt family's home to ask them for guidance and prayer.[81] Their home and the meetings held in Torvgaten 7 became the center for the revival and its spread.

T. B. Barratt soon received invitations to preach both in Norway and other countries, and he spent much of the following three years as a travelling evangelist. In addition to preaching, he wrote many texts advocating for and defending the theology and praxis of the Pentecostals.[82] These were spread to many parts of the world, among other things leading to an invitation to come to India in 1908. T. B. Barratt was hesitant to go on such a long trip leaving Laura and the children again, but Laura encouraged him to go saying there would be little joy in staying if God wanted him to be elsewhere.[83] Barratt wanted Laura to accompany him when he travelled, but she only did so on a few occasions since they had six children.[84] Thus, Laura spent much of this time as a leadership figure within the newly formed Pentecostal community in Christiania, managing their increasingly important periodical *Byposten*, and being in charge of their household.[85]

Laura was viewed as a wise leader, and she received many of the Pentecostal preachers (especially women) in her home. She also led meetings and spoke occasionally. Evidence of Laura's standing as one of the main leaders in the emerging Pentecostal revival was that she represented Norway at the first international Pentecostal conference in Sunderland in 1908.[86] Her husband was in India, but she went there together with the Norwegian evangelists Dagmar Gregersen and Agnes Thelle.[87] Reports

---

80. Barratt, *When the Fire Fell*, 142–49; Bundy, *Visions of Apostolic Mission*, 176–78, 190. Several of the leaders eventually became leaders in the Pentecostal revival in their home countries, such as Emil Meyer and Jonathan Paul in Germany, Alexander Boddy in England, Lewi Pethrus in Sweden, and A. Christensen in Denmark.

81. Barratt, "Om Laura Barratt," 3.

82. See Alegre, "Pentecostal Apologetics of T. B. Barratt," 84–274.

83. T. B. Barratt was gone from April to December 1908, stopping to preach in Sweden, Denmark, Germany, Switzerland, Italy, and Palestine. Barratt, *When the Fire Fell*, 159.

84. Lange, "Hjemme hos oss i vekkelsens første tid," *KS* (December 8, 1956) 754.

85. Barratt, "Tale om Laura Barratt," 3; Ski et al., *Fram til Urkristendommen*, 1:136.

86. "The Whitsuntide Conference," *Confidence* (June 30, 1908) 4–5. Barratt, "Konferensen i Sunderland," *Byposten* (June 27, 1908) 50–51. Ski et al., *Fram til Urkristendommen*, 1:136. The conference was arranged by Alexander Boddy.

87. Dagmar Gregersen and Agnes Thelle were instrumental in the Pentecostal revival's start in Germany and Switzerland. They were on their way to the US to attend

on the three women's participation at the conference were recorded in Boddy's periodical *Confidence* and it mentions Laura speaking.[88]

In the first years of the revival T. B. Barratt experienced massive opposition and ridicule both at home and abroad. Laura witnessed her husband being the victim of many lies and exaggerations and being accused of a variety of things in secular and Christian papers.[89] Among the accusations were that he was driving people insane, that he was hypnotizing people and manipulating the crowds, that he was transferring demonic spirits when he prayed for people, and/or that he was doing the work of the devil and not God. Some even argued that he should be put in an asylum for the mentally ill.[90] It was difficult for Laura to see her husband being portrayed in such a way, but she defended and encouraged him.[91]

According to their daughter Solveig Barratt Lange, Laura was a very important support for Barratt during the first trying years of the revival. She writes: "With her he could talk about everything, as with no one else. She understood him, and he in turn greatly esteemed her wisdom and abilities."[92] Barratt said that he could endure the opposition and ridicule as long as he knew Laura was with him.[93] Esther Barratt said that their mother had a cheerful personality and there was a "light and cheerful" atmosphere in their home. She also made efforts to let her husband find rest and peace in his home during the "storm." According to Esther, Laura "fought and suffered with her beloved Tom, shared the misunderstandings, mockery and contempt, but also the many and great glorious experiences."[94] Her companionship and support of her husband through the opposition was of great importance.[95]

A. B. Simpsons mission school. In 1910 they became missionaries to India. (See chapter on them by Glenn Gohr and Rakel Ystebø Alegre.)

88. "The Whitsuntide Conference," *Confidence* (June 30, 1908) 4, 8, 10–11.

89. Barratt, *Minner*, 66–70.

90. Bloch-Hoell, *Pinsebevegelsen*, 145–53, 201–5; Alegre, "Pentecostal Apologetics of T. B. Barratt," 66–75, 209–14, 280–85.

91. Barratt, *Minner*, 67.

92. Lange, "Barndomsminner," *KS* (July 14–21, 1962) 444.

93. Orlien, "Fru Barratt fyller 80 År," *KS* (November 23, 1946) 750.

94. Barratt, "Om Laura Barratt," 2.

95. Orlien, "Pastor T. B. Barratt som forkynner og kristen leder," *KS* (July 12, 1991) 17; Ski, *T. B. Barratt*, 150; Lange, "Hjemme hos oss i vekkelsens første tid," *KS* (December 8, 1956) 754; Gulbrandsen, "Tale holdt for gullbrudeparet Pastor T. B. Barratt og frue paa menighetens fest tirsdag 11. Mai 1937."

LAURA BARRATT'S LEADERSHIP IN THE EMERGING NORWEGIAN PENTECOSTAL MOVEMENT

From 1907–1909 Laura and other early "Barratt-Pentecostals" had worked together with Erik Andersen Nordquelle's community in Torvgaten 7.[96] The cooperation between him and T. B. Barratt was good while Barratt was primarily traveling as a revivalist preacher, but some differences between the two were becoming increasingly visible. In 1910 Barratt decided to rent a separate hall and organize his own community of believers. This represented a division between the followers of Barratt and Nordquelle in the city, a split that would gradually widen and lead to two separate Pentecostal denominations in Norway.[97] The meeting hall Barratt rented was Møllergaten 38, and in 1910 he presented the statutes of the community.[98]

The Barratts did not think of this as starting a church, but more like a "mission." However, the activities became regular and organized and the community did function as a church in many ways. They started children's ministries, held regular meetings, and stated their beliefs, but there was a relatively loose affiliation of its adherents. They did not have requirements for membership or a specific view on water baptism. The community in Møllergaten 38 was "alliance-minded" with an emphasis on the core Pentecostal beliefs and practices such as salvation, sanctification, Spirit-baptism, and healing.[99] From then on T. B. Barratt started to spend more time in Christiania and gradually functioned more as a pastor and strategic leader than as an evangelist.[100] However, he still travelled frequently though on shorter trips, and Laura had the largest responsibility when he was away.[101] Among other occurrences she received Frank Bartleman when he visited Norway in 1913 and translated for him at their meetings.

One of the disagreements between early Pentecostal leaders in Norway was the issue of water baptism.[102] Laura had from a young age

---

96. Bloch-Hoell, *Pinsebevegelsen*, 139–44; 175–78, 199–204.

97. Bloch-Hoell, *Pinsebevegelsen*, 116–218.

98. Bloch-Hoell, *Pinsebevegelsen*, 208–13.

99. Bloch-Hoell, *Pinsebevegelsen*, 208–13.

100. Bloch-Hoell, *Pinsebevegelsen*, 209; T. B. Barratt, "Fra vort utkigstaarn," *KS* (October 1, 1912) 150.

101. Barratt, *Erindringer*, 201.

102. Pethrus, "T. B. Barratt—Høvdingen," *KS* (December 8, 1956) 757–58.

believed in the Baptist view of water baptism, but T. B. Barratt was baptized as an infant after the Methodist pattern. He did not wish water baptism to be a dividing issue. However, some Pentecostals in Norway were strongly against infant baptism. Since the issue was of such importance to them, he decided to research the matter in depth in 1912. After months of research, he decided that the Baptists were right and that the biblical model for baptism was believer's baptism with full submersion.[103] Some authors argue that it was Laura who had the strongest influence on Barratt in this issue.[104] As mentioned above she was not satisfied with the "sprinkling" in her Methodist baptism and wished to have a baptism of full immersion. When her husband came to the same conclusion, she was happy with his decision, and they were both baptized by Lewi Pethrus in Stockholm on September 15, 1913.[105] The Barratts' baptism became an important moment in early Norwegian Pentecostal history, and even though it first made some of their followers leave, their baptism eventually enabled stronger uniformity and unity.[106]

In 1916, T. B. Barratt decided to reorganize his community in Møllergaten 38 and officially establish a Pentecostal church in Oslo. The church started with 200 members and was in 1921 named *Filadelfia*. It grew rapidly and by 1926 it had almost 1,500 members.[107] The leadership was organized with Barratt as pastor and a group of elders, deacons, and deaconesses. The members of all these groups were elected and together constituted the leadership group of the church.[108] Laura became a deaconess and was in this way a part of the formal leadership of the church. However, she was also considered a "mother" in the church, and they seem to have been thought of as a "pastor couple."[109] From 1916 until T. B. Barratt passed away in 1940, Laura maintained her position as a

---

103. Barratt, *Erindringer,* 203–4; see Barratt, *Den kristne daap og hvorfor jeg lot mig døpe.*

104. Ski, *T. B. Barratt*; 152; Bloch-Hoell, *Pinsebevegelsen,* 226.

105. Barratt, *Minner,* 18–19; Pethrus, "T. B. Barratt—Hövdingen," *KS,* December 8, 757–58.

106. Bloch-Hoell, *Pinsebevegelsen,* 226–27.

107. Bloch-Hoell, *Pinsebevegelsen,* 237.

108. Ski et al., *Fram Til Urkristendommen,* 1:201; 3:40–42.

109. Orlien, "Fru Barratt fyller 80 År," *KS,* (November 23, 1946) 750; Ski et al., *Fram Til Urkristendommen,* 2:130; "Hun var en mor i Israel," *KS* (November 26, 1966) 5. Orlien wrote she was a mother for the Filadelfia church. Laura was called "a mother in Israel."

deaconess and in the formal leadership, and she was actively involved in many branches of the church's ministries.

In 1910 the Barratts renamed their periodical *Byposten* to *Korsets Seir* (Victory of the Cross).[110] This change of name was meant to reflect the changed nature of the periodical. Now it was an organ of the Norwegian Pentecostal revival uniting "friends" all over the country, as well as Norwegian Pentecostals in North America and on the mission fields.[111] Laura continued to do much of the management and editorial work of the periodical from their home as they saw the periodical's subscription rate and reach increase rapidly. The children helped her pack and send out letters.[112] At this time Laura also began focusing more on the production and sale of Christian literature. This had been an important interest since childhood, and she used the paper to promote a variety of books and pamphlets, several of which her husband had authored, but also from other Christian traditions.

One of the Barratts' close friends after the Pentecostal revival broke out was grocer Thorvald Plum from Denmark. He published a periodical called *Kirkeklokken* that was very popular among Christians in Denmark, and he supported the revival.[113] Plum also published a large variety of Christian books and Laura started a cooperation with him that spread hundreds of the books in Norway. She advertised and wrote recommendations for them, in addition to her husband's books, in *Byposten*.[114] These were the small beginnings of what eventually became the publishing house *Filadelfiaforlaget*.[115] Many of the books they published were biographies of holy men and women. Laura often came under conviction while reading their stories and prayed for more holiness in her own life. She later wrote: "It is safe to say that our publishing company was started with the aim of spreading scriptural holiness."[116]

---

110. The periodical was named *Korsets Seir* from 1910–1919. The spelling of the last word was changed, and it was afterwards named *Korsets Seier*.

111. Barratt, "Godt Nytaar!," *KS* (January 1, 1910) 1.

112. Ski, et al. *Fram til Urkristendommen*, 2:60; Barratt, "Om Laura Barratt," 3.

113. Bundy, *Visions of Apostolic Mission*, 190–204.

114. Barratt, *Minner*, 93; "Hun var en mor i Israel," *KS* (November 26, 1966) 5.

115. "Hun var en mor i Israel," *KS* (November 26, 1966) 5.

116. Barratt, *Minner*, 93; Lange, "Hjemme hos oss i vekkelsens første tid," *KS* (December 8, 1956) 754, 757; "Laura Barratt—som redaksjonsmedhjelp og ekspeditør," *KS* (December 3, 1949) 596.

In 1910, Laura inspired her husband to write a new hymnal for the Pentecostal revival and she also came up with a name for it: "Maran Ata." Upon his wife's recommendation, Barratt, who also was a musician and song writer, dedicated himself to the task of collecting, translating, and writing new songs.[117] The result was the *Maran Ata* songbook published in 1911, which became an immediate and lasting success.[118] Laura promoted it in *Korsets Seir* and organized the sales. In some ways, she was Barratt's right hand in their publishing endeavors, but she also was a strategist and had her own separate initiatives.[119] Much of the production of literature seems to have been run like a family business, with T. B. Barratt writing and producing much of the content, but with Laura administrating, editing, translating texts, creating ideas, and promoting the content. As one writer says: "She loved to read and had an almost passionate desire to spread good literature [...]. In her and Barratt's many travels around the country she always brought a large and heavy package of books and hundreds of *Korsets Seier* for distribution."[120]

After renaming their periodical Laura and T. B. Barratt also renamed their small publishing company to *Korsets Seir/Seier Forlag*. Laura was the driving force of the company and would often function as "editor, publisher, head of expedition, and sales manager."[121] They ran this privately until the establishment of *Filadelfiaforlaget* in December 1924.[122] With this the Filadelfia church in Christiania formally took ownership of the publishing enterprise and the workload was shared by more people. T. B. Barratt remained the leader of the board until he passed away in 1940, and Laura was a member of the board until she wished to leave the position.[123] Then she continued as an "honorary member" of the board.[124]

---

117. Barratt, *Minner*, 111; Barratt, *Erindringer*, 200.

118. Bloch-Hoell, *Pinsebevegelsen*, 228; Farstad, *Pinsemusikken*, 68. In 1942 it had been published in eight editions.

119. "Laura Barratt—Som redaksjonsmedhjelp og ekspeditør," *KS* (December 3, 1949) 596; Orlien, "Fru Barratt Fyller 80 År," *KS* (November 23, 1946) 750.

120. "Hun var en mor i Israel," *KS* (November 26, 1966) 5.

121. Ski et al., *Fram til Urkristendommen*, 2:129.

122. Østby, "Fra Pastor T. B. Barratts privatforlag til hele pinsevekkelsens fellestiltak," *KS* (December 7, 1974) 5.

123. Østby, "Fra Pastor T. B. Barratts privatforlag," *KS* (December 7, 1974) 5. Their daughter Solveig Barratt Lange became an important contributor at Filadelfiaforlaget.

124. "Hun var en mor i Israel," *KS* (November 26, 1966) 5.

Her important role as a pioneer in Pentecostal publishing was widely acknowledged by the first generations of Pentecostals in Norway.[125]

Laura had from a young age been very interested in foreign mission work. The first Pentecostals in the Barratt-led revival who were "sent out" with a call to missions were the evangelists Dagmar Gregersen and Agnes Thelle.[126] In 1908 they went to the US to study at A. B. Simpson's Missionary School and in 1910 they were sent to India from Norway.[127] Laura accompanied them on the first step of their journey to the US in May 1908, and they set off for England together. More than a thousand people showed up at the harbor to wave goodbye to them.[128] The three women went to Alexander Boddy's conference in Sunderland as Norwegian representatives, and Gregersen and Thelle thereafter went to the US while Laura returned home. Laura kept in close contact with the women through letters while they were in America and in India and published many of their letters in *Byposten* and *Korsets Seir*. She also encouraged people to support them financially and both collected and reported on the donations sent to the missionaries.[129]

From 1910 there were Norwegian Pentecostal missionaries in India, China, Argentina, and South Africa, and the number of candidates and countries steadily increased. In *Korsets Seir* Laura managed the correspondence and published/edited the letters from many of the missionaries in addition to registering the offerings collected for each missionary. She maintained a large correspondence and showed great interest in their work and concern for their well-being and financial situation.[130] This is evident by the many letters published in *Byposten/Korsets Seir* that were addressed to her, as well as the testimonies of early missionaries. Berger Johnsen, who went as a pioneer missionary to Argentina in 1910,

125. Ski, "Verdig feiring av forlagsjubileet," *KS* (December 14, 1974) 8–9; Kornmo, "Filadelfiaforlaget—et Guds Verk gjennom 50 År," *KS* (December 18, 1974) 13; Barratt, "Laura Barratt—som redaksjonsmedhjelp og ekspeditør" *KS* (December 3, 1949) 596; "Hun var en mor i Israel," *KS* (November 26, 1966) 5; Orlien, "Kostelig i Herrens øyne er Hans frommes død: Tale ved Fru Barratts båre av forstander O. Orlien," *KS* (January 27, 1951) 41, 44.

126. See Glenn Gohr and Rakel Ystebø Alegre's chapter on Dagmar Engstrøm and Agnes Thelle Beckdahl.

127. "PYM en misjonsvirksomhet i vekst," *KS* (July 25, 1970) 10; Engstrøm, *Ha Tro Til Gud*, 45, 49.

128. "Fra Kristiania," *Byposten* (May 30, 1908) 43.

129. Engstrøm, "Minneord om fru Laura Barratt," *KS* (February 10, 1951) 66–67.

130. Tollefsen, "Fru Barratts bortgang," *KS* (January 27, 1951) 43; Barratt, "Om Laura Barratt," 3.

highlighted how well Laura received the new young missionaries and encouraged them.[131]

With the rapid increase of foreign missionaries and mission candidates, the early Pentecostals decided to start a missions organization in 1915. At the time there were few Pentecostal churches and both the Barratts and several of the missionaries felt the need for a more organized effort to send out and fund more missionaries.[132] The organization they started was called *Norges Frie Evangeliske Hedningemisjon* (NFEH) and T. B. Barratt was elected chairman, M. H. Sæther treasurer, and Laura Barratt secretary.[133] In this role Laura continued the work she had already started doing with managing correspondence and encouraging people to support the missionaries, in addition to new administrative tasks. She often advocated for missionaries to other Norwegian Pentecostals, actively engaged in fundraising, and encouraged them through letters and prayers.[134] Laura also maintained correspondence and cared for missionaries who were not part of their organization.[135] Parley and Chrissie Gulbrandsen, pioneer missionaries to China, remembered her as a "mother for all of us," and a "spiritual mother" that cared for them.[136] She held the position of missions secretary until 1922 but continued to be actively involved in encouraging and caring for the missionaries after this.[137] Congo-missionary Gunnerius Tollefsen commented that maybe Laura would have become a missionary had she not married Barratt. He believed, however, that she likely did more

---

131. Bratlie, *Pinsevekkelsen i Norge*, 175.

132. Bundy, *Visions of Apostolic Mission*, 315–51.

133. "Missionskonferansen," *KS* (May 15, 1915) 10; Ski, *T. B. Barratt*, 175. The other members of the council were C. M. Seehuus, M. B. Backe, Esther Tellefsen, H. Birkeland, Edw. Gasman, and Aldred Annensen. The organization was originally named *Norges frie evangeliske missionsforbund* but was later renamed after the Mission Covenant Church protested that their name was too similar to theirs.

134. Engstrøm, "Minneord om Fru Laura Barratt," *KS* (February 10, 1951) 66–67; Ski, "Noen minner om Fru Barratt," *KS* (February 17, 1951) 74; Tollefsen, "Fru Barratts bortgang," *KS* (January 27, 1951) 43; Gulbrandsen and Gulbrandsen, "En varm Herrens tjenerinne!," *KS* (January 20, 1951) 27; E. Barratt, "Om Laura Barratt," 3.

135. Tollefsen, "Fru Barratts bortgang," *KS* (January 27, 1951) 43; Bundy, *Visions of Apostolic Mission*, 327.

136. Gulbrandsen and Gulbrandsen, "En Varm Herrens Tjenerinne!" *KS* (January 20, 1951) 27. India-missionary Dagmar Engstrøm called her "a Mother in Israel." Engstrøm, "Minneord Om Fru Laura Barratt," *KS* (February 10, 1951) 66–67.

137. Ski, *T. B. Barratt*, 176.

for foreign missions through her work alongside her husband than if she had become a missionary herself.[138]

By 1929, T. B. Barratt had become convinced that the biblical way to send missionaries was not through a centralized organization but should be the responsibility of local churches. By then there were many more Pentecostal churches, and it was possible for local churches to take over the responsibility for the missionaries. It was also increasingly difficult for the organization to provide funds for the many new missionaries. Many disagreed with T. B. Barratt, but in 1931 the NFEH was dissolved.[139] Most missionaries were able to find a sending church and several additional churches that supported them. The Barratts' Filadelfia church took over the responsibility of a large portion of the missionaries.[140] In 1945 Congo-missionary Gunnerius Tollefsen was elected missionary secretary for the Pentecostal movement. Laura still showed great interest and involvement in foreign missions, often stopping by Tollefsen's office to discuss problems and give him advice.[141] Laura regularly emphasized the important role and work of the female missionaries and seems to have been important as a role model for many of the women who went to the mission field.[142]

THE BARRATTS' SUPPORT FOR WOMEN IN MINISTRY

Laura was from the beginning of the Pentecostal revival a very important support for the female Pentecostal evangelists, preachers, and missionaries and continued to be so until she passed away in 1951.[143] She rejoiced in the work of the "dear evangelist sisters" who would "go to places no one else would go."[144] That Laura and T. B. Barratt supported female ministers

138. Tollefsen, "Fru Barratts bortgang," KS (January 27) 1951, 43.

139. Bundy, *Visions of Apostolic Mission*, 437–45.

140. Bundy, *Visions of Apostolic Mission*, 445.

141. Tollefsen, "Fru Barratts bortgang," KS (January 27, 1951) 43; Barratt "60 år," KS (August 21, 1948) 448; Ski, "Ytremisjonens virksomhet søkes tilrettelagt," KS (July 21, 1945) 209–10.

142. Engstrøm, "Minneord om Fru Laura Barratt," KS (February 10, 1951) 66–67; Ski, "Noen minner om Fru Barratt" KS (February 17, 1951) 74.

143. Schjander, *To liv- to Fedreland*, 45; Ski, "Profiler," KS (June 10, 1948) 337; Barratt, "Bare førti dager til jul," KS (December 2, 1950) 758. In her article she encouraged Pentecostals to send donations to Alma Halse's work at the orphanage and the home for elderly (see chapter on Alma Halse by Kristina Undheim).

144. Barratt, "75 År," 45; Ski, "Profiler," KS (June 10, 1948) 337.

was among other things evident in the publication of enthusiastic texts in *Korsets Seier* on women such as Catherine Booth, Maria Woodworth-Etter, and Aimee Semple McPherson.[145] They both worked to mobilize women as evangelists, preachers, and missionaries, and encouraged the ministries of female pioneers such as Dagmar Gregersen, Agnes Thelle, and Anna Larssen. Their views on women in ministry and roles as spiritual mother and father for many women were likely of great importance for the movement's expansion, especially since the majority of early Pentecostals were women.[146]

Both Laura and T. B. Barratt had an egalitarian view of women in ministry which was influenced by their milieu and upbringing, as well as their experiences in ministry.[147] After they married, T. B. Barratt repeatedly encouraged Laura to preach and lead, saying: "you should not hide away the talents God have given you."[148] Their daughter Solveig Barratt Lange said the children grew up thinking it was "the most natural thing in the world that their mother preached or led a meeting."[149]

In 1933 T. B. Barratt made his views on women in ministry widely known when he published the book *Kvinnens stilling i menigheten* (The Position of Women in the Church). Laura agreed with her husband's arguments for women in ministry, and Martin Ski argues that she was the "driving force in the couple's years-long and highly prominent effort to provide more room for women in the church."[150] In the book T. B. Barratt laid out his (and his wife's) egalitarian views and went through scriptural and rational arguments to support this position.[151] Some of the arguments and interpretations of Bible verses were very similar to those of Fredrik Franson.[152] Most Norwegian Pentecostal men at the time seem to have accepted that women were evangelists, preachers, and missionaries, but

---

145. Bundy, *Visions of Apostolic Mission*, 417–18; "Et brudstykke av Herrens tjenerinde fru Booths liv" *KS* (September 1, 1916) 134–35.

146. Schjander, *To liv- to Fedreland*, 46; Ski, "Profiler," *KS* (June 10, 1948) 337.

147. T. B. Barratt was brought up as a Wesleyan Methodist and very influenced by the Holiness Movement, which had important female leaders such as Catherine Booth, Phoebe Palmer, and Hanna Withall Smith. He also witnessed the strong ministry of his mother, Mary, and the capabilities of his sisters Mary and Louise.

148. Lange, "Barndomsminner," *KS* (July 14–21, 1962) 444.

149. Lange, 444.

150. Ski et al., *Fram til Urkristendommen*, 2:129.

151. Barratt, *Kvinnens Stilling i Menigheten*, 5–38; Alegre, "Women in Pentecostalism in Europe," 268–69.

152. Franson, *Eders døtre skulle profetere*.

many thought women should not be pastors or elders.[153] In his book T. B. Barratt argued that women could hold any position in the church but did not mention the titles of pastor and elder. Martin Ski later claimed that Barratt did in fact believe they could be pastors and elders, but that he may have avoided using the titles to not cause too much controversy.[154]

Laura did not write her own book on her views of women in ministry, but the testimony of various Pentecostal pastors demonstrate that she held the same views as her husband. After T. B. Barratt passed away, the new pastor of the Filadelfia church, Osvald Orlien, said that he many times discussed the role of women with Laura. According to Orlien she "used any occasion she had" to tell the men who took over the leadership after her husband what "the correct view" on women in ministry was.[155] Laura argued that women could be pastors and elders, and that the Pauline verses that were used to argue against this were just a question of semantics: women and men were equal before God.[156] She said women were just as capable as men and would be of great blessing in leadership positions. According to Laura, many intelligent Pentecostal women did not dare to demonstrate their skills and talents since there was no room for them in the movement and they were not allowed to grow.[157] Several of the male Pentecostal ministers in the 1940s considered Laura "radical" in her views on women in ministry. She, on the other hand, accused them of being even more restrictive than the apostle Paul in their views on women.[158] Orlien stated that Laura was the foremost advocate for female ministers in the Pentecostal movement, but explained that they (the male leaders) did not agree with her on the issue of female pastors and elders, though they highly respected her "and admired her zeal."[159]

---

153. Pethrus, "T. B. Barratt—Hövdingen," *KS* (December 8, 1956) 758. It is difficult to assess what most women believed about these issues at the time. Lewi Pethrus mentions that he disagreed with Barratt on several issues and women in ministry was likely one of them. But he said this did not cause division between them and Pethrus considered Barratt one of his best friends.

154. Ski et al., *Fram til Urkristendommen*, 2:9–11; Alegre, "Women in Pentecostalism in Europe," 269.

155. Orlien, "Fru Barratt fyller 80 År," *KS* (November 23, 1946) 751.

156. Schjander, *To Liv- to Fedreland*, 46; Orlien, "Fru Barratt fyller 80 År," *KS* (November 23, 1946) 751.

157. Orlien, "Fru Barratt fyller 80 År," *KS* (November 23, 1946) 751.

158. Schjander, *To Liv- to Fedreland*, 46.

159. Orlien, "Fru Barratt fyller 80 År," *KS* (November 23, 1946) 751; Schjander, *To Liv- to Fedreland*, 46.

In the 1980s there was a new debate on the role of women in the Norwegian Pentecostal movement, and as a part of this, T. B. Barratt's book on women in ministry was republished.[160] In this climate one female minister wrote: "We are many sisters who miss T. B. Barratt and Laura Barratt's attitude towards women."[161] Another female evangelist wrote, "I think the last time I heard someone encourage the sisters among us was in Mrs. Laura Barratt's days. She was very good at this (....) Today we miss sisters that break new ground."[162] The Barratts' view that women could be pastors and elders was not shared by most Norwegian Pentecostals. It also seems that the lack of a strong leader advocating for and encouraging female ministers contributed to the decline of women's role as evangelists and preachers, at least domestically, from the 1940s.

THE BARRATTS' PARTNERSHIP IN MINISTRY AND LAURA'S FINAL YEARS

Laura and T. B. Barratt were partners in ministry from their earliest days at Voss, through their Methodist years in Christiania, and then as Pentecostals. T. B. Barratt highlighted on many occasions Laura's important role and ministry, and how much he valued "the help and blessing he had in her."[163] He said they occasionally disagreed on things but that it "is usually because I do not see things clearly enough," and that his wife was "quite a prophetess."[164] The two had different personalities and strengths, but they shared values and worked as a team.[165] When they started the Methodist diaconal ministry T. B. Barratt was the pastor and Laura was the secretary. When the Pentecostal mission organization NFEH was founded T. B. Barratt was chair of the board and Laura was the secretary. T. B. Barratt was a talented preacher and evangelist and an avid writer in their periodical and of books and music. Laura was strong administratively and she managed many practical affairs such as secretarial work, publishing, advertising, and distribution. Osvald Orlien highlighted

---

160. Alegre, "Women in Pentecostalism in Europe," 271.

161. Kvale, "Barratt, Gilbrant og kvinnen," *KS* (June 4, 1980) 12. Kvale further wrote: "It is difficult to experience the discrimination that characterizes many Pentecostal churches. But after a while one gives up."

162. Frøyshov, "Etterlysning," *KS* (January 16, 1980) 2.

163. Orlien, "Fru Laura Barratts høytidsdag 30. novbr," *KS* (July 12, 1941) 556.

164. Lange, *T. B. Barratt*, 278–79.

165. Ski et al., *Fram til Urkristendommen*, 2.129; Lange, *T. B. Barratt*, 278–79.

Laura's visionary, strategic and "practical" sense, and that she often was the one who first saw how problems could be solved and ministries efficiently built.[166] He also said that she had been interested and involved in all the branches of work of the church and the movement such as "inner mission, foreign mission, nursing home, Sunday school, social relief work, song and music, etc." But her great passion he considered to be the literary and publishing work.[167]

The early Norwegian Pentecostals considered Laura a wise woman with a very good judgment, and her husband had great trust in her assessment and opinions about practical matters.[168] In the Filadelfia church T. B. Barratt was the pastor, but he usually consulted with his wife on all matters of importance. Their daughter Solveig Barratt Lange had heard that if she was not present at a leadership meeting at the Filadelfia church and a decision was taken, "the brothers" would jokingly say "Let's wait to see what Mrs. Barratt says about it."[169] T. B. Barratt always discussed church matters with Laura and if she did not approve of a decision the leaders had made, he did not hesitate to reverse it. On one occasion he asked her from the pulpit if he could preach on the topic of "holiness" that day, and she answered from her seat "Yes, Tom, preach about holiness."[170] Seeing T. B. Barratt consult his wife in front of the large congregation made a strong impression on the young Pentecostals who were present.[171]

The Barratts experienced many trying times in ministry and their personal lives, and they stood together in adversity. The most difficult part of their life was the loss of four of their eight children.[172] One of their close friends, missionary Parley Gulbrandsen, said that the many hardships in their life seemed to have prepared them for the important role they had on the front lines of the (spiritual) battlefield, and highlighted how much they had been able to do together for the Pentecostal

---

166. Orlien, "Fru Barratt hjemme hos Gud," *KS* (January 20, 1951) 26–27.

167. Orlien, "Fru Barratt fyller 80 År," *KS* (November 23, 1946) 750–51.

168. Lange, *T. B. Barratt*, 278–79; Orlien, "Fru Barratt fyller 80 År," *KS* (November 23, 1946) 750.

169. Lange, *T. B. Barratt*, 278–79.

170. Minos, "Hellighet og vekkelse hører sammen," *KS* (March 10, 1973) 2.

171. Minos, "Hellighet og vekkelse hører sammen," *KS* (March 10, 1973) 2.

172. "Pinsemenighetens forstander, Barratt og hans hustru feirer gullbryllup i dag," *Tidens Tegn* (May 10, 1937). The four children they lost were Laura Jacobea (1893–1894), Susanna "Sussie" Wesley (1892–1904), Frances Gullbjørg (1899–1925), and Thomas "Tom" Eivind (1902–1926). The effect the loss of four children had on Laura Barratt will be discussed in a future article.

movement.[173] Several of the Barratts' coworkers and their children also highlighted the domestic felicity that the Barratts seemed to enjoy, and how this helped them persevere in trying times, especially during the strongest opposition against the Pentecostal revival.[174] They were both very fond of their children and each other; and in the storms, they found joy in the simple pleasures of domestic life. Their strong marital bond, unity in the face of adversity, unity on theological issues, and unity of goals made them an effective team and, in many ways, an effective "pastor couple" of their church and the Pentecostal movement in Norway.

T. B. Barratt passed away in 1940, but Laura continued to be actively involved in the church's work, though in a different way. To her great disappointment, the pastors and elders reorganized the leadership structure of the church after Barratt's death and excluded the deacons and deaconesses from the main leadership meetings. This meant that the pastors and elders, who were all male, were now in charge, and women (including Laura) were no more part of the formal leadership of the church.[175] However, Laura's informal influence seems to have remained in the church, and large parts of the Pentecostal movement, both young and old, had great respect for her, even though many had restrictive views on women in ministry.

As the Barratts' children became older Laura started to preach more frequently, especially when she was travelling with her husband. From 1927 to 1928 the couple had a long preaching tour in the US and Canada, and she almost always spoke before her husband entered the pulpit.[176] Her favorite text was Hebrews 3:8, "Jesus Christ is yesterday and today the same, yes forever."[177] Laura preached even more frequently after losing her husband, and "many thought she became better and better the older she got," and that she preached with "fire."[178] The last fifteen years

---

173. Gulbrandsen, "Tale holdt for Gullbrudeparet."

174. Lange, *T. B. Barratt*, 278–79; E. Barratt, "Om Laura Barratt," 2.

175. Ski, *T. B. Barratt*, 201; Ski et al., *Fram til Urkristendommen*, 3:42.

176. Barratt, "Om Laura Barratt," 4. See also Alegre, "Trans-Atlantic Influence from Norway."

177. Orlien, "Fru Barratt hjemme hos Gud," *KS* (January 20, 1951) 26.

178. Orlien, "Fru Barratt fyller 80 År," *KS* (November 23, 1946) 750; Orlien, "Fru Barratt hjemme hos Gud," *KS* (January 20, 1951) 26–27. Her health was frail, and her vision started failing so she could not read anymore, but she would regularly preach "with fire." Orlien also said that hearing her speak at various anniversaries and events was a "great experience" since she remembered so many details of people's families and the events that took place.

of her ministry Laura also dedicated much time to visiting the elderly and sick in the congregation and she was an important force in the establishment of the Filadelfia church's first home for the elderly, which was inaugurated in 1950.[179] Evidence of Laura's continued standing in the church and the movement was seen when she was invited as one of eleven delegates from Norway, and a guest of honor, at the world Pentecostal conference in Switzerland in 1947.[180]

When Laura Barratt passed away on January 6, 1951, the Pentecostals honored her in *Korsets Seier* and with a large funeral at the Filadelfia church. She was buried by her husband's side at the cemetery, *Vår Frelsers gravlund*, in Oslo.[181] At Laura's funeral pastor Osvald Orlien commented on her work and impact at the Filadelfia church and the movement at large:

> Mrs. Barratt has been in the front line the whole time, not just as her husband's companion, but as an active warrior in the Lord's army (. . . .) As the Chief's[182] wife she had a strong indirect influence on the development [. . .] but Mrs. Barratt could not settle for indirect influence, her rich personality had to lead to direct contact and influence (. . . .) With a sound practical perspective on things, a memory without comparison, and a boldness to be envied, she engaged in the tasks that came along. And her name is connected to almost all our branches of activity. She had the perseverance to see many of our endeavors grow and succeed.[183]

FINAL THOUGHTS

Laura Barratt was a gifted woman who had a strong influence on early Norwegian Pentecostalism, and she became known as the most prominent female Pentecostal leader in the country.[184] She was a pioneer in

179. Orlien, "Fru Barratt hjemme hos Gud," *KS* (January 20, 1951) 26–27; Barratt, "Om Laura Barratt," 3; Filadelfia, *Filadelfia Oslo 75 år*, 25.

180. Tollefsen, "Misjonsnytt," *KS* (April 26, 1947) 266; Ski and Orlien, *Kristus eller Kaos*. The world conference in Switzerland in 1947 had the following delegates from Norway: Dagmar Engstrøm, Oddbjøg Tollefsen, Willy Rudolph, Arthur Cornelius, Gunnerius Tollefsen, Laura Barratt, Solveig Barratt Lange, Osvald Orlien, Martin Ski, Leif Joelson, and Grønning.

181. Ski, "Fra Laura Barratts begravelse," *KS* (January 27, 1951) 42–43.

182. In Norwegian: "Høvdingen."

183. Orlien, "Fru Barratt hjemme hos Gud," *KS* (January 20, 1951) 26.

184. Orlien, "Fru Barratt fyller 80 År," *KS* (November 23, 1946) 750–51.

publishing, foreign missions, and Pentecostal church leadership together with her husband. Laura was also a strong supporter of and advocate for women in ministry. The steadfast support for her husband in the face of opposition was key in the first years of the revival, and they both had a strong and lasting impact on the Pentecostal movement in Norway and abroad.

Histories of Norwegian Pentecostalism and biographies about T. B. Barratt sometimes recognize that Laura was her husband's most important coworker, but her contribution has received little attention in recent decades.[185] Osvald Orlien believed that it was difficult to assess if it was T. B. Barratt or Laura that had the most significance for the Norwegian Pentecostal movement, and it seems that the Barratts' contemporaries were much more aware of Laura's important role and work.[186] Several of the Barratts' coworkers believed that if Laura had joined the Salvation Army she would have reached the highest positions, or if she had chosen politics she would have made a strong impact.[187] Laura chose to channel her energy into Pentecostal ministry, and she had a husband who valued her abilities and encouraged her to use them as much as she could. However, the views of women in ministry of other Norwegian Pentecostals frustrated her, and she lamented the restrictions put on women's public ministry.

When couples work together in pioneer ministry, such as in the case of pastors and missionaries, it seems that the husband often is portrayed as the protagonist and the wife as the supporter of his ministry. This way of telling the story can obscure the important role of many female pioneers, whose efforts were recognized in their time but may disappear in the historical narrative. In the case of the Barratts, this may be part of the reason that Laura has received little attention in the historical records. Her husband's legacy is long-lasting due to his important authorship and role as "apostle of Pentecostalism to Europe," but Laura's contribution and work should not be lost or simply attributed to her husband.

---

185. Orlien, "Pastor T. B. Barratt som forkynner og kristen leder," *KS* (July 12, 1991) 17; Ski et al., *Fram Til Urkristendommen*, 2:128–29.

186. Orlien, "Fru Barratt hjemme hos Gud" *KS* (January 20, 1951) 26–27; Ski et al., *Fram Til Urkristendommen*, 2:128–29; Tollefsen, "Fru Barratts bortgang," *KS* (January 27, 1951) 43; Gulbrandsen, "Tale holdt for Gullbrudeparet."

187. Ski, "Profiler" *KS* (June 10, 1948) 337; Orlien, "Kostelig i Herrens øyne er Hans frommes død," *KS* (January 27, 1951) 41, 44.

Laura became a role model for young Norwegian Pentecostal women and a mother figure for both men and women in the movement. In the first decades of Norwegian Pentecostalism a large majority of the adherents were women, and a majority of the evangelists and missionaries were also women. This mobilization of women seems to have had a strong impact on the movement's growth, and while the Barratts were the leaders many women flourished. Telling this part of history is important and demonstrates that women "were central and not peripheral" in the early Norwegian Pentecostal movement.[188]

BIBLIOGRAPHY

Alegre, Rakel Ystebø. "The Pentecostal Apologetics of T. B. Barratt: Defining and Defending the Faith 1906–1909." Virginia Beach, VA: Regent University, 2019.

———. "Trans-Atlantic Influence from Norway on Scandinavian-American Pentecostalism, 1906–1930." In *Revising Pentecostal History: Scandinavian-American Contributions to the Development of Pentecostalism*, edited by Rakel Ystebø Alegre et al. Eugene, OR: Pickwick, 2024.

———. "Women in Pentecostalism in Europe." In *Global Renewal Christianity: Spirit-Empowered Movements Past, Present and Future*, edited by Vinson Synan and Amos Yong, 4:259–73. Lake Mary, FL: Charisma, 2017.

Barratt, Esther. "Om Laura Barratt." Oslo: National Library Barratt archive: Ms.4 3341:X, n.d.

Barratt, Laura. *Minner*. Oslo: Filadelfiaforlaget, 1946.

Barratt, Thomas Ball. *Den kristne daap og hvorfor jeg lot mig døpe*. Kristiania: Korsets Seir, 1915.

———. *Erindringer*. Edited by Solveig Barratt Lange. Oslo: Filadelfiaforlaget, 1941.

———. *Kvinnens Stilling i Menigheten*. Oslo: Filadelfiaforlaget, 1933.

———. *When the Fire Fell, and an Outline of My Life*. Oslo: Alfons Hansen & Sønner, 1927.

Bloch-Hoell, Nils. *Pinsebevegelsen: En undersøkelse av Pinsebevegelsens tilblivelse, utvikling og særpreg med særlig henblikk på bevegelsens utforming i Norge*. Oslo: Universitetsforlaget, 1956.

Bratlie, Josef, ed. *Pinsevekkelsen i Norge gjennem 30 År 1907–1937*. Oslo: Filadelfiaforlaget, 1937.

Bundy, David. *Visions of Apostolic Mission: Scandinavian Pentecostal Mission to 1935*. Uppsala: Uppsala Universitet, 2009.

Centralkirkens Menighet Bergen: 60 Års Jubileum 1890–1950. Bergen: Aron Kallekleivs Trykkeri, 1950.

Chapman, Diana. "The Role of Women in Early Pentecostalism 1907–1914." *Journal of European Pentecostal Theological Association* 28 (2008) 131–44.

Diesen, Ingulf. *Veiryddere*. Oslo: Ansgar, 1980.

---

188. Wacker, "Are the Golden Oldies Still Worth Playing?" 95; Alegre, "Women in Pentecostalism in Europe," 259–60, 272–73.

Engstrøm, Dagmar. *Ha tro til Gud: Alt er mulig for den som tror*. Oslo: Filadelfiaforlaget, n.d.

Farstad, Per Kjetil. *Pinsemusikken: En undersøkelse av norsk pinsebevegelsens sang- og musikkliv 1907-2013*. Cape Town: Portal, 2014.

Gulbrandsen, Parley. "Tale holdt for Gullbrudeparet Pastor T. B. Barratt og frue paa menighetens fest tirsdag 11.Mai 1937." Oslo: National Library Barratt archive: Ms.4 3341:X, 1937.

Filadelfia. *Filadelfia Oslo 75 år*. Oslo, 1991.

Franson, Fredrik. *Eders døtre skulde profetere*. Christiania: Bibelkvindehjemmets, 1890.

Foreign Mission Headquarters. "American Baptist Foreign Mission Society 1930." N.d.: New York, 1930.

Hassing, Arne. *Religion and Power: The Case of Methodism in Norway*. Lake Junaluska, NC: General Commission on Archives and History, The United Methodist Church, 1980.

Lange, Solveig Barratt. *T. B. Barratt: Et Herrens Sendebud*. Oslo: Filadelfiaforlaget, 1962.

Palmqvist, Efraim. *Fredrik Franson*. Oslo: Ansgar, 1948.

Petri, Laura. *Hanna Cordelia Ouchterlony: Banbrytare för Frälsningsarmén i Skandinavien*. Stockholm: Frälsningsarméns Högkvarter, 1962.

Schjander, Fredrik. *To Liv—to fedreland*. Oslo: Rex, 1986.

Ski, Martin. *T. B. Barratt—Døpt i Ånd Og Ild*. Oslo: Filadelfiaforlaget, 1979.

Ski, Martin, et al. *Fram Til Urkristendommen: Pinsevekkelsen Gjennom 50 År. Volume I*. Oslo: Filadelfiaforlaget, 1956.

———. *Fram Til Urkristendommen: Pinsevekkelsen Gjennom 50 År. Volume II*. Oslo: Filadelfiaforlaget, 1957.

———. *Fram Til Urkristendommen: Pinsevekkelsen Gjennom 50 År. Volume III*. Oslo: Filadelfiaforlaget, 1959.

Ski, Martin, and Osvald Orlien. *Kristus eller kaos: Pinsevennenes verdenskonferanse i Sveits 1947*. Oslo: Filadelfiaforlaget, 1947.

Sødal, Helje Kringlebotn. *Norsk Kristendomshistorie 1800-2020: Fra selvsagt tro til mangfold*. Oslo: Cappelen Damm, 2021.

Wacker, Grant. "Are the Golden Oldies Still Worth Playing? Reflections on History Writing among Early Pentecostals." *Pneuma* 8 (1986) 81-100.

Image #4. Dagmar Gregersen Engstrøm and Agnes Thelle Beckdahl.

3

Dagmar Gregersen Engstrøm and Agnes Thelle Beckdahl

Pioneer Evangelists and Missionaries[1]

RAKEL YSTEBØ ALEGRE AND GLENN GOHR

INTRODUCTION

Dagmar Gregersen and Agnes Thelle became known as the "Norwegian sisters" when the young women set out to preach the Pentecostal message in several European countries in 1907 and 1908. They were an inseparable team for several years and two of the most impactful Norwegian Pentecostal pioneers. When T. B. Barratt brought the Pentecostal revival to Christiania (now Oslo), Dagmar and Agnes became two of the first Norwegians to be baptized in the Spirit and speak in tongues and the first evangelists to be sent abroad to spread the Pentecostal message, apart from Barratt.[2] The two women have especially become known for

---

1. This chapter is an edited and expanded version of Glenn Gohr's paper "Agnes Thelle Beckdahl: A Witness of God's Faithfulness in Europe and India." This paper was presented at the 44th Annual Meeting of the Society for Pentecostal Studies in 2015. All translations in this chapter are the authors' own.

2. In addition to T. B. Barratt who preached in Sweden in April/May 1907 and Denmark in June/July 1907, his wife, Laura, accompanied him on parts of these trips.

their role in the beginnings of German Pentecostalism in 1907, but they also had an impact in Switzerland, Denmark, England, Scotland, and the United States in the first years of the revival. Dagmar and Agnes were also the first foreign missionaries to be sent out by the Pentecostals in Norway when they left for India in 1910.[3] Most of their lives would become dedicated to their mission work in India, and the women had a lasting impact in the areas where they ministered.

In this chapter, we will tell the story of how Dagmar Gregersen and Agnes Thelle became Pentecostal evangelists and missionaries and describe their impact on early Pentecostalism in several countries. Pentecostal revivals seemed to follow wherever they went, and they set off "chain reactions" in many places.[4] These women are important examples of the many female evangelists and missionaries who spread the Pentecostal movement in its first decades.[5] By describing their ministry, we wish to shed light on the role of female traveling evangelists and how they sparked revivals and were instrumental in many people's Spirit baptism and healings. To limit the scope of this chapter, the emphasis will primarily be on their pioneer ministry as evangelists and missionaries in the period 1907–1911, spreading Pentecostalism in Europe, the United States, and India. After they became missionaries to India in 1910 both married and changed their names to Dagmar Engstrøm and Agnes Thelle Beckdahl.[6] To avoid confusion and repetition, we will therefore most often refer to them by their first names in this chapter.

DAGMAR'S AND AGNES'S PATHS TO PENTECOSTAL MINISTRY

Dagmar Gregersen was born in Christiania, on December 4, 1881. She was the youngest of seven siblings, and she lost her father at a young age. Gregersen said she had a happy childhood and a strong spiritual mother who took her children to Sunday school in the local Lutheran state church. She was baptized there and was taught about the faith as

---

3. Meier, "Fra Kristiania Til Kassel," 97–104; Nilsen, *Ut i All Verden*, 24–33; Mikaelsson, "Norwegian Pentecostal Foreign Mission," 56–59.

4. For examples of women who spearheaded chain reactions of ministry just after Azusa Street, see Cavaness, "Spiritual Chain Reactions," 24–29.

5. See Alvarsson's "Introduction" in this volume.

6. Dagmar Gregersen married the Norwegian missionary Henrik Engstrøm in 1910 and Agnes Thelle married the Danish missionary Christian Beckdahl in 1915.

a child. Sometimes Dagmar attended the state church, but she said she had not heard messages of the need for personal conversion until she turned nineteen and attended a New Year's Eve meeting at a chapel ("*bedehus*") on December 31, 1899.[7] A Seamen's pastor, Søren Pedersen, had just returned to Norway and was preaching that night. He challenged all present to commit to God before midnight since they did not know if something dramatic would happen and there would be no year 1900. Gregersen fell to her knees and "shouted to the Lord for salvation and liberation."[8] This was her conversion experience, and she became dedicated to the Christian faith.

From then Gregersen was active in different ministerial activities in Christiania. She also studied to become a teacher and obtained a position as a teacher in the city. To keep her position as a teacher, she had to remain a member of the Lutheran State Church. When Laura and T. B. Barratt started the Christiania City Mission in 1904, she joined the mission and could do so without leaving the state church.[9] When T. B. Barratt decided to build a building for the mission and embarked on his fundraising tour in the United States from 1905–1906, Gregersen assisted Laura in different tasks such as publishing the Barratts' periodical *Byposten*. She was an active coworker in the City Mission when Barratt returned with the Pentecostal message from New York in December 1906.[10]

Agnes Nikola Thelle was born on September 27, 1876, at Andøya, an island near Kristiansand off the Southern coast of Norway.[11] Her father, Carl Thelle, was a sea captain on a whaling ship, and he died soon after she was born. Agnes and her brothers and sisters were left solely in the care of their mother. According to her own account, Agnes was dedicated to her belief in God and the church from an early age but gave less importance to the faith in her teen years.

At age twenty, Agnes had two spiritual experiences that impacted her strongly. Her account of this was as follows: on Sunday, November 16, 1896, she went to church where the sermon had been on the separating

---

7. Engstrøm, *Ha tro til Gud*, 13; NRK, "Dagmar Engstrøm." The chapel was on *Teatergata 12* but was later demolished.

8. Engstrøm, *Ha tro til Gud*, 14.

9. Engstrøm, "Opplevelser og minner fra 1906–1907," *KS* (December 8, 1956) 752; Breistein, *Har staten bedre borgere?* 85–86.

10. Engstrøm, "Opplevelser og minner fra 1906–1907," *KS* (December 8, 1956) 752. See Rakel Ystebø Alegre's chapter on Laura Barratt.

11. Spence, *On the Borders of Nepal*, 4.

of the sheep from the goats. After the meeting, while she was sitting at the dinner table, she had a vision.[12] In this vision, she saw herself standing atop a high mountain and Jesus on top of another mountain peak. There was a deep chasm between them. Immediately she dropped her eating utensils and cried out in a loud voice, "Oh mother, I am lost, forever lost." Her mother brought the Bible and read her the story of the prodigal son. This seemed to calm her fears. That evening she attended a young people's meeting where the message was about Jesus being "the Way, the Truth, and the Life." Agnes then whispered, "Jesus, I accept you as my Way, my Truth, and my Life," and this became a definite conversion experience for her.[13] Agnes would later as a Pentecostal frequently speak of having visions.

The following Sunday, Agnes went to another young people's meeting, and as she sat and listened to the message, she wrote that someone saw a large tongue of fire descending upon her. From that point on, she decided she would enter full-time ministry. Agnes heard several missionaries speak during this time, and she started to feel a strong urge to go to the mission field. However, the following ten years she continued to stay at home, where she worked as a milliner, and she doubted she could ever become a missionary.[14] Her health was fragile, and she questioned how she could preach since she was a woman. Agnes described her struggle with her calling during these years in the following way:

> The enemy always brought before me my weak body and that God does not use women to preach on the foreign field, "so do not talk about your call to anybody." This was a great hindrance in my young Christian life. However, it was the lack of spiritual light in teaching those days.[15]

In 1906, Thelle finally decided to leave her home to serve full-time in Christian ministry. In December she moved to Christiania to help in a slum mission and jail services in the city, and she studied at a Bible School.[16] It was during this time that she heard Barratt speak about Spirit baptism and became part of the Pentecostal revival.

---

12. Beckdahl, *Witness*, 2.
13. Beckdahl, *Witness*, 3.
14. Beckdahl, *Witness*, 4.
15. Beckdahl, *Witness*, 4.
16. It is not clear whether the mission where she served in December 1906 was connected to the Barratts' City Mission.

Right before Christmas, 1906, Agnes Thelle went to a meeting at the Barratts' City Mission. It was a gathering where they distributed clothes to poor children, and she had felt God tell her to go there to donate some money. T. B. Barratt had just come home from America and was speaking.[17] She writes the following about the meeting:

> There I heard a powerful testimony about the victory on Calvary, and as I sat and listened, the Spirit said to me, "This is the full Gospel which you hear, and there is power in the blood to live an overcoming life." I went home to my room and believed that the promise of the Father was for me to receive power from on high for service.[18]

Agnes then prayed and "tarried" for ten days. During these ten days, she had several experiences. She felt her calling to missions renewed and she said she would go "even if it means to go to the darkest corner of the earth."[19] One day while she was reading the Bible, she came under conviction that her infant baptism was not enough and that she had to be baptized with full immersion. She was soon baptized. Agnes also writes that she experienced healing of digestive problems, something she had prayed for to enable her to eat anything on the mission field.[20] After ten days she writes she was baptized in the Spirit and spoke in tongues at a small prayer meeting. She also had a vision of herself preaching the gospel to a crowd of "brown faces on the missions field."[21] To Agnes Thelle the gift of the Holy Spirit gave her a new courage that enabled her to speak freely to everyone about Christ.[22] She continued to seek God, and in the Barratts' mission, on March 14, 1907, she again sensed a calling to become a missionary and that she was supposed to go to India.[23]

Dagmar Gregersen had already been a part of the City Mission for a while when T. B. Barratt came home with the Pentecostal message. She participated in all the early Pentecostal meetings and saw children, youth, and the elderly be baptized in the Spirit and speak in tongues. She observed that many fell to the floor and that several were convicted of

17. Bloch-Hoell, *Pinsebevegelsen,* 140–41; Barratt, *Erindringer,* 134.
18. Beckdahl, *Witness,* 5.
19. Beckdahl, *Witness,* 6.
20. Beckdahl, *Witness,* 10. She writes that a young girl who had prayed for many that had been healed was led to her house and came in and prayed for her.
21. Beckdahl, *Witness,* 8.
22. Beckdahl, *Witness,* 10–11.
23. Beckdahl, letter to Foreign Missions Department, Assemblies of God.

their sins and repented.[24] After three weeks of witnessing this, she studied the baptism in the Spirit in the Bible and prayed to God to show her if this really was his work. She became convinced that it was and started "tarrying" for the Spirit baptism. The following days she felt the "blood of Jesus Christ the Son of God cleansed me from all sin," which she described as a powerful experience of sanctification.[25] On January 26, 1907, Dagmar went to a Barratt-led revival meeting in Christiania and had an overwhelming experience of Spirit Baptism. Gregersen writes that she fell to the floor and that "a strong power fell over me and I started to scream and shout to the Lord."[26] She lay for a while on the floor in peace, then rose and danced and celebrated. To Dagmar, it was like she was intoxicated and she spoke in what she believed were several different languages. The experience was transformational, and she now felt a "fire in her heart" that did not cease.[27]

Though the timeline is a bit unclear, it seems it was either during these early weeks of the Pentecostal revival or the following year that Dagmar felt a calling to foreign missions. In addition to the public meetings, the early Pentecostals in Christiania held many smaller prayer meetings in different homes, and according to Dagmar, the following happened at one of these prayer meetings: "A young sister came under the power of the Spirit and shouted out while under prophetic inspiration: 'Dagmar, Dagmar, I send you to the dark place Banda.'"[28] Gregersen felt this as a direct call from God and decided to become a missionary to Banda. However, she did not know where it was, and none of the people she asked knew either. Dagmar then decided to visit her cousin Kinni Gundersen, who had a great interest in foreign missions, to tell her about her new calling. Her cousin had prayed for a while that God would show her a mission in India that she could pray for. She also had an encyclopedia and there she found an entry on the place called Banda. It said that Banda was a district in Northern India with about one million inhabitants. The young women

---

24. Engstrøm, *Ha tro til Gud*, 17.
25. Engstrøm, *Ha tro til Gud*, 17.
26. Engstrøm, *Ha tro til Gud*, 18.
27. Engstrøm, *Ha tro til Gud*, 18.
28. Engstrøm, *Ha tro til Gud*, 16. In a later article in *KS* Dagmar writes that she received this message during Christmas 1907. So, this prophecy could have been given one year later. D. Engstrøm, "Indien" *KS* (September 1, 1911) 134.

then laughed and cried, and they took the incident as a confirmation that Dagmar was to become a missionary in Banda, India.[29]

Like Agnes, Dagmar after some time concluded that her baptism as an infant was not biblical, and she decided to be baptized with full immersion. In June of 1907, she and thirty-eight others were baptized at Holmsbu. Since she now had become a "dissenter," she lost her job as a teacher.[30] In retrospect she believed this was when she learned that she should only depend on God and his provision in her life.[31]

SPREADING THE PENTECOSTAL REVIVAL IN EUROPE IN 1907

News of the Pentecostal revival in Christiania spread nationally and internationally in January 1907. This led several pastors from Sweden, Denmark, Germany, and England to visit the city and decide to become Pentecostals.[32] Dagmar and Agnes had both become "bold witnesses" after their Spirit Baptism and they were active participants in the meetings. One of the foreign visitors was the German Lutheran Emil Meyer. He was the leader of the *Hamburger Strandmission* (Hamburg Beachmission) and he came to Norway in May 1907.[33] Dagmar writes that Meyer heard her speak in German at a meeting and was surprised to later learn that she did not know the language.[34] When he asked T. B. Barratt to send Pentecostal evangelists from Christiania to Germany, it was decided that Agnes Thelle and Dagmar Gregersen would be the ones to go. Both women felt this was a call from God and they set out for Germany in late June 1907.[35] There they became known, and referred to, as "the

---

29. Engstrøm, *Ha tro til Gud*, 16. The information on inhabitants in Banda was likely incorrect.

30. Engstrøm, *Ha tro til Gud*, 19; NRK "Dagmar Engstrøm"; Breistein, *Har staten bedre borgere?*, 85; Mikaelsson, "Norwegian Pentecostal Foreign Mission," 58.

31. Engstrøm, *Ha tro til Gud*, 18–19. She spoke with Erik Andersen Nordquelle about the baptism before making her decision.

32. Bloch-Hoell, *Pinsebevegelsen*, 268; Alegre, *Apologetics of T. B. Barratt*, 84–85; Bundy, *Visions of Apostolic Missions*, 176–78, 190.

33. Alegre, *Apologetics of T. B Barratt*, 101–2; Meier, "Fra Kristiania Til Kassel," 96–97; Barratt, *Erindringer*, 148; Bundy, *Visions of Apostolic Missions*, 204–5.

34. Engstrøm, *Ha tro til Gud*, 23.

35. Engstrøm, *Ha tro til Gud*, 23; Meier, "Fra Kristiania til Kassel," 97; Beckdahl, *Witness*, 11–12.

Norwegian sisters."[36] Dagmar Gregersen, Agnes Thelle, and T. B. Barratt became the first Norwegians who were part of the revival in Christiania to travel abroad to spread the Pentecostal message.[37]

When Dagmar and Agnes arrived in Hamburg, they immediately started speaking about the Pentecostal message at Emil Meyer's mission. One of the leaders at the mission, Anna,[38] spoke Danish and therefore became the translator for the Norwegian evangelists. According to Agnes, their interpreter was a nurse.[39] Dagmar and Agnes believed they could not have an interpreter who was not baptized in the Spirit and told Anna this. According to Dagmar, she responded: "I want all that the Lord has for his people. Pray for me!" After three days Anna and two other women were baptized in the Spirit and spoke in tongues, and Dagmar believed that they were the first to have this experience in Germany.[40]

At the meetings at Meyer's mission, Agnes and Dagmar preached, prayed, spoke in tongues, interpreted messages in tongues, prophesied, and prayed with people for healing and Spirit baptism.[41] One night in Hamburg, Agnes writes that she sang in tongues in German and that a man listening to her declared, "This Norwegian sister who has just come amongst us does not know the German language, so I am convinced from this moment that this work is of God."[42] While the women were in Hamburg, Meyer had a large meeting to inaugurate a new building. Many ministers were in the city for a conference and came to the inauguration. There they heard Dagmar and Agnes speak and several were baptized in the Spirit.[43]

---

36. Simpson, "Pentecostal and Charismatic Movements in the Germanic Countries," 62–63; Simpson, *Revered and Reviled*, 118; Alegre, *Apologetics of T. B Barratt*, 103. Sometimes they are also referred to as "The Norwegian ladies," see Röckle and Kay, "Born in Difficult Times," 2–4.

37. Barratt, *Erindringer*, 164.

38. In some source her last name is said to be Smith, while in others Albrechtsen.

39. Beckdahl, *Witness*, 14.

40. Engstrøm, *Ha tro til Gud*, 24, 29; Gregersen and Thelle "Ilden er faldt i Tyskland," *Byposten* (July 13, 1907) 66; Gregersen and Thelle, "Ilden falder vedblivende i Tyskland," (*Byposten*, July 27, 1907) 68.

41. Engstrøm, *Ha tro til Gud*, 25; Beckdahl, *Witness*,14–15; Gregersen and Thelle "Ilden er faldt i Tyskland," *Byposten* (July 13, 1907) 66. Engstrøm and Beckdahl said they were part of a conference, and many leaders came from different parts of Northern Germany to the meetings in Hamburg.

42. Beckdahl, *Witness*,13.

43. Gregersen and Thelle, "Ilden falder vedblivende i Tyskland," *Byposten* (July 27, 1907) 68.

At their meetings in Hamburg Agnes and Dagmar met the Lutheran evangelist Heinrich Dallmeyer.[44] According to Agnes, Dallmeyer was "cleansed" (sanctified), healed, and baptized in the Spirit at the meetings and was fascinated by the women and their gift of speaking in tongues and interpretation.[45] Dallmeyer then invited the "Norwegian sisters" to come with him to the city of Kassel and hold meetings with him there. Beginning on Sunday, July 7, daily meetings were held in the temperance hall of a large Christian Teetotal Society, the *Blaukreuzhaus* (Blue Cross House), in Kassel.[46]

Agnes and Dagmar wrote that they had "powerful" meetings in Kassel and that the Holy Spirit "fell like lightning."[47] According to the women's testimony, people in the assembly were strongly "touched" by the Holy Spirit.[48] Dagmar claimed that at one meeting fifteen people fell to the ground and all started speaking in tongues at the same time.[49] The revival started to attract crowds, and according to Dagmar, many were baptized in the Spirit and spoke in tongues, and some received the gift of prophecy.[50] She also wrote that she had "had never witnessed something as wonderful" as the revival meetings in Kassel.[51] The "Norwegian sisters" stayed in Dallmeyer's home and seem to have had a good partnership with him, and many conversations with him and other ministers around the breakfast table.[52]

In the beginning, the local newspapers and Christian periodicals in general reported favorably of their meetings in Kassel. As the news spread, German holiness pastors and evangelists arrived from many parts of Germany to observe the meetings.[53] One evening Agnes and Dagmar

---

44. Meier, "Fra Kristiania til Kassel," 97–98; Beckdahl, *Witness,* 13–14.

45. Beckdahl, *Witness,* 13–15; Gregersen and Thelle, "Ilden er faldt i Tyskland," *Byposten* (July 13, 1907) 66.

46. Meier, "Fra Kristiania til Kassel," 97–98; Simpson, *Revered and Reviled,* 118.

47. Engstrøm, *Ha tro til Gud,* 25–27; Beckdahl, *Witness,* 15–16; Gregersen and Thelle, "Ilden falder vedblivende i Tyskland," *Byposten* (July 27, 1907) 68.

48. Engstrøm, *Ha tro til Gud,* 25–27; Beckdahl, *Witness,* 15–16; Gregersen and Thelle, "Ilden falder vedblivende i Tyskland," *Byposten* (July 27, 1907) 68.

49. Engstrøm, *Ha tro til Gud,* 26; Gregersen, "Guds ild falder i Tyskland," *Byposten* (August 10, 1907) 71.

50. Engstrøm, *Ha tro til Gud,* 26; Beckdahl, 15–16; Gregersen, "Guds ild falder i Tyskland," *Byposten* (August 10, 1907) 71–72.

51. Gregersen, "Guds ild falder i Tyskland," *Byposten* (August 10, 1907) 71–72.

52. Gregersen, "Guds ild falder i Tyskland," *Byposten* (August 10, 1907) 72.

53. Alegre, *Apologetics of T. B Barratt,* 103; Meier, "Fra Kristiania til Kassel," 97–98.

entered and saw many of the German Holiness leaders there. The young women felt nervous and intimidated. Agnes wrote:

> Sister Dagmar and I said to each other, "Now it is with us as it was with Luther in Worms; we can only say, God help us, Amen." He Himself will advance His own cause. "But God hath chosen the foolish things of the world to confound the wise, and God hath chosen the weak things which are mighty."[54]

According to the women, some prominent Christian leaders accepted their message and sought the baptism in the Spirit, and they rejoiced in this.[55] However, criticism and opposition against the meetings soon emerged and came from both the secular press and leaders within the German Holiness Movement (*Geimenschaftbewegung*).[56] Some of the German Holiness leaders who visited the meetings started to warn strongly against the Pentecostal revival and the "Norwegian sisters" in publications. This was especially the case with Elias Schrenk, who first had assessed the meetings and the message of Spirit Baptism positively.[57] Dagmar and Agnes told the readers of *Byposten* that he was shaking at one of the meetings in Kassel.[58] Schrenk and others soon argued that the meetings were under the influence of "a lying spirit," and after a few months, many German Christians turned against the Pentecostal revival in Kassel.[59]

Dagmar and Agnes believed that the revival in Kassel had started well, but that problems and excesses emerged. They experienced increased criticism and mockery from the press and the crowds who gathered at their meetings.[60] The women argued that the primary cause of

---

Simpson, *Revered and Reviled*, 120–21. Among the leaders in the *Geimeinschaftbewegung* that came were Theodor Haarbeck and Elias Schrenk.

54. Beckdahl, *Witness*, 15; Gregersen and Thelle, "Ilden falder vedblivende i Tyskland," *Byposten* (July 27, 1907) 68.

55. Beckdahl, *Witness*, 15–16; Gregersen, "Guds ild falder i Tyskland," *Byposten* (August 10, 1907) 71.

56. Meier, "Fra Kristiania Til Kassel," 100–104; Alegre, *Apologetics of T. B Barratt*, 102–5; Beckdahl, *Witness*, 17–18; Thelle and Gregersen, "Fra Zürich," *Byposten* (August 24, 1907) 76.

57. Gregersen and Thelle, "Ilden falder vedblivende i Tyskland," *Byposten* (July 27, 1907) 68.

58. Gregersen, "Guds ild falder i Tyskland," *Byposten* (August 10, 1907) 71.

59. Meier, "Fra Kristiania Til Kassel," 97–104; Alegre, *Apologetics of T. B Barratt*, 104–7; Simpson, *Revered and Reviled*, 121–23; Schrenk, *Was Lehrt Uns Die Kasseler Bewegung*.

60. Beckdahl, *Witness*, 17; Simpson, *Revered and Reviled*, 121–23.

the excesses was that Heinrich Dallmeyer "failed to keep things under control."[61] They objected against what they considered his lack of spiritual discernment and leadership. Apparently Agnes and Dagmar decided to withdraw from the meetings because Dallmeyer did not intervene to keep unspiritual influences in check.[62] They left Germany and went to Switzerland, where they had been invited to Zurich, while Dallmeyer continued the meetings in Kassel.

The meetings in Kassel were eventually shut down by the police on August 2, 1907.[63] Many German Holiness leaders thereafter spoke strongly against the revival at Kassel and the Pentecostal movement at large. This culminated in the Berlin Declaration in 1909, where it was declared that the revival at Kassel and Grossalmerode came "from below."[64] Sommer Gottfried summarizes one of the objections against the Pentecostal revival in the declaration as follows: "The evil spirit's primary entry point are prophecies, which gradually seek to replace Scripture. What makes matters worse: these prophetic words are given mainly by women, who usurp authority over men."[65] The authors of the Berlin Declaration pointed out that they believed the role women had in the Pentecostal revival was unbiblical and listed this as further evidence that the movement was not from God.[66] Among the leaders in the *Gemeinschaftbewegung* there had been mixed assessments of the ministry of Agnes and Dagmar. During the Kassel revival, several had viewed them in a positive light as godly and sober witnesses who were ministering

61. Meier, "Fra Kristiania til Kassel," 99; Alegre, *Apologetics of T. B Barratt*, 103; Barratt, "I Tyskland," *Byposten* (January 15, 1909) 8; Barratt, "Lidt lys," *Byposten* (January 25, 1908) 7–8. This was also T. B. Barratt's view of the situation. Carl Simpson also agrees with this assessment and writes that the women tried to guide Dallmeyer. Simpson, *Revered and Reviled*, 122.

62. Meier, "Fra Kristiania til Kassel," 98–99; Giese, 67. See also Hollenweger, *Pentecostals*, 223.

63. Meier, "Fra Kristiania til Kassel," 98.

64. Alegre, *Apologetics of T. B Barratt*, 256–59; Meier, "Fra Kristiania til Kassel," 101–5. Examples of critical texts are: Dallmeyer, *Satan Unter Den Heiligen* and Schrenk, *Was Lehrt Uns Die Kasseler Bewegung*.

65. Gottfried "Pentecostalism in Germany," 114–15.

66. Meier, "Fra Kristiania til Kassel," 97–105; Simpson, *Revered and Reviled*, 374;Alegre, *Apologetics of T. B Barratt*, 258. The declaration commented concerning prophetic messages: "In the manner of their transmission they are very similar to the messages of Spiritualist Mediums. Mostly the messengers are women. This has led to women, even young girls, taking on leadership roles in many places within the Movement, against the clear teaching of Scripture." Quote from Berlin Declaration in Simpson, *Revered and Reviled*, 374.

after a biblical pattern, but after some time many started warning against the two Norwegian women.[67]

Heinrich Dallmeyer also soon turned against the revival he had first led and declared he had been deceived by a "lying spirit."[68] This caused Dagmar and Agnes great pain, and they believed he had done so due to strong pressure from German Holiness leaders and under the threat of losing his income.[69] Even though the revival at Kassel ended and became controversial, it continued to be considered as the great catalyst for the Pentecostal revival in Germany.[70] The role of Dagmar and Agnes played in this was widely recognized by many German Pentecostals.[71] When the German Pentecostal movement celebrated its seventieth anniversary in 1977 the then ninety-six-year-old Dagmar Gregersen was invited to the conference as a speaker and guest of honor.[72]

Following their meetings in Germany, Agnes and Dagmar went to Zurich, Switzerland. A small group of people interested in the Pentecostal revival had invited them and they arrived on August 2, 1907.[73] While they had ministered among Lutherans in Germany, the group that invited them to Zurich according to Dagmar called themselves "Dowie's Followers."[74] The women had not heard about John Alexander Dowie and were initially a bit skeptical. But they found a community that longed for a new revival and that wanted to know if it was true that Christians could speak in tongues as on the day of Pentecost. Their translator from Germany, Anna, accompanied them and she also spoke to the group of her own experiences and gave messages in tongues.[75]

The women's meetings in Zurich attracted many people and according to Dagmar a revival started, and many were saved and baptized

---

67. Meier, "Fra Kristiania til Kassel," 99–100.

68. Giese, *Und flicken die Netze*, 209–10; Penn-Lewis, "The Hour of Peril," *The Christian* (January 9, 1908) 12; Alegre, *Apologetics of T. B Barratt*, 121–22.

69. Engstrøm, *Ha tro til Gud*, 31–32; Mikaelsson, "Norwegian Pentecostal Foreign Mission," 57.

70. Meier, "Fra Kristiania Til Kassel," 95–105.

71. Sommer, "Pentecostalism in Germany," 113; Röckle and Kay, "Born in Difficult Times," 3; Schmidgall, *European Pentecostalism*, 126–27; Simpson, *Revered and Reviled*, 118–23; Meier, "Fra Kristiania Til Kassel," 95–105.

72. Engstrøm, *Ha tro til Gud*, 143.

73. Bundy, *Visions of Apostolic Missions*, 219.

74. Engstrøm, *Ha tro til Gud*, 28.

75. Engstrøm, *Ha tro til Gud*, 29.

in the Spirit.[76] Some also experienced healing, and several would fall to the ground or jump for joy. The Swiss that became Pentecostals during these meetings came from different church backgrounds, and during Dagmar and Agnes's three-week stay "they laid the foundation for the first Pentecostal church in Switzerland."[77] According to Dagmar the group was no longer a "Dowie" congregation when they left and later became a Pentecostal church.[78] However, in the community there also arose some confusion and hesitation about the "Norwegian sisters" and the Pentecostal revival. They had started to hear the claims from voices in Germany declaring that the revival was from the devil, and seemed to especially have been affected by the critique of the Swiss Holiness preacher Otto Stockmayer.[79] T. B. Barratt visited the community several times later and was instrumental in appointing leadership at the church and guiding them in the face of opposition.[80] The Pentecostals in Switzerland still trace their origins to the arrival of Dagmar Gregersen and Agnes Thelle in Zurich in 1907.[81]

After Dagmar and Agnes's stay in Switzerland they briefly returned to Germany, but soon had to leave due to the rising opposition against the Kassel revival.[82] They continued to Copenhagen, Denmark, where they arrived on September 3, 1907.[83] They were received at the train station by several of T. B. Barratt's supporters in the country: merchant Thorvald Plum, Lutheran pastor H. J. Mygind, Mr. and Mrs. Rasmussen, and a Mrs. Hansen.[84] Mygind was a missionary in Syria and F. Rasmussen was the editor of a widely distributed Christian periodical named

---

76. Engstrøm, *Ha tro til Gud*, 27–30; Bundy, *Visions of Apostolic Missions*, 219–21; Plüs, "Swiss Pentecostals," 99; "Ilden er faldt i Zürich, Sveitz," *Byposten* (September 7, 1907) 80–81.

77. Plüss, *Vom Geist bewegt*.

78. Engstrøm, *Ha tro til Gud*, 30.

79. Bundy, *Visions of Apostolic Missions*, 219–21; Alegre, *Apologetics of T. B Barratt*, 198–201.

80. Bundy, *Visions of Apostolic Missions*, 220–21; Alegre, *Apologetics of T. B Barratt*, 198–201.

81. Simpson, "Pentecostal and Charismatic Movements in the Germanic Countries," 80–81; Schmidgall, 154–55; Plüss, "Swiss Pentecostals," 99.

82. Engstrøm, *Ha tro til Gud*, 31–32; "Iden er faldt i Zürich, Sveitz," *Byposten* (September 7, 1907) 80–81.

83. Christensen, *Unorganized Religion*, 62.

84. Engstrøm, *Ha tro til Gud*, 33.

Kirkeklokken.⁸⁵ They all gathered in Rasmussen's home, and they were eating when Mrs. Hansen suddenly started speaking in tongues. Dagmar writes that she interpreted what Mrs. Hansen said. It was a message for Mygind to encourage him in his missionary work, but also a message to all of them "to stand firm in the belief in the *power of God and victory*."⁸⁶ According to Dagmar the following happened thereafter:

> [. . .] pastor Mygind stood up and said: "Tonight the Lord has convinced me that this revival is from him. I have had so many doubts when I have seen the outer manifestations and have been thinking to withdraw from it all. But friends, Mrs Hansen spoke perfect and fluently in the Syrian language, and sister Dagmar interpreted it so correctly and word-by-word that if I had tried to translate it myself it wouldn't have been as perfect. Pray for me and that I will receive this gift of the Spirit!" For me it was overwhelming that the gift of interpretation had been tested and was shown to be real.⁸⁷

While in Copenhagen, the Danish Pentecostals arranged for Agnes and Dagmar to hold several meetings, among others at the large concert hall *Koncertpalæet* on October 6, 1907. The reports from the women's meetings in Copenhagen were varied, as they had been in Germany, and some controversy arose over their ministry.⁸⁸ After their meetings they returned to Norway where they continued to minister at meetings in Christiania. The ladies became some of Laura and T. B. Barratt's closest coworkers in the revival, and they became well-known preachers and evangelists among early European Pentecostals.⁸⁹

MINISTRY WHILE PREPARING FOR FOREIGN MISSIONS

After Agnes and Dagmar's preaching tour in Europe, they felt it was time to prepare to become missionaries. Both sensed a call to India, and they

---

85. Bundy, *Visions of Apostolic Missions*, 190–91. Rasumussen and Mygind had visited Barratt and the revival in Christiania in the spring of 1907.

86. Engstrøm, *Ha tro til Gud*, 33.

87. Engstrøm, *Ha tro til Gud*, 33; Christensen, *Unorganized Religion*, 85–86.

88. Christensen, *Unorganized Religion*, 62–63; Bundy, *Visions of Apostolic Missions*, 195–96, 202–3.

89. "The Whitsuntide Conference," *Confidence* (June 30, 1908) 5. Barratt later went to visit and minister in the places Agnes and Dagmar had preached and kept especially a close connection to the Pentecostals in Switzerland and Denmark. Bundy, *Visions of Apostolic Missions*, 189–204, 219–21. See also Christensen, *Unorganized Religion*.

decided to continue their partnership in ministry. The young women wished to prepare for the mission field by studying at A. B. Simpson's Missionary Training Institute in Nyack, New York.[90] In addition to classes in missions and theology Dagmar and Agnes both needed to study English. In the Northeast, there were large Norwegian communities, especially in Brooklyn, and the women had family and friends in the region.[91] There were also several Norwegian-American Pentecostal communities that would receive the women with open arms. Pentecostals in Norway started to raise funds for Dagmar and Agnes, who became their two first missionary candidates. However, the funds that came in were small and sporadic in the beginning and the women set out for the mission school in the United States in faith that God would provide the money they needed along the way.[92]

In April 1908, Agnes and Dagmar left Norway together with Laura Barratt, who accompanied them on the first leg of their journey to England. More than a thousand people came to the harbor to wave farewell to them as they embarked on their journey.[93] The three women were on their way to Sunderland, England, to participate in Alexander Boddy's first international Pentecostal "Whitsunday Conference."[94] At Monkwearmouth in Sunderland Agnes, Dagmar, and Laura Barratt stayed with Alexander and Mary Boddy and took part in special meetings held at All Saints' Church.[95]

90. Engstrøm, *Ha tro til Gud,* 38–46; Beckdahl, *Witness,* 33; Barratt, *When the Fire Fell,* 101; "Fra Kristiania: Søstrenes Gregersen og Thelles afsked," *Byposten* (May 30, 1908) 43–44. This may have been on T. B. Barratt's recommendation since he knew the school well after his stay at A. B. Simpson's mission home in 1906.

91. Engstrøm, *Ha tro til Gud,* 38–46. See also, Alegre, "Transatlantic Influence."

92. Engstrøm, *Ha tro til Gud,* 38–39; Bundy, *Visions of Apostolic Missions,* 237; Barratt, *When the Fire Fell,* 200. See Bundy, *Visions of Apostolic Missions,* for more on the "faith mission" philosophy and practice of early Norwegian Pentecostal missionaries.

93. "Fra Kristiania: Søstrenes Gregersen og Thelles afsked," *Byposten* (May 30, 1908) 43–44.

94. "The Whitsuntide Conference," *Confidence* (June 30, 1908) 4–5, 8. Whitsunday is the name of a church celebration in the British Isles. It is equivalent to Pentecost Sunday. This was the first of the Sunderland International Conventions hosted by A. A. Boddy. Approximately 120 visitors from abroad attended. T. B. Barratt did not participate this year because he was in India. His five-month-long stay in India in 1908 would also prepare the way for Agnes and Dagmar to arrive and be welcomed by other Pentecostal ministers and missionaries there.

95. "The Whitsuntide Conference," *Confidence* (June 30, 1908) 4–11, 15–22; Barratt, "Konferensen i Sunderland," *Byposten* (June 27, 1908) 50–51; Thelle and Gregersen, "Kjære venner!" *Byposten* (June 13, 1908) 45–46.

Agnes and Dagmar participated actively in several of the meetings at the conference and they sang, gave testimonies, spoke of their visions and dreams, prophesied, spoke in tongues with interpretation, prayed for people, and were part of conversations on different topics.[96] An account of this was recorded in Boddy's Pentecostal periodical *Confidence*, and it gives us a sense of what their preaching and practices were like as early traveling Pentecostal evangelists. The women's interpreter for the conference was Mrs. Beruldsen from Scotland. In one meeting Agnes said that she in a vision had seen stars in the sky form into a circle with the capital letters "V. V" in the center.[97] Then it was revealed to her that the letters "V. V" stood for "*Verdens Vaekkelse*," which in Norwegian means "Worldwide Revival." She had also seen an angelic figure appear saying: "Victory, Victory, Victory," and then Jesus himself came near with the message: "Behold, I come quickly, hold fast that thou hast, that no man take thy crown."[98] The day after her vision she sensed the Lord gave her the following message to the church:

> The Spirit saith to the Churches: As heaven was near the earth, revealed in the vision, so near is My coming, saith the Lord. Never has the Spirit been poured out on the whole earth as in these days; therefore, stand together as one band, that ye may be found ready when I come. I am coming soon.[99]

At another meeting, both Dagmar and Agnes talked about their visions and dreams, and then Agnes gave a message in tongues. This was interpreted by Dagmar into Norwegian and then by Mrs. Beruldsen into English. A part of that message was as follows: "The Lord shall be your Star, and you shall walk in His Light. Let your Light be shining, then the darkness will go because of the Light. VICTORY, VICTORY—This I give to everyone that trusts in ME."[100] Their messages at the conference were

---

96. "The Whitsuntide Conference," *Confidence* (June 30, 1908) 4–5, 8; "Whit-Sunday," *Confidence* (June 30, 1908) 7; "The Social Gathering," *Confidence* (June 30, 1908) 9–10; "The World-Wide Revival: A Dream-Prophecy," *Confidence* 1 (June 1908) 11; Beckdahl, *Witness*, 20–21; Gregersen, "Brev fra søster Gregersen," *Byposten* (September 12, 1907) 69–70.

97. "The World-Wide Revival: A Dream-Prophecy," *Confidence* 1 (June 1908) 11.

98. "The World-Wide Revival: A Dream-Prophecy," *Confidence* 1 (June 1908) 11; Beckdahl, *Witness*, 20–22; Thelle, "Brev fra søster Thelle," *Byposten* (August 29, 1908) 65–66.

99. "The World-Wide Revival: A Dream-Prophecy," *Confidence* 1 (June 1908) 11; Thelle, "Brev fra søster Thelle," *Byposten* (August 29, 1908) 65–66.

100. "The World-Wide Revival: A Dream-Prophecy," *Confidence* 1 (June 1908) 16–17; Gregersen, "Brev fra søster Gregersen," *Byposten* (September 12, 1907) 69–70.

widely circulated through the periodicals *Confidence* and *Byposten*. At the conference at Sunderland, Agnes and Dagmar were able to further expand their network and have personal contact with other important leaders in the Pentecostal movement.[101]

Agnes and Dagmar traveled on the ship "Saxonia" from Liverpool to Boston in June 1908.[102] They did not have any promise of funds while in the United States and set out on their journey "in faith" that God would provide what they needed to attend the Missionary Training Institute in Nyack, NY. The women used any occasion they had to evangelize, and they sang and preached many times also onboard the ship. On the final day, they were invited to sing and share their testimony at the "Captain's dinner." Agnes and Dagmar also spoke about their calling to foreign missions, and the leader of the party arranged for an offering to be collected for the women. The result was an offering of seventy-five dollars, and the women took this as a confirmation that "God would provide" for them.[103]

The women were not able to enroll at A. B. Simpsons Missionary Training Institute before January 1909, and when they arrived in the United States in the summer of 1908 they first stayed for a while in Boston, where Dagmar's sister, M. Gregersen lived. She worked as a nurse in a private home and had arranged for the women to rent a room in the house.[104] Soon after they arrived in Boston, Agnes got severely sick. They believed she had pneumonia and that it was affecting both lungs. Agnes had a high fever, was in much pain, and had difficulties breathing.[105] Their host family and Dagmar's sister insisted they find a doctor, but Dagmar and Agnes refused. They believed in divine healing and that it was against their faith to go to the doctor. That she was so sick was something they interpreted as a test of their faith, and Dagmar was convinced that Agnes would be healed if their faith did not falter.[106] The

---

101. "The Whitsuntide Conference," *Confidence* (June 30, 1908) 4–11, 15–22; Barratt, "Konferensen i Sunderland," *Byposten* (June 27, 1908) 50–51; Thelle and Gregersen, "Kjære venner!" *Byposten* (August 15, 1908) 63–64. Some of the participants were Gerrit R. Polman and Arie Kok of Amsterdam, A. A. and Mary Boddy, Andrew Murdoch of Scotland, Elizabeth Sisson, H. S. Mogridge, James Techner, and Smith Wigglesworth.

102. "Passenger Lists of Vessels," Liverpool-Boston, departure June 16, 1908.

103. Engstrøm, *Ha tro til Gud*, 39–40.

104. Engstrøm, *Ha tro til Gud*, 39–40.

105. Engstrøm, *Ha tro til Gud*, 39–40; Beckdahl, *Witness*, 22–25. Agnes writes she also had dysentery. She was in extreme pain.

106. Engstrøm, *Ha tro til Gud*, 40–41; Beckdahl, *Witness*, 24–25. According to Agnes, Dagmar was at some point worried she had died and that she would go to jail for not taking her to the hospital.

owner of the house said they were fanatical and that they had to leave if they would not call for a doctor. Consequently, they left and took the tram to her cousin and aunt's home, where they carried Agnes into the house. Everyone present thought she was about to pass away, but Dagmar made everyone leave the room and anointed Agnes and shouted: "In the name of Jesus, live!" According to Dagmar, Agnes instantly felt better and exclaimed: "Dagmar, I can breathe, and the pain is gone. I am healed!"[107] Shortly after, they were able to move back to the room they rented, and Agnes recovered her strength. Dagmar, at least, seems to have kept her conviction for many years that seeking help from a doctor demonstrated a lack of faith.[108]

By the time Dagmar and Agnes arrived in the United States, they were already quite well-known by many Norwegian-American Pentecostals, especially through many reports in the Barratts' periodical *Byposten* of their evangelistic ministry in Europe. While in Boston, the women received an invitation from Pastor Gabriel Nelson to minister in the Danish Evangelical Free Church in Hartford, Connecticut, which also had Norwegian members.[109] At the same time a Norwegian Pentecostal evangelist in Brooklyn, Oscar Halvorsen (known in the United States as Oscar Hall), had recently moved to Bridgeport, Connecticut to open a Pentecostal mission there. Hall and Nelson arranged for the Norwegian and Danish Pentecostals in Brooklyn and Hartford to come together for a week-long conference at Halvorsen's mission in Bridgeport. Agnes and Dagmar joined the conference, and after the experience of Agnes's healing, they felt even more bold in their public ministry.[110] In addition to healings, sanctification experiences, and Spirit baptism, young people also felt called to foreign missions at the conference.[111] Agnes and Dag-

107. Engstrøm, *Ha tro til Gud*, 40–41.

108. It seems so in her autobiography that she still had this conviction at an old age, but this is a bit unclear.

109. Engstrøm, *Ha tro til Gud*, 43; Beckdahl, *Witness*, 26–27; Gregersen and Thelle, "Brev fra søstrene Gregersen og Thelle," *Byposten* (October 24, 1908) 81–82. Engstrøm writes that his name was Enok Nelson, but she likely did not remember his first name correctly. In her autobiography some dates and chronology are incorrect. For further information on the connection between Norwegian Pentecostals in Norway and the US see Alegre, "Transatlantic Influence from Norway."

110. Gregersen and Thelle, "Brev fra søstrene Gregersen og Thelle," *Byposten* (October 24, 1908) 81–82; Engstrøm, *Ha tro til Gud*, 44; Skibsted, *Oscar Halvorsen*, 56–57; Beckdahl, *Witness*, 26–27. The meetings were held at a place called Black Rock in Bridgeport.

111. Gregersen and Thelle, "Brev fra søstrene Gregersen og Thelle," *Byposten* (October 24, 1908) 81–82; Engstrøm, *Ha tro til Gud*, 44; Skibsted, *Oscar Halvorsen*, 56.

mar may have played an important role in this emphasis on missions since they were preaching and were planning to go to India. Two of the Scandinavian missionaries that came from this group in the Northeast were Berger Johnsen and Ellen Nilsen. Johnsen became a pioneer missionary in Argentina and Nilsen in India.[112]

Dagmar and Agnes helped strengthen the connection between early Norwegian-American Pentecostals in the Northeast and the early Pentecostal movement in Norway.[113] After the conference the "sisters" went to Hartford where they stayed with pastor Nelson and his family. They were not able to enroll at the Missions School until January and stayed with Pastor Nelson for several months. In Hartford, they made many friends who supported them financially and promised them a place to stay when they needed this.[114] The church in Hartford also sent two missionaries to India within a few years who aided Dagmar and Agnes in their work.[115]

In January 1909 Agnes and Dagmar enrolled at A. B. Simpson's mission school in Nyack, New York, where they studied with more than two hundred students.[116] They were very content with the school and especially enjoyed their classes with A. B. Simpson. The language was a challenge, but they worked hard to improve their English. Dagmar and Agnes also appreciated the opportunities and freedom they had to minister at the school. According to Dagmar, many students who had difficulties came to them for prayer, and they started holding prayer meetings in the basement of the school.[117] After learning about the difficulties on the mission field, Dagmar and Agnes became convinced that the many future missionaries at their school needed to be baptized in "Spirit and fire," to be effective witnesses. They started to pray for students to experience this and in March 1909 sent their first account of a fellow student who had been baptized in the Spirit and started speaking in tongues.[118] Dagmar writes that a revival started at the school, and many were baptized in the

112. Skibsted, *Oscar Halvorsen*, 56–57.

113. For further information on this see Alegre, "Transatlantic Influence."

114. "Fra andre lande," *Byposten* (March 15, 1909) 23.

115. The two missionaries were Ellen Nilsen and Gunder Beruldsen. "Fra missionsmarken," *KS* (February 15, 1913) 27; "Br. Gunder Beruldsen," *KS* (August 15, 1914) 125. Beruldsen died of Cholera in Banda, India in 1914, at age 24.

116. "Fra andre lande," *Byposten* (March 15, 1909) 23.

117. Engstrøm, *Ha tro til Gud*, 45; "Fra andre lande," *Byposten* (March 15, 1909) 23.

118. Gregersen and Thelle, "Amerika," *Byposten* (April 15, 1909) 31–32. They were also concerned that the students be cleansed before their baptism in the Spirit.

Spirit. She clearly had the impression that A. B. Simpson and the other teachers were happy about the revival and "the growth in the students' spiritual lives."[119]

Agnes and Dagmar did well at the school and spent almost a year there. When the year ended Dagmar writes that the teachers thanked them for being a blessing to the school and the students. Before returning to Norway, they visited the Norwegian Pentecostals in Brooklyn and Hartford again and rejoiced that their communities had grown significantly.[120] Many had joined Nelson's new Pentecostal church in Hartford, where they by then only practiced believer's baptism. Dagmar's sister had also joined the church and been baptized in the Spirit. They wished they could have stayed longer, but now felt the urgency of returning to Norway so they could leave for India. That was after all their main goal.[121]

DAGMAR AND AGNES BECOME MISSIONARIES IN INDIA

Since Agnes and Dagmar first had to take a ship to England, they decided to stay there for some time to minister before going home to Norway. While in England they were also invited to Scotland to preach. The women came home to Norway during the fall of 1909 and had a few months to visit with family and friends before leaving for India.[122] At some time during their stay Dagmar became engaged to the young Pentecostal evangelist Henrik Engstrøm, who was a part of the early Pentecostal revival in Christiania, and who also wished to become a missionary to India. It was decided that Dagmar would go to India first and that they would be married when he arrived there later.[123] Dagmar and Agnes were to be sent out as missionaries by Norwegian Pentecostals in Christiania, with Banda as their final destination. In faith, they sailed from Norway in January 1910 with about two hundred Norwegian crowns, which was only enough money to get to England.[124] They were forced to remain in England for several weeks, and while they waited for funds to appear, they

119. Engstrøm, *Ha tro til Gud,* 45.
120. Engstrøm, *Ha tro til Gud,* 46–47.
121. Engstrøm, *Ha tro til Gud,* 46–47.
122. Gregersen and Thelle, "Elskede venner!," *Byposten* (December 1, 1909) 94.
123. Engstrøm, *Ha tro til Gud,* 48–49, 61–62.
124. Beckdahl, *Witness,* 40; Gregersen and Thelle, "Reisebreve," *KS* (March 15, 1910) 44–45.

participated in several Pentecostal meetings. Agnes wrote her mother: "I told you that the Lord would send us in His own time. A way opened so we can now purchase second-class tickets on a P. and O. steamer, buy new outfits, and pay our board in India for the coming hot season."[125] It was the wealthy British Pentecostal leader Cecil Polhill who had felt God tell him to send them out, and he paid for their tickets and other expenses.[126] The women were able to leave England in February and start their long journey to India.[127]

When the women arrived in Bombay on March 4, they experienced how T. B. Barratt had prepared the way for them through his four-month stay there in 1908. They were warmly received first by the English missionaries in Bombay and at Pandita Ramabai's Mukti Mission.[128] They stayed at the Mukti Mission for about six months and were very impressed by Ramabai and their work there, such as weaving, printing, and translation.[129] One day while at Mukti, an American missionary named Albert Norton visited the Norwegian women. He had a mission station in the close by city of Poona and had heard of Dagmar's calling to Banda. Norton had opened an American Pentecostal mission in the city of Faizabad in Northern India and said he had traveled by train through the district of Banda on his way there. Soon there was a convention in Faizabad, and Norton invited Dagmar and Agnes to join them there. The women took this as a sign from God since Banda was in Northern India.[130]

In Faizabad, Dagmar and Agnes rented a house together, and they decided to stay there for some time while they were studying Hindi. They called their house the "Mission Mizpah." According to Dagmar both

---

125. Beckdahl, *Witness*, 39; Gregersen and Thelle, "Gud er trofast!" *KS* (March 1, 1910) 36.

126. Engstrøm, *Ha tro til Gud*, 49–50. See Usher, *Cecil Polhill* for more on Polhill. See Alegre, *Apologetics of T. B Barratt*, 238–51, 274 for more information on the connection between Laura and T. B. Barratt and Cecil Polhill.

127. Gregersen and Thelle, "Reisebreve," *KS* (March 15, 1910) 44–45.

128. Gregersen and Thelle, "Reisebreve," *KS* (April 15, 1910) 60; Engstrøm, *Ha tro til Gud*, 50–51; Gregersen and Thelle, "Reisebreve," *KS* (July 1, 1910) 100; Gregersen and Thelle, "Reisebreve," *KS* (August 15, 1910) 125–26. Schoonmaker received them in Bombay and they stayed at Miss Orlebar's Beluah mission in the city. Alegre, *Apologetics of T. B Barratt*, 159–62, 169–95.

129. Engstrøm, *Ha tro til Gud*, 50–51; Gregersen and Thelle, "Brev fra søstrene Gregersen og Thelle," *KS* (September 15, 1910) 140–42; Gregersen and Thelle, "Brev fra søstrene Gregersen og Thelle," *KS* (October 15, 1910) 154–55.

130. Engstrøm, *Ha tro til Gud*, 55–56; Spence, *On the Borders of Nepal*, 6–7; Barratt, "De bortdragende missionærer" *KS* (November 1, 1910) 161.

missionaries and many natives were baptized in the Spirit during the conference held in October 1910.[131] After the conference, the women stayed in Faizabad, where they studied the language and helped missionaries in the region with evangelism. Dagmar also explained that their house was open to missionaries and Indian evangelists to come and seek Spirit baptism, and that Mrs. Norton helped them greatly in this ministry.[132]

On December 2, 1910, Henrik Engstrøm, Dagmar's fiancé, arrived in India. Twelve days later they were married in the presence of several missionaries, and the wedding became a Pentecostal meeting with messages in tongues and prophecies about their future ministry in Banda.[133] After Dagmar's marriage her partnership with Agnes continued for almost a year in Faizabad, until they expanded their mission work in different places. The three Norwegians evangelized, held weekly prayer meetings with British soldiers and studied the language.[134] J. H. King visited their mission in Faizabad and held meetings, which greatly encouraged them.[135] The newlywed Engstrøms still planned to go to Banda, but missionaries in the region had told them that it would be very difficult to get permission to be missionaries there, and the Engstrøms were waiting for the right time to try to enter the area. They decided to first go to Darjeeling in Northern India for a few months during the worst heat and then to help a German Lutheran missionary couple in Chopra, with the last name of Bantel, who had joined the Pentecostal revival.[136] The Engstrøms stayed at their mission in Chopra for three months, and then they traveled to Banda, the place Dagmar had received a prophecy about in Christiania.[137]

131. Engstrøm, *Ha tro til Gud*, 56; Gregersen and Thelle, "Indien: Fyzabad," *KS* (November 15, 1910) 172–73; Gregersen and Thelle, "Indien: Ilden falder i Fyzabad," *KS* (December 15, 1910) 189–90.

132. Engstrøm, *Ha tro til Gud*, 60; Gregersen and Thelle, "Indien: Ilden falder i Fyzabad," *KS* (December 15, 1910) 189–90.

133. Engstrøm, *Ha tro til Gud*, 61–62; "Gregersen and Thelle Indien," *KS* (January 15, 1911) 10–12; H. Engstrøm, "Indien," *KS* (February 1, 1911) 22–23.

134. Thelle and Engstrøms, "Indien," *KS* (April 1, 1911) 53.

135. Thelle and Engstrøms, "Indien," *KS* (May 1, 1911) 71; "Indien" *KS* (April 15, 1912) 62. King was one month in Faizabad and they also spent two months with him in Darjeeling. According to Barratt, King spoke very highly of the Engstrøms.

136. Engstrøm, *Ha tro til Gud*, 65–66; Engstrøms, "Indien," *KS* (August 15, 1911) 125; Engstrøm, "Indien" *KS* (September 1, 1911) 134. In *KS* they name the place "German Mission" in Chopra. It seems one of the main reasons to stay there was that it was inexpensive.

137. Engstrøm, *Ha tro til Gud*, 66. They went there in August 1911.

From the beginning, Agnes had been clear with Dagmar that she did not feel that God had called her to Banda. Dagmar was prepared to go there alone, but she was happy that God had provided her with a husband "who also had been called to the same place."[138] Right after the Engstrøms' wedding, Agnes had gone to Northern India to participate in a conference in Nanpara, about twenty kilometers from the border to Nepal.[139] Then in the summer of 1911 she was with the Engstrøms for three months in Darjeeling, close to the borders of Nepal and Tibet, and they were all impressed by the missionaries' efforts to evangelize the Tibetans who sometimes crossed the border.[140] Agnes stayed behind for a while when the Engstrøms left, and from then the two "Norwegian sisters" began working more separately, though they still felt they stood together in the missions work in India and had a mission base in Faizabad for some more time.[141] By 1912 the offerings were collected separately for them and designated to either "sister Thelle" or the Engstrøms.[142]

After having spent time in Northern India, Agnes felt that God was calling her to permanent evangelistic work along the border of Nepal with the hope of also evangelizing the Nepalese who occasionally crossed the border.[143] The country was closed for missionaries, but the Nepalese came to the train stations in Northern India. "A door opened" for Agnes when two female missionaries in Nanpara invited her to stay with them in the Spring of 1912. They had bought a building and were to establish a mission station there.[144] Agnes joined the two women's mission, and her goal was to reach Nepal.[145] From there she could see the Himalayan mountains rise in the distance.

---

138. D. Engstrøm, "Indien" *KS* (September 1, 1911) 134.

139. H. Engstrøm, "Indien," *KS* (February 1, 1911) 23; "Indien," *KS* (February 15, 1911) 32.

140. "Indien" *KS* (May 15, 1911) 78. According to a letter to T. B. Barratt, Agnes Thelle became engaged to Max Moorhead and was to marry him in Darjeeling in 1911. However, they did not marry.

141. "Indien," *KS* (July 15, 1911) 112; "Indien," *KS* (November 1, 1911) 162–63; Engstrøms, "Banda" *KS* (March 1, 1912) 37–38. After some time in Darjeeling Agnes went to Bombay, while the Engstrøms were in in Chopra. They met again in Faizabad before they again went their separate ways.

142. "Indien," *KS* (April 15, 1912) 62. Before this, it had been sent to them as a team and divided between them.

143. "Indien" *KS* (June 1, 1912) 85–86.

144. "Indien," *KS* (June 1, 1912) 85–86.

145. "Indien," *KS* (December 15, 1912) 187–88.

While Agnes and Dagmar were at Pandita Ramabai's mission in Mukti, the two met a Danish Salvation Army missionary by the name of Christian Beckdahl. Shortly after they met, he wrote to Agnes saying that he had been baptized in the Spirit and that he felt God call him to a place where the gospel had "never been heard." He decided to leave the Salvation Army and the mission station in nearby Gorakhpur and began missionary work "by faith."[146] Beckdahl was then asked to build a chapel near the border of Nepal for the American Pentecostal Mission.[147] By 1913 he was stationed in Uzka Bazar and had received *Korsets Seir* for two years, which included many reports from Agnes and the Engstrøms' work in India.[148]

At the time that Christian Beckdahl began working for the American Pentecostal Mission, Agnes Thelle and two coworkers were at the mission station at Nanpara, which was also on the border of Nepal. Their roof leaked badly, so they decided to write to Christian Beckdahl and ask him to come and repair it, which he did. When the time came for Agnes's scheduled furlough, Christian proposed.[149] Agnes left India in March 1914, made a short visit to preach in England and Scotland, and then traveled to Norway to visit her family and raise funds for her mission work. She told of their plans to marry and then return to India and open a new mission in Bilaspur in Northern India.[150] After a year in Norway, Agnes Thelle went to the United States where she married Christian Beckdahl on August 14, 1915, in the Scandinavian Evangelical Mission in Brooklyn, New York.[151] Two days later they were both ordained as missionaries at Wells Memorial Gospel Assembly in Tottenville, New York.[152] After some deputational work, the couple sailed for India in December 1915. They arrived in Bombay and then traveled to Bilaspur where they established a mission.

By the 1920s the Beckdahls had moved to Nanpara, on the border of Nepal, close to the place where Agnes had previously worked. According

---

146. Beckdahl, "Gorakhpur," *KS* (March 15, 1911) 46; Spence, *On the Borders of Nepal*, 6–7.

147. Spence, *On the Borders of Nepal*, 6–7.

148. Beckdahl, "Fra brevmappen," *KS* (May 15, 1913) 79–80.

149. Spence, *On the Borders of Nepal*, 7.

150. "Missionsmarken," *KS* (September 15, 1914) 142–43; "Missionsmarken," *KS* (May 1, 1915) 68.

151. "Missionsmarken," *KS* (June 15, 1915) 90–91; "Andre missioner," *KS* (October 15, 1915) 158; "Andre missioner," *KS* (February 15, 1916) 31.

152. Christian and Agnes Beckdahl, ordination certificates, Wells Memorial Gospel Assembly, Tottenville, New York, August 16, 1915. Flower Pentecostal Heritage Center.

to her account, the nationals made a path to their door. They had never seen a white woman before, and many wanted to touch "this peculiar being," as they called her.[153] Agnes also proved quite a novelty as she sang and played the guitar. One day about fifty sick people came to her for help, some traveling as many as forty miles. Rumors had spread that the missionary had brought a magic charm with her. This was a large bottle of castor oil with which she anointed the sick and prayed for their healing. That evening, the people were still there in a crowd, so Christian Beckdahl and an Indian evangelist preached to the people and prayed for the sick.[154]

From this beginning the Beckdahls attempted to evangelize in neighboring Nepal. The country was closed to the gospel, and missionaries could not enter without permission. The Beckdahls remained in Northern India, traveled constantly, held open-air meetings, and witnessed to whoever would listen. They endured attacks of malaria and had to climb steep cliffs on a regular basis. Once Agnes was poisoned and near death, but after five hours of suffering, she wrote that God had healed her. Three times her husband was near death, but she also believed that God intervened and saved him on all these occasions.[155]

Agnes and Christian Beckdahl served together as appointed Assemblies of God missionaries to India from June 1919 until Christian's death thirty-one years later.[156] The Beckdahls never settled down in one place for very long, as they constantly wished to reach new territories with their message. They often lived in small mud houses where they encountered such things as squirrels, rats, cobras, and poisonous lizards. It took them more than twenty years to cover the entire district of Bahraich, preaching the gospel in every village at least once. The Beckdahls had one son, Samuel, who was born in 1921. He was raised on the mission field in India, and as his parents, he also became a missionary to India.[157]

Christian Beckdahl did not wish to retire, and the couple were missionaries in North India for over forty years. One afternoon he was involved in a serious motorcycle accident. He went into a coma, pneumonia

153. Spence, *On the Borders of Nepal*, 10; Beckdahl, "Along the Nepal Border," *Pentecostal Evangel* (April 9, 1967) 22–23. A testimony and a synopsis of Agnes's ministry in India appeared in the *Pentecostal Evangel* in 1967.

154. Spence, *On the Borders of Nepal*, 10.

155. Beckdahl, "Paying Her Vows to God on the Borders of the Closed Lands," *Latter Rain Evangel* (September 1923) 8.

156. Christian and Agnes Beckdahl, missionary file, Assemblies of God World Missions.

157. Samuel and Ruth Beckdahl, missionary file. Assemblies of God World Missions.

set in, and malaria developed into blackwater fever. He passed away on November 12, 1950, at the age of seventy-three and was buried on the compound in the District of Bahraich.[158] After this, Agnes was advised to return to the United States and retire. She did retire as far as her foreign missionary service was concerned, but she continued to preach and be involved in tract ministry in the United States.[159] Agnes went to live at Pinellas Park Home in 1954 and spent her final days at Bethany Retirement Home in Lakeland, Florida. She passed away on January 17, 1968, at the age of 91.[160]

On September 27, 1911, Dagmar and Henrik Engstrøm had their first son, Victor. Four months later, in January 1912, they were able to enter the region of Banda in Uttar Pradesh together with an Indian evangelist couple, Hanka and Hanzu.[161] They immediately established a Pentecostal mission. The local British government official rented them a large building that had previously served as a hospital, and this became their home and mission station. From the city of Banda, they started an evangelistic ministry to the villages in the region. They received important help when Indian evangelists connected to other Swedish and American Pentecostal missions arrived to aid them in their new pioneer work.[162] An American mission sent a young Indian evangelist named Georg. Henrik and Georg daily walked to the villages nearby to preach. According to Dagmar no "spiritual work of any kind" had been done in Banda before, and she interpreted this as a confirmation of the prophecy she received that God would send her "to the dark place Banda."[163]

Like many other missionaries in India, the Engstrøms became increasingly involved in social work, especially in caring for children who had been abandoned and were begging by the roads. They rented a building that became a home for the children and invited homeless widows to live there and care for the children.[164] A new Norwegian missionary,

---

158. Spence, *On the Borders of Nepal*, 15. More than 2,000 people from all the nearby villages came to his funeral.

159. And her burden for the land of Nepal never lessened with the advancing of years.

160. "Four Missionary Ladies Go To Be With the Lord," *Pentecostal Evangel* (May 12, 1968) 28.

161. Engstrøm, *Ha tro til Gud*, 66–67; Engstrøms, "Banda," *KS* (March 1, 1912) 37–38.

162. Engstrøm, *Ha tro til Gud*, 68–71.

163. Engstrøm, *Ha tro til Gud*, 69.

164. Engstrøm, *Ha tro til Gud*, 91.

Anna Jensen, became an important help at the orphanage. The conditions in Banda were hard on the three Norwegian missionaries' health and in March 1921 Henrik Engstrøm passed away. This was a great sorrow for Dagmar. She was now left with all the responsibility for the mission, the children, and their own three sons.[165] Dagmar felt the responsibilities she now had to carry alone were too great for her, and in grief, she returned to Norway with her three sons, Victor, Josef, and Stefan.

After some time in Norway, friends suggested that Dagmar travel to the United States for a while thinking the change might help her recover her strength.[166] She heeded their advice and spent time among Scandinavian Pentecostals in Hartford and Brooklyn.[167] Dagmar returned with renewed strength to Norway and decided to return to India with her sons to continue their work in Banda.[168] Several new young missionaries from Norway came to Banda to help her at the mission. When Norway was invaded by Germany in 1940, Dagmar's son Stefan, who was with her in India at the time, was drafted for military service. He was sent to Canada to receive training as a pilot and one month before the war ended in 1945, he passed away when the Germans shot down his airplane over Norway.[169] After a stay in the United States during the war she was able to return to Norway on the first ship from the United States to Oslo in 1945. She then returned to India where she continued her mission work in Banda until 1948.

Dagmar lived a long life after she permanently returned to Norway from India in 1948.[170] At the age of ninety-three Dagmar was honored with the Medal of St. Olav by the king of Norway for her mission work.[171] Three years later, she was invited to speak at the German Pentecostal

---

165. Engstrøm, *Ha tro til Gud*, 92–93.

166. Engstrøm, *Ha tro til Gud*, 94–96. Thus, Dagmar travelled to the United States with her youngest son and Dagmar Jacobsen who wished to go as a missionary to Banda.

167. Norwegian Pentecostals in Hartford had supported them in India, and her financial support from the US increased greatly after this visit. Dagmar rejoiced at seeing how their communities had grown since her stay in the Northeast in 1908/1909.

168. Engstrøm, *Ha tro til Gud*, 96–97.

169. Engstrøm, *Ha tro til Gud*, 125–27, 132–33; Engebretsen, "Stefan Engstrøm død," *KS* (September 22, 1945) 342; Tollefsen, "Misjonsveteran 75 år," *KS* (November 24, 1956) 726.

170. Tollefsen, "Misjonsveteran 75 år," *KS* (November 24, 1956) 726. In 1973 she was able to visit the mission in Banda again, as well as the Norwegian mission in Nepal.

171. Engstrøm, *Ha tro til Gud*, 158; Hegertun, "Ukens Portrett: Dagmar Engstrøm," *KS* (January 20, 1979) 5, 7.

movement's seventieth anniversary in Hamburg. She went there and spoke of the early revival she and Agnes had been a part of in 1907.[172] In her eighties Dagmar left the Filadelfia church in Oslo and joined the Maranatha movement in Norway where she was an active preacher until she was over one hundred years old. In 1984 she passed away and she is remembered as one of Norway's most important Pentecostal evangelists, missionaries, and preachers.[173]

DAGMAR'S AND AGNES'S THEOLOGICAL THINKING

From their testimonies and early preaching and practices it seems clear that Dagmar and Agnes held the classical five-fold gospel of many early Norwegian Pentecostals: Jesus as Savior, Sanctifier, Spirit-Baptizer, Healer, and Coming-King.[174] They preached the need for personal conversion; they wrote about holiness and prayed for people to be cleansed; they preached and prayed for Spirit baptism and healings; and they spoke of the imminent return of Christ. The women also frequently spoke in tongues and interpreted messages in tongues, spoke of their dreams and visions, and delivered prophetic messages.[175] They had high regard for prophetic messages, as is evident in how Dagmar acted after having received a message about God calling her to Banda. Especially Dagmar argued for the importance of sanctification, and she believed that many of the problems the Pentecostals were having in the early revival could be due to people not being "cleansed" before their Spirit Baptism.[176] Agnes later joined the Assemblies of God, and this may have affected her views on sanctification.

From the moment Agnes and Dagmar joined the Pentecostal revival, they thought it was of utmost importance that Christians, and especially ministers and missionaries, be baptized in the Spirit. When they traveled as evangelists in Norway, Europe, and the United States, they

---

172. Engstrøm, *Ha tro til Gud*, 143–50.

173. NRK, "Dagmar Engstrøm." Emanuel Minos called her in 1981 for "the grand old lady" of the Pentecostal movement.

174. See Dayton, *Theological Roots of Pentecostalism*, on the fivefold gospel.

175. See Alegre, *Apologetics of T. B Barratt* for details on Barratt's theology. Their prophetic messages were sometimes recorded, as at the Sunderland convention in 1908.

176. Gregersen, "Brev fra søster Gregersen," *Byposten* (January 15, 1909) 6–7; Gregersen and Thelle, "Ilden er faldt i Tyskland," *Byposten* (July 13, 1907) 66. In their meetings in Hamburg in 1907 they prayed for cleansing.

frequently preached about this and prayed for people for Spirit baptism. When they became missionaries in India, they also emphasized Spirit baptism and spoke to both missionaries and Indian evangelists about the importance of this experience. They both experienced many hardships related to health, the climate, and finances in India, and they believed Spirit baptism would empower missionaries to persevere and be effective witnesses amid difficult circumstances. From their letters, it seems that especially Indian evangelists were receptive to their message on Spirit baptism and came to them for prayer.[177] Dagmar and Agnes brought the Pentecostal message from Christiania to people in many different parts of the world. The Norwegian "sisters" also practiced speaking in tongues during prayer and prayer meetings and wrote about their joy in praying with other Pentecostals at home and abroad.

T. B. Barratt was the two women's most important guide in Pentecostal theology, but they were also independent thinkers from the beginning. Evidence of this is that they both decided to be baptized by full immersion six years before Barratt did. In their early years, the women were also more radical than Barratt on the issue of only trusting God for healing and refused to call on medical doctors.[178] This is evident when Agnes was sick in Boston in 1908. The women would often anoint with oil when they prayed for the sick, as when Dagmar anointed and prayed for Dagmar in Boston, and the rumors surrounding Agnes's "magic bottle" that circulated in Northern India. The women were also committed to the practice of "faith mission," and to go as evangelists and missionaries without a budget, but "in faith" that God would provide what they needed. Often, they received what they needed as donations arrived, but they also saw the need for more organized efforts to raise funds and to go to Norway and the United States to raise interest for the mission cause. On the role of women in ministry they both seem to have agreed with Laura's and T. B. Barratt's egalitarian vision.[179] Agnes believed for many years that being a woman limited her ministry, but as a Pentecostal, she did not seem to think there were any restrictions. When Dagmar's husband passed away, she continued leading their mission station alone. Both T. B. and Laura Barratt encouraged the women in their work as evangelists and missionaries.

177. Thelle, "Indien," *KS* (July 15, 1913) 110–11.

178. See Kimberly Alexander's *Pentecostal Healing* for early Pentecostal views of healing and doctors.

179. See Rakel Ystebø Alegre's chapter on Laura Barratt.

FINAL THOUGHTS

Dagmar Gregersen Engstrøm and Agnes Thelle Beckdahl stand out as two of the most significant Norwegian Pentecostal pioneer evangelists and missionaries. Their ministry is an example of the freedom of women to preach and to be traveling evangelists and missionaries in the early years of the Pentecostal revival. They are also examples of the great impact young female Pentecostals had in the expansion of the revival, especially in praying for others to receive their baptism in the Spirit and healing.[180] Together Agnes and Dagmar spread the message of Spirit baptism to communities in Norway, Denmark, Germany, Switzerland, England, Scotland, the United States, and India, and their ministry set off chain reactions in many places. Dagmar and Agnes were also the first and most prominent missionaries in the early Norwegian Pentecostal movement, and they inspired and mobilized many for foreign missions. The fact that they were female preachers does not seem to have been an issue in any place but in Germany, at least in the first decades of the revival, and they had strong support for their ministry by Laura and T. B. Barratt.

BIBLIOGRAPHY

Alexander, Kimberly Ervin. *Pentecostal Healing: Models in Theology and Practice*. Dorset, UK: Deo, 2006.

Alegre, Rakel Ystebø. *The Pentecostal Apologetics of T. B. Barratt: Defining and Defending the Faith 1906–1909*. PhD diss., Regent University, 2019.

———. "Women in Pentecostalism in Europe." In *Global Renewal Christianity: Spirit-Empowered Movements Past, Present and Future*, edited by Vinson Synan and Amos Yong, 4:259–73. Lake Mary, FL: Charisma, 2017.

———. "Trans-Atlantic Influence from Norway on Scandinavian-American Pentecostalism, 1906–1930." In *Revising Pentecostal History: Scandinavian-American Contributions to the Development of Pentecostalism*, edited by Rakel Ystebø Alegre et al., 87–117. Eugene, OR: Pickwick, 2024.

Barratt, Thomas Ball. *Erindringer*. Oslo: Filadelfiaforlaget, 1941.

———. *When the Fire Fell, and an Outline of My Life*. Oslo: Alfons Hansen & Sønner, 1927.

Beckdahl, Agnes N. T. Letter to Foreign Missions Department, Assemblies of God, April 1961.

———. *A Witness of God's Faithfulness*. Lucknow: Lucknow, n.d.

Bloch-Hoell, Nils. *Pinsebevegelsen: En undersøkelse av pinsebevegelsens tilblivelse, utvikling og særpreg med særlig henblikk på bevegelsens utforming i Norge*. Oslo: Universitetsforlaget, 1956.

---

180. See Alvarsson's introduction.

Breistein, Ingunn Folkestad. *Har Staten Bedre Borgere?: Dissenternes Kamp for Religiøs Frihet 1891–1969*. Trondheim: Tapir, 2003.
Bundy, David. *Visions of Apostolic Mission: Scandinavian Pentecostal Mission to 1935*. Uppsala: Uppsala Universitet, 2009.
Cavaness, Barbara. "Spiritual Chain Reactions: Women Used of God." *Assemblies of God Heritage* 25 (2005–2006) 24–29.
Christensen, Nikolaj. *Unorganized Religion: Pentecostalism and Secularization in Denmark, 1907–1924*. Leiden: Brill, 2022.
"Dagmar Engstrøm—forkynner og misjonær i 75 år." NRK TV-program May 20, 1982. https://tv.nrk.no/program/FOLA01000482.
Dallmeyer, August. *Satan Unter Den Heiligen: Die Casseler Bewegung—Im Lichte Der Erfahrung*. Neumünster: Vereinsbuchhandlung G. Ihloff & Co, 1907.
Dayton, Donald. *Theological Roots of Pentecostalism*. Peabody, MA: Hendrickson, 1987.
Engstrøm, Dagmar. *Ha tro til gud: alt er mulig for den som tror*. Oslo: Filadelfiaforlaget, 1980.
Giese, Ernst. *Und Flicken de Netze: Dokumente Zur Erweckungsgeschichte Des 20. Jahrhunderts*. Metzingen/Württ: Ernst Franz Verlag, 1987.
Gohr, Glenn. "Agnes Thelle Beckdahl: A Beacon of Pentecost in Europe and India." *Assemblies of God Heritage* 17 (1997) 11–15.
Gohr, Glenn. "Agnes Thelle Beckdahl: A Witness of God's Faithfulness in Europe and India." Paper presented at the 44th Annual Meeting of the Society for Pentecostal Studies, 2015.
Hollenweger, Walter J. *The Pentecostals*. Minneapolis: Augsburg, 1977.
Meier, Ralph. "Fra Kristiania til Kassel: Pinsebevegelsens begynnelse i Tyskland og forholdet til Gemeinschaftsbevegelsen." In *Pentekostale Perspektiver*, edited by Knut-Willy Sæther and Karl Inge Tangen, 91–110. Bergen: Fagbokforlaget, 2015.
Mikaelsson, Lisbeth. "Norwegian Pentecostal Foreign Mission: A Survey of Mission History with an Emphasis on Organization, Expansion, and Gender." In *Charismatic Christianity in Finland, Norway, and Sweden: Case studies in Historical and Contemporary Developments*, edited by Jessica Moberg and Jane Skjoldli, 49–77. New York: Palgrave Macmillan, 2018.
Nilsen, Oddvar. *Ut i All Verden: Pinsevennenes ytre misjon i 75 år*. Filadelfiaforlaget, 1984.
"Passenger Lists of Vessels Arriving at Boston, Massachusetts, 1891–1943." National Archives Microfilm Publication T843, roll 123, line number 1, record id 005104065_00230_0; Digital Folder Number 005104065, Image Number 00230-s.
Plüss, Jean-Daniel. "Swiss Pentecostals: A Journey Between Corporate Identity and Christian Unity." In *Global Renewal Christianity: Spirit-Empowered Movements Past, Present, and Future, vol. IV: Europe and North America*, edited by Vinson Synan and Amos Yong, 99–111. Lake Mary: Charisma, 2017.
———. *Vom Geist bewegt. Die Geschichte der Schweizerischen Pfingstmission*. Kreuzlingen, 2015.
Röckle, Bernhard, and William K. Kay. "Born in Difficult Times: The Founding of the Volksmission and the Work of Karl Fix." *Journal of the European Pentecostal Theological Association* 23 (2003) 72–101.
Schmidgall, Paul. *European Pentecostalism: Its Origins, Development, and Future*. Cleveland, TN: CPT, 2013.
Schrenk, Elias. *Was Lehrt Uns Die Kasseler Bewegung*. N.d.: Kassel, 1907.

Simpson, Carl. "The Development of the Pentecostal and Charismatic Movements in the Germanic Countries." In *European Pentecostalism*, edited by Anne Dyer and William Kay, 61–83. Leiden: Brill, 2011.

———. *Revered and Reviled in a Quest for Pentecostal Holiness: Jonathan Paul and the German Pentecostal Movement*. Lambert, 2012.

Skibsted, Werner. *Oscar Halvorsen: Liv og Virke*. Oslo: Filadelfiaforlaget, 1947.

Sommer, Gottfried. "Pentecostalism in Germany: Historical and Theological Perspectives." In *Global Renewal Christianity: Spirit-Empowered Movements Past, Present, and Future*, edited by Vinson Synan and Amos Yong, 4:112–29. Lake Mary: Charisma, 2017.

Spence, Inez. *On the Borders of Nepal*. Springfield, MO: Foreign Missions Department, Assemblies of God, n.d.

Usher, John Martin. *Cecil Polhill: Missionary, Gentleman and Revivalist*. Leiden: Brill, 2020.

Image #5. Anna Larssen Bjørner.

4

Anna Larssen Bjørner
A Drama of Institutionalization and Independence[1]

Nikolaj Christensen

INTRODUCTION

The early Danish Pentecostal movement had several female pioneers: Ellen Hansen, the first person in Denmark known to have spoken in tongues; Johanne Mollerup, the "mother" of the early Danish Pentecostals; the many women missionaries who took up the call to go abroad very early on, including two to China by 1909 and four to modern-day Lebanon by 1911, followed by many more, including the remarkable Anna Lewini who became the first Western Pentecostal missionary in Sri Lanka; and not least the "Thomsen sisters," Frederikke and Frida, two young evangelists who happened to share a last name and who brought the Pentecostal message to towns all over Denmark.[2]

However, one name stands out above the rest: Anna Larssen Bjørner, née Halberg (1875–1955), the most famous representative of Danish Pentecostalism ever. Before her, the most well-known face of Pentecostalism

---

1. All translations in this chapter are the author's own.
2. On all these, see Christensen, *Unorganized Religion*. The present chapter also incorporates elements of my PhD thesis: Christensen, "Flickering Flames."

in Denmark had been T. B. Barratt, but though this extensively travelling preacher's involvement with Denmark was particularly great, he decided to keep his home base in Norway. After he began to divert his efforts away from Denmark around 1911, the most visible leader of the Pentecostal movement there was the celebrated former actress Anna Larssen, from 1912 accompanied by her new husband Sigurd Bjørner (1875–1953) who had joined the movement more recently.

Still, Denmark plays a humbler part in the history of Scandinavian Pentecostalism than the movements in Sweden and Norway. This led earlier historians to believe that there was a lack of a Great Man to lead the Pentecostals in Denmark. For example, Nils Bloch-Hoell wrote that Anna Bjørner "did not possess the eloquence necessary to bridge the gap between the different cultural levels which she and the majority of the audience represented."[3] It is true that, though she had been an actress, Bjørner struggled for a while to find her own voice—but behind this struggle lies the fact that she and other early female Pentecostal leaders were treated differently from men, and historians prone to focus on the works of Great Men have continued to treat them unfairly because of their gender.

There is, however, a risk of simply morphing this into an almost equally problematic Great Woman theory. This is tempting in a research study where archival material, such as letters and scrapbooks, is a cornerstone, since typically only papers pertaining to the most prominent leaders such as T. B. Barratt and Anna Bjørner have been preserved. But such materials still reveal details of who their most important contacts were, which is not always clear from published periodicals and memoirs. A broader range of perspectives is also available in certain long-forgotten published materials, such as short-lived, small-circulation periodicals. Nonetheless, here I will mainly rely on the perspective of leaders—Bjørner in particular, but also Barratt—in order to perceive the experience of their followers.

EARLY LIFE AND CAREER

Six-year-old Anna Halberg had her first role on stage in Henrik Ibsen's *A Dollhouse*, directed by her half-Italian, half-Danish father in Trondheim, in her mother's native Norway. She had her first major role at the age of

---

3. Bloch-Hoell, *Pentecostal Movement*, 180.

12, back in her own hometown of Copenhagen, in Émile de Girardin's *Le supplice d'une femme*. But shortly after, her father, Johan Halberg, had a nervous breakdown and was confined to a mental hospital for eighteen months before dying there in 1888. Her mother, Georgine, was left with five children and no stable income. She was only able to support the two oldest, Anna and her sister; of the rest, one was adopted by relatives, one by strangers, and one was sent to an orphanage. Her mother was devasted and soon she too was taken to a mental institution. However, she was able to return home and instead looked to the church for guidance. This gave her daughters their first experience of Christianity.

Despite a well-meaning church member's attempt to steer young Anna in a different direction, she was drawn to the same business that had been fatal for her father. At the theater, this young talent soon also became an object of often much older men's interest. She warded off aggressive advances from some, but nonetheless by the age of sixteen she was engaged to the author Gustav Wied who was twice her age. When he tried to take advantage of her, this engagement was broken off; instead, she had a breakthrough on stage, and soon found in Herman Bang (1857–1912) a director she could trust. From here, triumph followed on triumph before culminating in her signature role as the protagonist in Alexandre Dumas *fils*' most famous play, *La Dame aux Camélias*. However, her private life was more turbulent. Shortly before her nineteenth birthday, she married a different author, Otto Larssen (1864–1910). The marriage was far from a happy one; she gave birth to a son, Finn, but nonetheless they split up and the marriage was dissolved in 1898.[4]

She kept the son but seems to have been somewhat negligent with him; eventually he was taken from her and adopted by the writer Gustav Esmann and his wife Fanny. Anna Larssen also often required financial help—usually from male acquaintances—when she encountered debt due to overspending. One of her lovers, her colleague Johannes Poulsen, gave her a copy of the New Testament in 1901; most others in Larssen's fashionable milieu had put religious faith definitively behind them.[5]

4. Bjørner, *Teater og Tempel*, 5–42; Neiiendam and Neiiendam, "Anna Larssen Bjørner."

5. Anna Larssen Bjørner collection, Theatre Museum at the Court Theatre, Copenhagen, miscellanea (uncatalogued).

TRANSFORMATION

In the years to follow, Larssen continued to occasionally accompany her mother to religious gatherings. Their favorite preacher was H. J. Mygind (1867–1949), a former Lutheran pastor and missionary turned independent revivalist. By early 1907, he had heard news of the emerging Pentecostal revival in Norway and visited to see for himself. The gatherings took on a Pentecostal character, and soon the leader of the Norwegian movement, T. B. Barratt, was in Copenhagen himself. Larssen's mother led her daughter to a conversion experience. Larssen also attended some of Barratt's meetings, and when the press caught on to this, she came under pressure to either distance herself from the movement or step into it completely. In December 1908, she let Barratt lead her to an experience of baptism in the Holy Spirit.[6]

Larssen did not speak in tongues on this occasion, but only several months later. She continued to frame her story in various ways, more or less conforming it to what emerged as the standard Pentecostal *ordo salutis* with tongues as the sign of Spirit baptism. This common narrative framework of the Pentecostal experience was an important basis for the subsequent building of Pentecostal institutions.[7] As an extreme case, one of Larssen's public testimonies even referred to the experience in December 1908 as her conversion, whereas she had previously described herself as already being a believer at that point.[8] Whatever it was, it gave her the courage to begin to witness directly to her colleagues in the theater and invite Barratt to speak to them. A less well-known actress, Anna Lewini, was converted and immediately became one of Danish Pentecostalism's most ardent evangelists. In the summer of 1909, Larssen finally spoke in tongues and both actresses resolved to leave the theater and follow their true calling. But the church historian Elith Olesen's claim that this happened "after [Barratt] had exploited the conversion of the two actresses to the utmost as a publicity stunt (a summer tour around Denmark in the summer of 1909)" is a complete misunderstanding; in fact they had been on an exhausting tour with their theater company.[9] Thus, the *push* away

6. Valdemar Willumsen, "Anna Larssens Afsked med Teatret," *Berlingske Søndags Magasin* (March 14, 1943); Bjørner, *Teater og Tempel*, 86–96; Olesen, *De frigjorte*, 428; Bloch-Hoell, *Pentecostal Movement*, 78.

7. For a general introduction to institutionalization, see Alberoni, *Movement and Institution*.

8. *KS* (October 1, 1911) 151.

9. Olesen, *De frigjorte*, 428–29; cf. Bjørner, *Teater og Tempel*, 101–2.

from the theater might have been felt more strongly than the *pull* from Barratt and other Pentecostals.

According to another Danish church historian, Michael Neiiendam, it was only after Larssen's Spirit baptism at the end of 1908—not after her conversion a few months earlier—that she experienced the "shrill disharmony" between the purification she had received and her life on the stage.[10] Neiiendam, who for his own part strongly disagreed with the view that the theater and Christianity are incompatible, seems to have conflated Larssen's position with that of other Pentecostals. However, Neiiendam treated Larssen sympathetically. Not all who loved the theater were on friendly terms with the new Anna Larssen, like the Neiiendam family was, as seen from the letters between her and Michael Neiiendam's uncle, the actor Robert Neiiendam.[11] In preparation for his book, Michael Neiiendam was in correspondence with Mygind and Barratt, but also politely solicited Anna Larssen Bjørner's confirmation of certain historical details.[12]

The decision to abandon the stage was met with disbelief. The theater threatened Larssen with financial ruin. It was felt that she would benefit from spending time in a mental institution—as both her parents had done—and she consented immediately. On the day of Larssen's admission, Lewini wrote a letter to Barratt, complaining that her colleagues—and Larssen's mother—were giving Lewini the "blame" for Larssen's breach of contract. The day before, when she had not yet been offered admission to the clinic, Larssen herself wrote to Barratt, expressing the worry that her physician would declare her "irresponsible"– if not downright insane—and that this would affect her witness.[13] Outsiders often branded Pentecostal women as "hysterics," as illustrated by Danish newspapers' caricatures of Pentecostal meetings.[14] This was of course a blatant attempt to rein in their exuberance, when radical evangelical movements like Pentecostalism, with their lack of hierarchical structure,

---

10. Neiiendam, *Frikirker og Sekter*, 210.

11. Anna Larssen Bjørner collection (Theatre Museum); see also Neiiendam, *Gennem mange Aar*, 195–203.

12. Anna Larssen Bjørner collection (Royal Library), I., letters August 11, 1926, October 3, 1926; T. B. Barratt Papers I.18, p. 55; XIII.a.

13. T. B. Barratt Papers, I.13, p. 11, letters August 5, 1909 and August 4, 1909 respectively.

14. See *Social-Demokraten* (November 21, 1909) front page.

provided a sphere in which they could operate more freely than in the rest of society.

The leader of the clinic, Professor Daniel Jacobson, had many connections with artistic and literary circles and a strong commitment to cultural radicalism, paired with a humorous but dismissive approach to religion.[15] Like in the case of his most famous patient, the Norwegian painter Edvard Munch, Jacobson was discrete enough to avoid divulging any further information about Larssen, a prominent public figure in a delicate situation.[16] It falls beyond the scope of this brief account to systematically apply a Foucauldian concept of "disciplinary institutions" to experiences such as Larssen's, but this would be recommendable for a future study. Jacobson seems, like his mentor Knud Pontoppidan, to have been somewhat cautious in defining a clear line between insanity and normality.[17] Nonetheless, he put Larssen in the latter category. After two months, she was allowed to go.[18]

During her time in the clinic, Larssen translated the popular English mystic Marie Corelli's *A Romance of Two Worlds*. Her Christian friends, including Barratt, were somewhat concerned about this apparent fondness for the esoteric.[19] But at the time, Larssen felt that this work encapsulated her dilemma. The American scholar David Bundy suggests that the alliterative title of Anna Larssen Bjørner's later autobiography, *Teater og Tempel* ("Theater and Temple") is meant to deliberately evoke the name of the trendsetting newspaper *Politiken*'s long-running review column *Teater og Tribune*—"Tribune" meaning a platform, either for spectators or performers.[20] Bjørner had been caught between two realms, with more striking parallels than most of their respective supporters would admit. But by embracing the "Temple," she was no longer merely a spectator in her own life. In an interview, she mentioned that the "last years at the theater were so terrible" for her because of the manager, Martinius Nielsen, and the poor quality of the repertoire, but only when this

---

15. Jacobson, *I Kittel*, 121, 139–40.

16. Therkelsen, "Edvard Munch," 285.

17. Jacobson, *Sindssyg—ikke sindssyg?*; Brinkmann and Triantafillou, *Psykens historier*, 55–57.

18. Bjørner, *Teater og Tempel*, 117.

19. *Byposten* (November 15, 1909) 92.

20. Bundy, *Visions*, 197.

conversation turned to her religious life did she unambiguously state her decision never to return to the stage.[21]

BEGINNINGS IN MINISTRY

Anna Larssen's farewell to the theater had drastically increased public awareness of the fledgling Pentecostal movement in Denmark. Barratt continued to return to Copenhagen frequently. The press was still hungry for a scandal. Larssen wrote a private letter to a newspaper editor complaining about a covert agenda and false allegations against Barratt.[22] The coverage meant that, for a time, the revival meetings became rowdy. After several weeks when things had begun to calm down, Larssen gave her public testimony, a year after her first direct experience of the Holy Spirit. She describes the admittedly very large hall as having been half-empty on this occasion.[23] This may have been due to an increased admission charge, apparently to raise more funds to help the unemployed who had been well represented at the meetings.

Larssen or Lewini would have been unconventional choices to lead the continuing Pentecostal assembly that sprang from this, not just because of their gender but because they were relatively recent converts with no leadership experience, very unlike most other early Pentecostal leaders. Instead, Barratt persuaded Larssen's old acquaintance Mygind to return from a stint in Lebanon. Nonetheless, Mygind gave a big platform to Larssen and other women leaders. What he perhaps did not know was that he was Barratt's second choice for this task. Barratt had first approached H.P. Mollerup (1866–1929), a popular Lutheran pastor. Though not directly involved with the Pentecostal movement himself, he was the stepson of Johanne Mollerup who had been a mentor to Larssen and Lewini. Barratt knew that Mollerup had a better reputation among Danish revivalist Lutherans than Mygind—and perhaps a more stable theology as well.[24]

Barratt was probably also hesitant to call Mygind home from an important task on the mission field. Nonetheless, perhaps the idea of finding a leader that he could "have full confidence in" came partly

---

21. *Aarhuus Stiftstidende* (October 12, 1909) 3.
22. T. B. Barratt Papers, I.13, p. 11, November 4, 1909.
23. Bjørner, *Teater og Tempel*, 135.
24. Christensen, *Unorganized Religion*, 86–87.

from regrets over the long shot that approaching Mollerup had been.[25] However, Mollerup too would undoubtedly have supported Larssen. It seems likely that Barratt was keen to secure a leader who would enable her to find her "higher platform."[26] The meetings were begun on February 23, 1910 after Barratt returned from a few days away in Gothenburg, where he had joined Larssen and Lewini who were speaking at a gathering there.[27]

Larssen's conversion and the upheaval that followed had caught the attention of Pentecostal leaders across the world. When Alexander Boddy visited the Pentecostals in Copenhagen, he commented on her appeal to the local citizenry: "It is to them so very wonderful to see the pet-actress of gay pleasure-loving Copenhagen—the Paris of the North—converted and giving thus to those present sincerely a Holy Message."[28] But though she was now speaking words that conveyed her own convictions, she was still relying on sermons, stories, poems, and songs written by others. Women were still barred from the state church's pulpits as well as from most other public roles, and thus Larssen had few models to emulate as over almost a decade she slowly found the confidence to preach without a script.[29]

SECOND MARRIAGE

At one of her speaking engagements, Larssen had met the evangelist and former lieutenant Sigurd Bjørner who was now working for the Danish YMCA. The two were married in July 1912. Sigurd Bjørner himself retrospectively outlined his spiritual development like this: awakened to the burden of sin at the age of 7, saved at the age of 19, but only baptized in the Spirit in 1919 at the age of 43, shortly after his adult baptism.[30]

---

25. T. B. Barratt Papers, I.13, p. 11, undated letter, circa November 1909.

26. Bjørner, *Teater og Tempel*, 130.

27. *KS* (March 1, 1910) 39; (April 1, 1910) 54–55.

28. *Confidence* (October 1910) 229; see also *Byposten* (December 15, 1909) 99; *Confidence* (January 1910) 3–5; *Glöd från Altaret* (February 1910) 11–13; *The Upper Room* (March 1910) 3.

29. Female preachers were not completely unprecedented even within the state church, but they may have been so rare that Larssen was unaware of them; see Martinsen, "Apostelinder."

30. Jensen, *Mindeskrift*, 11–13.

Anna Bjørner later described her husband as "my best friend on Earth."[31] Her personal papers, including photographs, witness to this.[32] But her work as a travelling evangelist in Denmark and beyond was well under way from a couple of years before she married Sigurd. Her background made her the most cosmopolitan of the Danish Pentecostals. And her independent travel activity continued after her marriage. Among the places she would visit to speak and share her testimony were larger towns in Western Denmark such as Aarhus, Holstebro, and Horsens.[33] But increasingly the Bjørners worked side by side, especially after Bjørner left the YMCA.

They were given a horse-drawn wagon and a large tent for meetings, probably by the butter merchant Thorvald Plum who was known to sponsor Pentecostal activities. Alternatively, the benefactor could have been the tobacco manufacturer C. W. Obel, who also donated the money for a large villa to them. The villa in Helsingør north of Copenhagen was used simultaneously as a residence and a meeting hall. But in their tent, they could go to where people were and had the time to go to revival meetings—a favored spot was the beaches near their home. Over the summer they would reside in their wagon.

During this time, Anna Bjørner continued to busy herself as a translator. Among the books she translated was T. W. Moore's critique of the Millennium Dawn movement—later known as Jehovah's Witnesses—probably wishing to ensure that there could be no confusion between this and the Pentecostal movement.[34] She was extremely interested in ensuring the Pentecostal movement had a strong public image. In 1913, she reported that the famous professor of theology Valdemar Ammundsen had stated that "The tongues we have heard . . . of late years, are surely the same as those heard in the days of the apostles."[35] The same year, her husband's former boss Olfert Ricard wrote to her that he himself "would like to possess the gift of tongues."[36] As late as 1927, to her surprise, she

---

31. Jensen, *Mindeskrift*, 16.

32. Anna Larssen Bjørner Collection (Royal Library), III.

33. *Aarhuus Stiftstidende* (December 15, 1912) 2; (December 17, 1912) 1; (May 5, 1913) 3; *Jyllandsposten* (December 17, 1912) 3; *Horsens Folkeblad* (November 24, 1913), 5.

34. Moore, *Milleniets Daggry*.

35. Barratt, *When the Fire Fell*, 184.

36. Bjørner, *Hørt, tænkt og talt*, 54.

heard an unnamed Lutheran pastor offer a cautious but positive appraisal of the Bjørners from his pulpit.[37]

During the winters, the Bjørners traveled other parts of the country. One particularly widely reported visit was to Sæby in Northern Denmark, where Anna Bjørner's prayers apparently healed a young woman of tuberculosis in December 1916.[38] By 1918, Anna Bjørner had definitively put her literary readings behind her in favor of a direct preaching ministry, which once again made her more independent of her husband, at least for a time.[39] Already in 1917, she felt able to comment on the typical preaching style of state church pastors, whom she likened to unctuous "ham" actors. She noted that the first principle she had learnt on stage should also apply to preaching: to "speak with the same voice that you speak in every day"—but she reasoned that state church pastors were not able to do this since they did not practice a "full gospel" on the other six days of the week.[40]

OVERCOMING DIVISIONS

It has been claimed that the Danish Pentecostal movement was "at a standstill" during the 1910s.[41] But in fact a slow and steady spread was still happening during this period, and there were theological and organizational developments under way, which would shape the Pentecostal movement in the years to follow. I make a distinction between *denominational* and *interdenominational* Pentecostalism, which is somewhat artificial. In fact, there was plenty of crosspollination and overlap between the two. The goal is not to present them as two different movements, but rather as two different strategies, sometimes adopted successively by the same leaders. The interdenominational group consisted of those most closely connected with Barratt's ministry, such as the Bjørners; these were hesitant to separate themselves from the existing churches and form their

---

37. Bjørner, *Hørt, tænkt og talt*, 55–56.

38. *Evangelii Härold* (December 28, 1916) 212; *Berlingske Tidende* (September 10, 1950) 9–10, cited in "Fru Anna Larssen Bjørners Liv og Levned," MS by Johannes Rasmussen, held in the Anna Larssen Bjørner collection (Theatre Museum), p. 3.

39. Anna Larssen Bjørner collection (Theatre Museum), letter to "H.P." dated September 14, 1918; cf. contemporary reports, e.g., *Evangelii Härold* (February 8, 1917) 27.

40. *Evangelii Härold* (March 1, 1917) 38, quoting from *Svenska Morgonbladet*.

41. Neiiendam, *Frikirker og Sekter*, 213.

own. But the 1910s saw the slow end of interdenominational Pentecostalism and the beginnings of a Pentecostal denomination in Denmark.

A significant leader in the interdenominational group was the Bjørners' friend Carl Næser (1875–1944). Little is known of his religious development before he first met Sigurd Bjørner; other members of his aristocratic family seem to have been committed Christians but not necessarily of the revivalist sort. The rupture with the YMCA, where Næser and Bjørner had been colleagues, did not mean an end to their collaboration; Håkon Hanssen's biography of Anna Bjørner describes Næser as the soul of their work in Helsingør, and he also helped with the tent meetings.[42] Næser's private guestbook confirms that, at least around 1915–1917 when the Bjørners were traveling most extensively, his home became an significant gathering place for Pentecostals who were not ready to associate themselves with any of the budding Pentecostal congregations, which required adult baptism for full membership.[43]

Unlike in some other contexts, division does not seem to have led to multiplication in Denmark, only confusion. There was a need for a new unifying leadership, and once again the person at the center would be Anna Larssen Bjørner. The road there was rocky—for a while she supported the controversial doctrine of universal salvation which sprouted among Danish Pentecostals at this time, possibly influenced by the American Pentecostal leader Joseph H. King who had visited Copenhagen in 1912 and whose theology tended somewhat in that direction.[44] This doctrine was principally promoted by another early Danish Pentecostal, Asmus Biehl, but in 1919, the Bjørners signaled a new, unified direction for the Pentecostal movement in Denmark, by being baptized in water themselves and forming a rapidly growing congregation of their own in Copenhagen.[45] The religious press was horrified. An editorial in *Kristeligt Dagblad* seemed to concede that it was the Bjørners' newfound success that made criticism necessary: "The present time is a time of decay in all areas, including the religious area. It is only a small number of weeks ago that the Bjørners were rebaptized, and they have already succeeded in baptizing quite a few."[46]

42. Hanssen, *Anna Larssen Bjørner*, 39–40.
43. Vincent Næser archive, III.D.2.
44. Jacobsen, *Thinking*, 178–79; Christensen, *Unorganized Religion*, 139.
45. Christensen, *Unorganized Religion*, 147–52.
46. *Kristeligt Dagblad* (August 27, 1919) quoted in Bjørner, *Hvad vi tror*, 5.

Anna Bjørner's memoirs, which have an apologetic aim, make no mention of the controversial topic of adult baptisms—neither her and her husband's nor their converts'. Bloch-Hoell considered the developments in 1919 a result of Barratt's "apostolic" influence—but Neiiendam, whom he cited, actually concurred with the interpretation that the main impulses at the time came from Sweden.[47] It was Swedish Pentecostals who had been consistent supporters of the denominational faction. The fact that the Bjørners were baptized by a Norwegian (in Sweden) is also not enough to stipulate a strong Norwegian influence at the time.

Jens Folkertsen, a fellow universalist, arrived from the island of Bornholm in 1919 to assist the Bjørners in their work in the Copenhagen area.[48] In December that year, the Bjørners gathered a Scandinavian Pentecostal conference in Copenhagen at a monumental hall known as *Koncertpalæet*, which had also been used for previous Pentecostal meetings, most recently by the Bjørners during the spring of 1919.[49] While the Pentecostals seem in general to have been ready to accept the new baptismal practice (which many local groups had already adopted years earlier), two other issues remained controversial enough that they had to be discussed at the conference: universalism and freedom of organization. Whereas unsurprisingly Lewi Pethrus took the lead in the discussions on ecclesiology, it was mainly Barratt who addressed the soteriological issue.[50] The outcome of the conference was that the Danish Pentecostals agreed to reject universalist teachings, and the Scandinavian congregational model of organization was cemented. It seemed that this form of organization enabled effective leadership to a greater degree than either more loosely organized assemblies or more hierarchical denominational structures. The first brief report in the Swedish periodical *Evangelii Härold* stated that "We hope to God that these days have been of great significance for the Lord's work in Denmark."[51]

There were only few negative reactions to the developments from inside the Pentecostal movement itself; it seems that those who insisted on infant baptism were relatively rare by 1919. Some, such as H. J. Mygind, may have already realized which way the wind was blowing and left quietly. An interesting case is the aforementioned Lutheran pastor H.

---

47. Bloch-Hoell, *Pentecostal Movement*, 79; Neiiendam, *Frikirker og Sekter*, 213.
48. Neiiendam, *Frikirker og Sekter*, 214–15.
49. *Korsets Budskab* (June 1919) 4.
50. *Korsets Budskab* (January 1920) 1–2.
51. *Evangelii Härold* (December 23, 1919) 201.

P. Mollerup, a friend and relative of numerous Pentecostals in Copenhagen. He had officiated at the Bjørners' marriage but his relationship with the movement had remained somewhat ambiguous. However, in December 1921 he is reported to have received Spirit baptism and spoken in tongues—but like Thorvald Plum and Mygind he remained in the state church. Infant baptism was the main question that separated him from the Pentecostal movement.[52]

THEOLOGIAN

The basic message of the early Pentecostals in Denmark seems in many ways to have been similar enough to that of the Lutheran revival movements that preceded them. Mygind emphasized in 1913 in a letter to Anna Bjørner that only faith is required—only empty hands and a childish receiving faith, which was one of the reasons he could not follow those Pentecostals who rejected infant baptism.[53] The early Pentecostals were Christocentric: Anna Bjørner recounts an Italian officer's reaction to a meeting in 1926: "To think that they only spoke of Jesus Christ all evening."[54]

When the Pentecostal movement had become more organized in 1919, it also became both more visible and more interconnected on the national level. The move away from the established church may have meant a loss of respectability in some sense, though it might be asked how widely respected it is possible to be for a movement that is simultaneously nearly anonymous—apart from the one name attached to it in the public imagination: Anna Larssen Bjørner herself, who retained her public profile. Moreover, any loss of respectability was not unambiguous, as the well-regarded H. P. Mollerup was finally drawn closer to the Pentecostal movement. Nonetheless, there was strong external opposition to the new developments. The fiercest Lutheran critic of the Pentecostals was Emil Steenvinkel (1892–1959). Aside from attacking their rejection of infant baptism, he furthermore claimed that the Bjørners were

---

52. KS (December 30, 1921) 4; Bjørner, Hørt, tænkt og talt, 23–24; Mygind, H.P. Mollerup, 67–68, 106–12.

53. Anna Larssen Bjørner Collection (Royal Library), I., dated September 17, 1913.

54. Bjørner, Teater og Tempel, 167.

rejecting the gospel of grace and preaching "sinlessness," though this accusation is given less weight and substance.[55]

In response, Anna Bjørner wrote a short book, the first by a Danish Pentecostal to present and defend Pentecostal doctrine as a whole. Though she attempted to show that many aspects of their teaching were a natural extension of Lutheranism, it becomes abundantly clear that the differences are very real, perhaps without her fully realizing it. As with the radical Holiness movements around the turn of the century, there was a disagreement over the words from Luther's Small Catechism: "we sin greatly each day."[56] Bjørner refused to believe that her Lutheran opponents believed this literally, though from encounters in the past, she was well aware that it was what they preached.[57] Bjørner rejected Steenvinkel's classically Lutheran reading of Romans 7.[58] At the same time, she also made sure to distance herself from the extremes of the earlier radical "sinless" movement. In a later piece, Anna Bjørner emphasized that though it was possible to achieve "perfection" in a certain sense (namely through Spirit baptism), this did not take away the need for a "daily struggle of faith and death to self" as some had previously believed, resulting in antinomianism.[59]

Anna Bjørner also defended the original "specialty" of Pentecostalism—Spirit baptism—on Biblical grounds, seeking to show that it is no specialty at all, but her arguments from experience are perhaps questionable when defending against that particular charge.[60] Her defense of divine healing, on the other hand, did not contest Steenvinkel's claim that the Pentecostals attach great importance to the outward signs; instead she attacked the Lutherans back for their lack of church discipline.[61] She defended the Pentecostal emphasis on the second coming of Christ with a barrage of Bible verses, but perhaps missed the point by not addressing

---

55. Steenvinkel-Svendsen, *Vær paa Vagt*, 9, 16.

56. From the explanation of the Lord's Prayer, fifth petition; see Luther, *Primary Works*, 12; for the controversy surrounding the same phrase within the Holiness movement, see Olesen, *De frigjorte*, e.g., 489.

57. Bjørner, *Hvad vi tror*, 7–10.

58. Bjørner, *Hvad vi tror*, 10–12; cf. Steenvinkel-Svendsen, *Vær paa Vagt*, 16.

59. *KS* (March 10, 1922) 4.

60. Bjørner, *Hvad vi tror*, 13–17.

61. Bjørner, *Hvad vi tror*, 17–23.

the actual charge, which was that the Pentecostals were proclaiming the *imminent* return of Christ.[62]

However, by far the longest section in Bjørner's book, as also in Steenvinkel's pamphlet, concerns the question of believers' baptism. It is clear that she was influenced by voices from abroad, where the practice of infant baptism was not as universally assumed, and that she was eager for Danish Christians to turn their gaze outward. One intriguing possibility is that she was inspired by the English pastor W. O. Hutchinson (1864–1928) who also provided part of the theological basis for the Welsh-led Apostolic Church, which the Bjørners would later join, though his doctrine of the five-fold ministry of apostles, prophets, etc. was not yet as fully developed or as central as it would later become. At the end of her book, Anna Bjørner formulated a statement of faith for the Danish Pentecostal movement using the same characteristic phrase that Hutchinson used—"What we believe and teach"—which was also the title of Bjørner's book:

> I gather together what we believe and teach in the following points:
>
> Firstly:
> We believe and teach that we are saved solely by the blood of Jesus Christ, the Son of God, poured out for our sins.
> (Acts 4:12; Matt 26:28; 1 Pet 1:18–19.)
>
> Secondly:
> That by the same blood we have healing, when we are sick.
> (Isa 53:4; Matt 8:18; 1 Pet 2:24.)
>
> That we as those who are dead with Christ must be buried in the water of baptism in the name of the Father, the Son and the Holy Spirit, as our pledge of a clear conscience towards God and our confession before the world.
> (Rom 6:4; Matt 28:19; 1 Pet 3:21.)
>
> That by the law of the Spirit of life in Christ Jesus we have been made free from serving under the yoke of sin, and that He is mighty to "keep us from falling," when we are walking in the light and the blood of Jesus is allowed to purify us from all sin and unrighteousness.
> (Rom 8:2; Jude 24; 1 John 1:7–9.)

---

62. Bjørner, *Hvad vi tror*, 23–25.

That the baptism of the Holy Spirit, in the same way as we read that the first Christians experienced it, is for us and should be desired and received if we are to be able to put on the full armor of God and "withstand in the evil day, having done all."
(Acts 2:4; Eph 5:18, 6:10–18.)

That all the gifts of the Spirit, as they are mentioned in 1 Cor 12:7–10, should continually be found in the churches according to the word of Jesus Christ and the Apostle Paul.
(Mark 16:17–20; John 14:12; 1 Cor 14:1; 13:8–12.)

That as saved and baptized one should belong to a congregation ordered according to the Biblical pattern.
(Acts 2:41; 14:24; 1 Tim 3:2, 8, 15; Eph 4:18.)

That communion or the breaking of bread is a congregational meal: that is, only for those who are saved and baptized.
(Acts 2:41–42; 20:7.)

That the second coming of Jesus Christ is near according to the prophecies of Scripture, and in line with what the Holy Spirit is testifying in the churches throughout the world through prophecy and the interpretation of tongues.
(Rev 3:11; 22:12, 17, 20; 1 Thess 5:6.)

And that there is an "eternal judgement," an eternal separation from God for all those who do not receive Jesus Christ as their savior.
(Heb 6:2; 9:27; Rev 14:11; 20:15; 22:15.)[63]

Bjørner's list shows especially strong similarities with the earliest form of Hutchinson's doctrinal statement from 1910. All but the first of Hutchinson's eight points have a direct equivalent in Bjørner's statement, in almost the same order—and she would hardly have rejected his first point of "Repentance, Confession and Restitution" either. Both emphasized the blood of Christ, including with reference to sanctification.[64] In Hutchinson's later statements sanctification and water baptism no longer appear in the same order.[65] Bjørner's statement has no equally obvious overlap

63. Bjørner, *Hvad vi tror*, 57–59. Translation my own.
64. *Showers of Blessing*, No. 1 (January 1910), 5; see also Cho, "Move to Independence," 119–20.
65. *Showers of Blessing*, No. 11 (undated, ca. 1913), 9; No. 12 (undated, ca. 1914), 9–10, repeated in No. 13 and 15.

with the "Eleven Tenets" of the Apostolic Church, which were only available in Welsh (in their complete form) until 1920.[66] There is also not a strong similarity to T. B. Barratt's statement of faith from 1911,[67] nor to his later version from 1919, which was instead reproduced in the Danish Pentecostal periodical *Korsets Budskab*.[68]

However, I have seen no indication of any contact with Scandinavia in Hutchinson's *Showers of Blessing* or other literature on his Apostolic Faith Church; the closest would be a letter from Finland.[69] It might be that Bjørner simply happened to be in possession of a years-old issue of the publication, which was distributed freely and usually undated. The Bjørners could have picked up a copy during their visit to England for the Keswick conference in 1913.[70] The Apostolic Church had already split from Hutchinson in 1916, but if Bjørner drew on his doctrinal statement then it would at least confirm that she was consciously taking a step away from the interdenominational strategy (including its air of respectability due to state church connections), since Hutchinson had been condemned by Anglican Pentecostal leaders a few years earlier.[71]

The main differences between the two statements are that Bjørner includes the gifts of the Spirit as a separate point (no. 6), as well as the precise prescriptions regarding baptism and congregational order (no. 7, inspired by a Swedish formula), and finally the possibility of eternal damnation (no. 10), which could be seen as an explicit rejection of her earlier universalism. Bjørner also places divine healing as high up as second place, which could confirm that this practice had held a central position in the Bjørners' ministry during the 1910s.

There is a certain irony in the fact that Anna—not Sigurd—Bjørner authored this doctrinal statement if it was based on one formulated by Hutchinson, who was an outspoken opponent of letting women "teach doctrines,"[72] though this also foreshadows the humbler role that Anna Bjørner would assume when they joined the Apostolic Church four years

---

66. Hollenweger, *Handbuch*, 2:1730–32; Burgess and van der Maas, *New International Dictionary*, 322–23. For an analysis of the Welsh Apostolic leader D.P. Williams's departures from Hutchinson's original formulation, see Worsfold, *Origins*, 102–7; and for background, see 91–95, 188–90.

67. *KS* (January 1, 1911) 1, also reprinted in Hollenweger, *Handbuch*, 2:1964.

68. Thomas Ball Barratt, "Klare Linier," *KS* (September 1, 1919); *Korsets Budskab* (October 1919) 1–2; (November 1919) 1–2.

69. *Showers of Blessing*, No. 14 (ca. 1914) 8.

70. Bjørner, *Teater og Tempel*, 148–51.

71. Walsh, *To Meet*, 194–98.

72. *Showers of Blessing*, No. 14 (ca. 1914) 12; see also White, *Word of God*, 148–50.

later. Whether there were outside influences or not at this point, the central point to note is that the criticisms that the Pentecostals encountered had now prompted them to clarify what they believed, making the new divide even sharper.

THE GOSPEL ASSEMBLY

Formally it was Sigurd Bjørner—not Anna—who took on the mantle of leadership with the formation of the Gospel Assembly in 1919. His ascendancy led to internal tensions, and after a couple of years came to a head in a conflict which is discussed at some length by Neiiendam, whereas it is entirely to be expected that Anna Bjørner would omit this in *Teater og Tempel*.[73] Sigurd Bjørner's opponents rejected pragmatic forms of organization in favor of what they thought had been divinely revealed to them—for example, through prophetic women. Anna Bjørner herself was attempting to push her husband into the foreground at her own expense, but perhaps his abilities were overstretched. Some looked elsewhere for leadership; a competition over national influence was brewing between the Gospel Assembly in Copenhagen and the congregations in Northern Denmark.

Meanwhile, the evangelistic activities centered around the Bjørners were continuing. Increasingly the main base for their "Gospel Tent" was the busy *Trianglen* intersection in Copenhagen, though this intensely public location also provided for a few troublemakers who mocked and occasionally disrupted the meetings.[74] Members of the Gospel Assembly also did their best to spread the belief in the power of the gospel, and specifically divine healing. Some of them visited hospitals to sing and speak to patients.[75] By the end of 1921, the congregation had reached five hundred members and was building itself a permanent home.[76] Before that, from the autumn of 1920 the Gospel Assembly had begun to hold its meetings in a hall which was shared with a pre-existing Pentecostal congregation, Filadelfia, many of whose members had already switched

---

73. Neiiendam, *Frikirker og Sekter*, 216–17.
74. *KS* (January 10, 1922) 5–6; Bjørner, *Teater og Tempel*, 155–56.
75. *KS* (December 20, 1921) 4–5.
76. *Evangelii Härold* (December 8, 1921) 223.

to the Gospel Assembly. Only occasionally would they hold joint meetings with the remaining members of Filadelfia.[77]

To reach and unite Pentecostals across the country—as well as across Scandinavia—the Bjørners began to edit their own pages in Barratt's periodical, *Korsets Seir*. Barratt had suggested the partnership to the Bjørners at the inauguration of the new hall for the Filadelfia church in Stockholm, in September 1921. The idea was realized only a month later—a snap decision.[78] Then followed a relatively successful period in the history of Pentecostalism in Denmark, which was however interrupted by a schism in 1924, at which point over half of the Pentecostal movement in Denmark, including the Bjørners, joined the Apostolic Church. This was a time of reorganization and institutionalization across the European Pentecostal movements, which also meant an end to formal public ministry for women, even the famous Anna Bjørner.

Growth had been good but also meant chaos. Now Denmark became the well-organized Apostolic Church's beachhead in continental Europe. This was one of the fastest-growing Pentecostal denominations in Europe, if only for a brief time during these years. The timing was exactly right for it to seem the obvious solution to the lack of organization that the Danish Pentecostals had been experiencing.[79]

EPILOGUE

In 1936, the Bjørners left the Apostolic Church behind and began afresh with a new congregation in Copenhagen. Perhaps the publicity garnered from Anna Bjørner's memoirs, published for her sixtieth birthday the previous year, had convinced them that they still had an independent influence to exercise. For the years to come until she died at the age of 79, Anna Bjørner remained the central public figure of the Danish Pentecostal movement, still remembered by the press for both her dramatic talent and her dramatic conversion.[80] Her charisma transcended any formal institutional hierarchies.

77. Neiiendam, *Frikirker og Sekter*, 215–16.
78. *KS* (October 20, 1921) 4.
79. Christensen, *Unorganized Religion*, 174–94.
80. E.g., *Berlingske Aftenavis* (March 24, 1942) 6, 8; (March 10, 1950) 4, 6; *Aarhuus Stiftstidende* (September 7, 1950) 3–4; *Sorø Amtstidende* (September 9, 1950) 4–5; *Berlingske Tidende* (September 10, 1950) 9–10; (March 6, 1955) 2; *Frederikshavns Avis* (October 2, 1952) 2, 7; *Politiken* (March 6, 1955) 7–8.

In a book published near the end of her life, she emphasizes more strongly than ever the disharmony she experienced after her Spirit baptism and concludes: "A follower of Christ must be found in his Father's work. His [sic] place is not in high society, not in the ballroom, and not in the theater."[81] Whether or not one believes this judgement is still equally relevant today, one cannot but admire the radical integrity that led her on her unexpected path.

BIBLIOGRAPHY

Alberoni, Francesco. *Movement and Institution.* Translated by Patricia C. Arden Delmoro. New York: Columbia University Press, 1984.
Anna Larssen Bjørner collection ("Efterladte papirer," Acc. 2012/175), Royal Library, Copenhagen.
Anna Larssen Bjørner collection, Theatre Museum at the Court Theatre, Copenhagen.
Barratt, Thomas Ball. *When the Fire Fell, and an Outline of My Life.* Oslo: Alfons Hansen & Sønner, 1927.
Bjørner, Anna Larssen. *Hørt, tænkt og talt.* Copenhagen: Facula, 1954.
———. *Hvad vi tror og lærer. En kort redegørelse til kristenheden i Danmark.* Copenhagen: V. Pios Boghandel, 1920.
———. *Teater og Tempel. Livserindringer.* Copenhagen: H. Hirschsprungs Forlag, 1935.
Bloch-Hoell, Nils E. *The Pentecostal Movement.* Oslo: Universitetsforlaget, 1964.
Brinkmann, Svend, and Peter Triantafillou, eds. *Psykens historier i Danmark: om forståelsen og styringen af sjælelivet.* Frederiksberg: Samfundslitteratur, 2008.
Bundy, David D. *Visions of Apostolic Mission: Scandinavian Pentecostal Mission to 1935.* Uppsala: Uppsala University Library, 2009.
Burgess, Stanley M., and Eduard M. van der Maas, eds. *The New International Dictionary of Pentecostal and Charismatic Movements.* Grand Rapids: Zondervan, 2002.
Cho, Kyu-Hyung. "The Move to Independence from Anglican Leadership: An Examination of the Relationship between Alexander Alfred Boddy and the Early Leaders of the British Pentecostal Denominations (1907–1930)." University of Birmingham, 2009. http://etheses.bham.ac.uk/421/.
Christensen, Nikolaj. "Flickering Flames: The Early Pentecostal Movement in Denmark, 1907–1924." PhD diss., University of Birmingham, 2017.
———. *Unorganized Religion: Pentecostalism and Secularization in Denmark, 1907–1924.* Global Pentecostal and Charismatic Studies 42. Leiden: Brill, 2022.
Hanssen, Håkon. *Anna Larssen Bjørner: Skuespillerinnen som valgte Kristus.* Oslo: Filadelfiaforlaget, 1950.
Hollenweger, Walter J. *Handbuch der Pfingstbewegung.* 10 vols. Geneva, 1965.
Jacobsen, Douglas Gordon. *Thinking in the Spirit: Theologies of the Early Pentecostal Movement.* Bloomington: Indiana University Press, 2003.
Jacobson, Daniel. *I Kittel og Kjole: Smaatræk af et Menneskes Liv.* Copenhagen: Hirschsprung, 1932.

---

81. Bjørner, *Hørt, tænkt og talt,* 116.

———. *Sindssyg—ikke sindssyg?: Foredrag holdt i Studenterforeningen 16. November 1918*. Copenhagen: E. Jespersen, 1918.
Jensen, Kristian. *Mindeskrift: Sigurd Bjørner 28.7.1875—18.2.1953*. Copenhagen: Vanløse Evangelieforsamlings Forlag, 1954.
Luther, Martin. *Luther's Primary Works: Together with His Shorter and Larger Catechisms*. Edited by C. A. Buchheim and Henry Wace. London: Hodder & Stoughton, 1896.
Martinsen, Lone Kølle. "Apostelinder: Grundtvig og spørgsmålet om kvindelige præster." In *Guds ord i kvindemund: om køn og kirke*, edited by Else Marie Wiberg Pedersen, 157–88. Copenhagen: Nord Academic, 2023.
Moore, T. W. *Milleniets Daggry eller International Forening for Bibelstudium's Lære: undersøgt i Lyset af Guds Ord*. Translated by Anna Larssen Bjørner. Copenhagen, 1915.
Mygind, Hans Jacob. *H.P. Mollerup: Kirkens Korshær Stifter*. Copenhagen: Lohse, 1944.
Neiiendam, Klaus, and Robert Neiiendam. "Anna Larssen Bjørner." In *Dansk Biografisk Leksikon*, edited by Svend Cedergreen Bech. Copenhagen: Gyldendal, 1979. http://denstoredanske.dk/Dansk_Biografisk_Leksikon/Kunst_og_kultur/Teater_og_film/Skuespiller/Anna_Larssen_Bjørner.
Neiiendam, Michael. *Frikirker og Sekter*. 1st ed. Copenhagen: G. E. C. Gad, 1927.
Neiiendam, Robert. *Gennem mange Aar*. Copenhagen: Branner og Korch, 1950.
Olesen, Elith. *De frigjorte og trællefolket: Amerikansk-engelsk indflydelse på dansk kirkeliv omkring år 1900*. Frederiksberg: Anis, 1996.
Steenvinkel-Svendsen, Emil. *Vær paa Vagt! En Redegørelse om de kristelige Livstegn i Anledning af den Bjørnerske Gendøber- og Syndfrihedslære*. Copenhagen: Christian F. Rømer, 1919.
T. B. Barratt Papers ("Etterlatte papirer," Ms.4° 3341). National Library of Norway, Oslo.
Therkelsen, Jørgen. "Edvard Munch og Daniel Jacobson." *Bibliotek for læger* 185 (1993) 285–303.
Vincent Næser archive (Vincent Næser, Privatarkiv 8014), Danish National Archives (Rigsarkivet), Copenhagen.
Walsh, Timothy Bernard. *"To Meet and Satisfy a Very Hungry People:" The Origins and Fortunes of English Pentecostalism, 1907–1925*. Studies in Evangelical History and Thought. Milton Keynes: Paternoster, 2012.
White, Kent. *The Word of God Coming Again: Return of Apostolic Faith and Works Now Due on the Earth. With a Sketch of the Life of Pastor W. Oliver Hutchinson*. Bournemouth: Apostolic Faith Church, 1919.
Worsfold, James E. *The Origins of the Apostolic Church in Great Britain: With a Breviate of Its Early Missionary Endeavours*. Wellington: Julian Literature Trust, 1991.

Image #6. Anna Lewini.

5

Anna Lewini
From a Radical Conversion to a Hidden Ministry[1]

MALENE KJÆR ERIKSEN AND NIKOLAJ CHRISTENSEN

Anna Lewini (1874–1951) was a Danish actress who converted to Pentecostalism and became an evangelist who traveled the world to preach the Gospel. She eventually became one of the first foreign Pentecostal missionaries in Sri Lanka and can be considered one of the founders of Pentecostalism in Sri Lanka.

CONVERSION

When it comes to Lewini's childhood, she lived a culturally Christian life. She was a member of the Danish Lutheran Church.[2] Anna Lewini wrote a short book about her time before and around her conversion in detail.[3] Although one should be cautious about autobiographical statements from recent converts, which tend to be framed in a very particular light, her book is a valuable first-hand source of not only the events of the early Pentecostal revival in Copenhagen but also the felt experience of it.

---

1. All translations in this chapter are the authors' own.
2. Somaratna, *Walter H. Clifford*, 11.
3. Lewini, *Min omvendelse*. An English version of her testimony was later published in *Confidence* (January–March 1922) 7, 10–12.

She also explains her early life in her book. She writes that she went to church and Sunday school throughout her childhood but after she had her confirmation, she turned away from the so-called "Christian life" and turned to the world instead. She describes that as the years went by, her aversion to religion was increasing. To earn a living, she started to do theatrical acting. She married a fellow actor, Carl Sigurd Lomholt, but became divorced, like Anna Larssen Bjørner, and went by her mother's last name. She, too, had been an actress. Anna Lewini's conversion happened while working in a theatre in Copenhagen around 1909. During this period of her life, she was happy, and her mind was stable. She explains that she was mostly in a good mood, so it was no hardship or misery that led her to God.[4]

It was a colleague at the Theatre, Anna Larssen, who made her come to a Pentecostal meeting in Copenhagen where she came to faith. The Pentecostal meeting, at which Lewini converted to the Pentecostal faith, was a revival meeting which was led by Pastor Thomas Ball Barratt in 1909. Sometime before the meeting and Lewini's conversion, Anna Larssen was "under the influence" of Pentecostalism because of Pastor Thomas Ball Barratt's preaching. Barratt came from Norway to lead several meetings in Copenhagen in 1907 and preached about the experiences he had had with the Spirit in New York in 1906. There was resistance from various church leaders, including Baptists and Lutherans. Despite this, some of their members were open to hearing about the new awakening. Lars Due Christensen, a former pastor at *Kirken i Kulturcenteret*, which has emerged from different Pentecostal churches in Copenhagen, thinks that the reason that the Pentecostal movement did not become as big in Denmark as in the rest of the Nordic countries is that there were no strong leaders in Denmark to go in front, like Norway's Thomas Ball Barratt or Sweden's Lewi Pethrus. He claims that there was a possibility for the movement to grow bigger. He rightly notes that Barratt "writes in his memoirs that what he experienced at the meetings in Denmark was some of the strongest in Scandinavia." He concludes on this basis: "If there had been stronger leaders in the beginning, who could get it organized, it would have looked different."[5] This is certainly one of the factors that influenced the development of early Danish Pentecostalism. But Barratt

---

4. Lewini, *Min omvendelse*, 4–7; "Anna Lomholt—dansk film database."
5. Hansen, "Da Helligånden."

did have an impact on Lewini when he held the meetings in Copenhagen in 1909.

At first, Lewini was reluctant to join the meeting since she believed that religion was not useful for modern living.[6] Lewini writes that she came to the meeting out of curiosity. She had heard a lot about Pentecostals and speaking in tongues and wanted to find out what it was. She had been invited to these meetings before but every time she had been confused about when the meeting was even though a lot of her friends had been there. This time she got to know when the meeting would be held.[7]

She went to the meeting, but she could not remember what was said, sung, or prayed. When she writes about the meeting, she points out that there was no speaking in tongues. She underlines that she was not captivated by what happened in the meeting itself, but two things stood out. First of all, the happiness which the people at the meeting seemed to be filled with and secondly the love she met there. She explains that she had never seen the love that these people had before. She had heard God speak with a loving voice to her before, but not as certain and captivating as at this meeting. She writes that she generally had a "light mind" but this happiness was something else.[8] The day after the first meeting, she went to another meeting. At the meeting, a special song was sung, and she felt as if it was sung directly to her. In her book, she explains that parts of her had a hard time understanding it, but she felt that it was for her. She believed that since the "ice was broken now," Satan himself was threatened and started to make her feel that all that had happened was not real. She felt that a battle was going on inside her. At the meeting, they recommended that you attend the subsequent tarrying service. Lewini stayed for this. She writes that she did not stay out of curiosity, but she also felt that she could not attend it in the way that was intended. Still, she felt like she could not walk away. She wanted to leave, but she felt that she could not. Instead, she hid behind a window.

At the tarrying service, the other attendees sang a song with their whole heart. Lewini envied their joy. She could see this was not something they had learned or mastered, but a true experience. She explains that she wanted to be able to bow down and turn to God, but she felt as if she could not.[9] She was confused about what happened inside of her at

---

6. Somaratna, *Walter H. Clifford*, 11–12.
7 Lewini, *Min Omvendelse*, 4.
8 Lewini, *Min Omvendelse*, 4–5.
9 Lewini, *Min Omvendelse*, 7–11.

the meeting. She felt that it was a battle between the light and the dark. She explains that this was "the calling" but it was hard for her to voluntarily choose it. The tarrying service was about to end when a young girl approached her. She asked Lewini whether she was saved and left afterwards. Lewini went home from the meeting, but she could not sleep. She describes it as "a horrible night." She did not feel at peace. The day after was a battle as well. She knew that she had to make a choice. She believed it was a question of life in eternity or death. These battles shaped her experience of becoming a Pentecostal.

On April 27, 1909, she went to a closed meeting. She explains that this evening was essential for her. She experienced a peace coming over her. When someone from the stage asked whether anybody needed prayer, a young girl suddenly stood beside her. Lewini thought that the girl noticed her internal battle. The girl pushed a chair in front of her and Lewini bowed down to join the prayer. It was at this moment that Lewini gave her heart to God and felt that when she let him into her life, he received her as she was. She states that in the morning she could with all truth and belief say that the old had passed and everything had become new.

After this, she explains that wherever she went, she felt as if she had to talk about it. At another tarrying meeting on the thirteenth of May, she received what she understood to be baptism with the Holy Spirit with speaking in tongues. At first, she felt that her jaws moved as if she was speaking but no sound emerged. She did not understand it and because she did not know anything about this she believed that it was the Holy Spirit which took her in possession. Then a man laid hands on her head, and she felt an indescribable joy and began to praise God in unknown tongues.[10]

FROM 1909 UNTIL LEWINI'S ARRIVAL IN SRI LANKA IN 1923

After her conversion, Lewini took an active part in the Pentecostal ministry in Copenhagen.[11] She soon began an itinerant ministry and evangelized for some years in Scandinavia, starting in Odense, Denmark.[12] In 1911, Lewini led several awakening meetings in this part of the country.[13]

---

10 Lewini, *Min Omvendelse*, 12–20.
11. Olesen, *De frigjorte*, 430–31.
12 *KS* (September 1, 1910) 136.
13 *KS* (January 15, 1911) 15.

Soon, most of her ministry was in Sweden but she also evangelized in Denmark and Norway.[14] In between evangelizing in Sweden she led meetings in Kristiania when Barratt was out of town. In September 1910, Barratt went to Zürich and he announced that while he was in Switzerland Lewini and Anna Ruud would be leading the meetings in his church. He writes, "The room was filled and they had a wonderful time." He also informs us that before Lewini came to lead the meetings there, she had been in Gothenburg and before that in Høvaag in Norway where she had been a blessing to the people there.[15] In 1911, Barratt went to Finland and during that time Lewini came back to lead the meetings in his church but also other places around the city to reach the people in the city who did not attend church.[16]

Lewini also visited Flekkefjord in Norway and held some meetings there. Barratt said that her testimony was simple but "spot on." Many people responded to her advice to receive the blessing of heaven. Barratt compares seeing her on stage sharing her testimony with the times she was on stage as an actress. "Now the cross is shining around her," he states.[17]

When she was evangelizing in Sweden, Norrköping was a special focus, where she stayed several times between 1916 and 1919 and became one of the principal figures of the Pentecostal revival there, although she also evangelized in other towns, including in the area around Linköping and further south in Halland as well as Stockholm.[18] Barratt writes in 1916 that Lewini had sent him a greeting from Sweden in which she writes that she had had great progress in her ministry. She had been praying for hundreds of people and was still praying for more breakthroughs.[19]

After her first stay in Norrköping, Lewini contacted Barratt who had mentored her after her conversion and who she referred to as her spiritual father.[20] She wrote to him that she and others had been laboring "almost all winter" for revival. She also wrote that a few hundred people had been converted and many of these people had received baptism in

14 Christensen, *Unorganized Religion*, 213–14.
15 *KS* (October 1, 1910) 151.
16 *KS* (September 15, 1911) 143–44.
17 *KS* (December 1, 1911) 183.
18 *EH* (May 31, 1916) 92; (January 24, 1918) 16; (April 11, 1918) 59; Gäreskog, *Pingstväckelsen inom Metodistkyrkan*, 165–66; Wahlström, *Andens dop*, 23. See also Christensen, *Unorganized Religion*, 213–14.
19 *KS* (May 15, 1916) 76.
20 Somaratna, *Walter H. Clifford*, 13.

the Holy Spirit. After her campaign ended, she probably returned to Denmark. In 1917, she came back to Norrköping. Since her last visit, a Pentecostal prayer group had been formed.[21] In announcements of meetings, her name would be mentioned alongside prominent pastors such as Barratt and Anton Taranger from Norway and the Methodist Pentecostal pastor Per Nilsson from Sweden.[22] It may have been Lewini who persuaded Barratt to participate. Lewini was sometimes described as the principal leader of revival meetings, ahead of male leaders.[23]

At a conference in Nyköping, she spoke alongside Gerda Åström, another protagonist of this book. Interestingly, Åström was described as an "evangelist" (along with a man, Albin Holmgren), while Lewini's title is consistently simply "Mrs" *(fru)*, as she would have been known in the theatre.[24] Later she returned to Örebro where she had ministered some years earlier. At this time, in the early 1920s, she was exhausted after several years of itinerant ministry. Here she met Smith Wigglesworth, a notable healing evangelist from England. Wigglesworth motivated her to go after her calling to foreign mission beyond Scandinavia. He encouraged her to move to London to prepare for this, and that was exactly what she did. In London, she was not only receiving training but again leading revival meetings and, remarkably, was pro tem superintendent of the PMU's Women's Training Home from February 1922 until June of the same year. After this, she went on her world tour.[25]

SRI LANKA

During her tour, she visited the Mukti Mission in Bombay, India, and found friends there among the workers, including Minnie Houck who would go on to assist Lewini in her work in Sri Lanka. Like several of Lewini's associates in Scandinavia, the sisters at Mukti also had a Methodist connection. About the meetings, Anna Lewini wrote: "At the first meeting some came forward for prayer that they might be saved, but in the afternoon a large number came forward for prayer that they might be saved, but in the afternoon a large number came forward for salvation

---

21 Christensen, *Unorganized Religion*, 214; Gäreskog, *Pingstväckelsen inom Metodistkyrkan*, 121.

22 EH (January 24, 1918) 16.

23. Gäreskog, *Pingstväckelsen inom Metodistkyrkan*, 122.

24 EH (August 29, 1918) 139; (October 17) 167.

25 Christensen, *Unorganized Religion*, 214.

and found forgiveness for their sins. At each subsequent meeting, a great many came asking that we may pray for them."[26]

After her stay in Bombay, Lewini went to Colombo in Sri Lanka. In the *Pentecostal Evangel*, September 8, 1923, Lewini wrote that she felt God telling her to go to Ceylon (Sri Lanka), but she doubted that she would be able to settle down in Ceylon. She went to start a Pentecostal mission station there. This mission station would be the first and, for some time, the only station run by foreign Pentecostal missionaries among the five million people in Ceylon. Lewini said: "We know 10 or 12 on the island who have received their "Pentecost" and a few who are really longing for it. God has given me the opportunity to proclaim this truth all over Colombo and in other parts of Ceylon and now we are preparing to open up a real Pentecostal Hall." Minnie Houck came from Nuwara Eliya to stay with Lewini. Because of her friendship with Minnie Houck, Lewini found a place in Colombo where she could stay.[27]

During her time in Sri Lanka, she adopted the lifestyle of the locals. This meant that she had to live without some of the luxuries she enjoyed in Europe. She always wore distinctive white clothes with no jewelry, adapting the traditional long gown for her missionary purposes.[28] In Sri Lanka, she contacted several people who were interested in her ministry.

The Pentecostal message had already been given to some Christians in Sri Lanka by previous ministers who were a part of the Assemblies of God. Nevertheless, the amount of people who had heard this message and can be noted as "Spirit-filled" was small. John Samuel Wickramaratne and J.J. B. de Silva played a major role in the start of her ministry in Sri Lanka. They were both connected to the Baptist Church in Sri Lanka, and they helped Lewini hold revival meetings around Colombo. Already in 1922, they had held meetings at the best-known theater hall in Colombo, which was the Tower Hall at Maradana. In 1923, they also rented a private house at Borella, which they named Glad Tidings Hall, where they could hold meetings for the public regularly. At one point, they had to move from the house in Borella to Bambalapitiya and later to Wellawatta. Many people who were passionate about the ministry of the Holy Spirit joined these meetings. Most likely, a missionary called Ram

26 *The Pentecostal Evangel* (June 9, 1923) quoted in Somaratna, *Walter H. Clifford*, 15.

27 *The Pentecostal Evangel* (September 8, 1923) quoted in Somaratna, *Walter H. Clifford*, 15–16.

28 Somaratna, *Walter H. Clifford*, 22.

Paul also attended these meetings. Ram Paul later founded the Ceylon Pentecostal Mission, which is a Pentecostal organization that later on had a huge impact on Sri Lanka and other countries. Anna Lewini also went to other big cities in Sri Lanka. She went by the railway system to the different cities to evangelize. Minnie Houck wrote in 1924 that during the Christmas holiday, a Pentecostal convention was held by J. B. de Silva and Lewini at Chilaw, which is a town near Colombo. After this Lewini felt called to start something new in Colombo. She started her ministry at Wellawatta alongside her work at Borella.[29]

While Anna Lewini was leading and managing services at Borella, the British Assemblies of God missionary Walter Clifford came to Sri Lanka. Lewini welcomed his contribution to the work she had started. Minnie Houck had stated: "Though Mrs. Lewini is still the missionary in charge, she is praying that someone may be led to take her place."[30]

The fact that Lewini wanted someone to take over for her is also underlined in a letter which Lewini wrote to an American friend in 1923: "Pray for her (Minnie Houck) and for me and if anyone, filled with the Spirit, feels led to Ceylon let them haste, for the time is short."[31] Lewini remained traditional in her view of gender roles in Christian ministry, even compared with her contemporaries, and was thankful that a man would take over to pastor her converts.[32] When Clifford arrived, Lewini humbly accepted a role in the background and gave him the main stage of the ministry which she had begun. She did not consider the ministry which she had started as her personal property. What she wanted was to obey the calling to extend the Kingdom of God.

After Clifford arrived on the island, Lewini did not take part in the preaching ministry, but her ministry continued until the 1940s. Instead of preaching, she focused on counseling and prayer ministries during this time. Her last furlough in Denmark was in 1935 when she met T. B. Barratt for the last time; he remained a mentor figure to her.[33] Back in Ceylon, during World War II, Lewini took part in setting up the mission station at Makewita alongside Samuel Wickramaratne and his wife and

---

29 Somaratna, *Walter H. Clifford*, 16–18.

30 *The Pentecostal Evangel* (June 28, 1924) quoted in Somaratna, *Walter H. Clifford*, 19.

31 *The Pentecostal Evangel* (June 8, 1923) quoted in Somaratna, *Walter H. Clifford*, 19.

32. Christensen, *Unorganized Religion*, 193.

33. *KS* (March 30, 1946) 207.

family. During these years of quieter and more hidden ministry after the 1920s, her work got less attention and the information to be found is far scarcer.[34]

In 1946, at the age of seventy-one, she concluded that her life's work was finished. She had seen conversions among both Sri Lankans and foreigners. She let Wickramaratne oversee the work, supported by other locals and travelled back to Denmark.[35] She helped the first Swedish Pentecostal missionaries to Sri Lanka to obtain visas.[36] Lewini died in 1951 in Aarhus, Denmark.[37]

CONCLUSION

In the book *Walter H. Clifford* by the Sri Lankan historian G. P. V. Somaratna, it is claimed that "Anna Lewini was the real founder of Pentecostalism in Sri Lanka."[38] This statement can be discussed since there were some native Pentecostals in Sri Lanka before Lewini arrived. She was one of the first foreign Pentecostal missionaries to be based there, but she worked with existing local evangelists who had been active for over a decade.[39] Lewini was independent and continued to be an independent missionary. She had had limited collaboration with the Assemblies of God, whereas when Swedish Pentecostal missionaries later arrived in Sri Lanka they eventually separated from them completely over theological differences.[40] Many of the later Sri Lankan leaders were continuously blessed by the foundation laid through the ministry that Lewini had been doing. Somaratna rightly concludes that: "The Christian church in Sri Lanka owes a great debt of gratitude to this woman missionary who accepted the call of God to come to an unknown country to offer the service of her lifetime."[41]

---

34 Somaratna, *Walter H. Clifford*, 17–23.
35 *KS* (March 30, 1946) 207; Christensen, *Unorganized Religion*, 215.
36 "Intervju med Majken Anthin."
37 "Anna Lomholt—dansk film database."
38 Somaratna, *Walter H. Clifford*, 23.
39 Christensen, *Unorganized Religion*, 214–15; Anderson, "Emergence," 18–19.
40 Andreasson, *Svensk Pingstmission*, 31.
41 Somaratna, *Walter H. Clifford*, 23.

BIBLIOGRAPHY

Anderson, Allan Heaton, "The Emergence of a Multidimensional Global Missionary Movement: A Historical Review." In *Pentecostal Mission and Global Christianity*, edited by Wonsuk Ma et al., 10–25. Regnum Edinburgh Centenary Series, Volume 20. Oxford: Regnum, 2014.

Andreasson, Barbro. *Svensk Pingstmission i Sri Lanka*. Huddinge: MissionsInstitutet PMU, 2001.

"Anna Lomholt—dansk film database." https://danskefilm.dk/skuespiller.php?id=8987.

Christensen, Nikolaj. *Unorganized Religion: Pentecostalism and Secularization in Denmark, 1907–1924*. Global Pentecostal and Charismatic Studies 42. Leiden: Brill, 2022.

Gäreskog, Roland. *Pingstväckelsen inom Metodistkyrkan i Sverige åren 1907–1922*. Stockholm: Insamlingsstiftelsen för pingstforskning, 2013.

Hansen, Mette Skov. "Da Helligånden flyttede i villakvarter." *Kristeligt Dagblad*, November 27, 2011.

"Intervju med Majken Anthin." IPS, Pingst—arkiv & forskning, 1993.

Lewini, Anna. *Min omvendelse og hvorledes jeg modtog Aandens daab med tungetale*. Copenhagen: Jensen & Rønagers Bogtrykkeri, 1910.

Olesen, Elith. *De frigjorte og trællefolket: Amerikansk-engelsk indflydelse på dansk kirkeliv omkring år 1900*. Frederiksberg: Anis, 1996.

Somaratna, G.P.V. *Walter H. Clifford: The Apostle of Pentecostalism in Sri Lanka*. Nugegoda: Margaya, 1995.

Wahlström, Magnus, ed. *Andens dop och nådegåvorna. Ett ekumeniskt "pingstmöte" i Stockholm 1918*. Stockholm: Insamlingsstiftelsen för pingstforskning, 2016.

Image #7. Gerda Åström.

6

Gerda Åström
Apostle and "Standing Witness" in Northern Sweden[1]

TOMMY H. DAVIDSSON

THE EARLY YEARS

Margareta (Gerda) Kristina Åström (1878–1940) was born on June 19, 1878 in the remote village of Södra Stortjärn, situated ca. sixty kilometers north of Umeå, in northern Sweden. She was the seventy-fourth child to be born in the parish that year.[2] Gerda was the fourth of twelve children born to her father, Johan Ulrik Åström (1842–1919), and her mother, Anna Magdalena Grenholm (1849–1926).[3] Johan came from a simple background and worked as a tenant farmer.[4] Not all her family members were of low standing, but some held positions of influence at the local commune.[5] Gerda's upbringing resembled a traditional Swedish Lutheran family in many ways. She was baptized as an infant by vicar H. G.

---

1. All translations in this chapter are the author's own.
2. *1878 års födelse och dopbok för Bygdeå moderförsamling*, 141.
3. Lars-Evert Jonsson states that Gerda only had seven siblings, but this discrepancy could be explained as a purposeful discounting of those who died at an early age. Jonsson, *Gerda Åström, Den trefaldiga nåden*, 8.
4. Bygdeå kyrkoarkiv, *husförhörslängder (1874–1884)*, 630.
5. Wendén, *Ett stort verk genom ett svagt redskap*, 59.

Westerlund and was confirmed in the Lutheran faith on June 10, 1893.[6] Her maternal grandmother, whom she called a true "child of God,"[7] had a special place in her life during her early years. She taught Gerda how to read and exemplified Christlike behavior.[8]

Gerda's father was a tenant of one-sixteenth plot of land, an area that could have been as little as three thousand square meters.[9] A crop failure in the early 1880s forced the family to move to Svartvik, a little town just south of Sundsvall on the east coast of central Sweden, in the county of Medelpad, in July 1883. The goal was most likely for Gerda's father to find employment in Svartvik's growing lumber industry. Mats Morell notes that it was common for tenant farmers in the nineteenth century to seize the chance of better-paid jobs when the opportunity arose. Relocating for work was thus a common experience for low-income families like the Åströms, especially when the land could not sustain them.[10] The stint in Svartvik was short-lived since Johan could not procure a permanent job in the city. The family returned to Södra Stortjärn after only six months.

The family's hardships were not limited to agricultural failures and unemployment but had a very personal dimension as well. Gerda lost her younger sister, Maria, in 1880 and her only brother, Anders, in December 1882, just a few months before their relocation to Svartvik.[11] Their family misfortunes continued after they returned to Södra Stortjärn, as her younger sisters, Ester and Hilda, suffered premature deaths in March 1886 and January 1888 respectively. Thus, Gerda experienced the loss of four siblings in her first decade of life.

The family undertook the 360-kilometer journey back to the Sundsvall area in July 1887. This time they did not settle in Svartvik but in the adjacent village of Vapelnäs. Gerda lived in the Sundsvall region from 1887 to 1899 and thus spent all her teenage years there.[12] The east

---

6. *1878 års födelse och dopbok för Bygdeå moderförsamling*, 141.

7. Åström, *Den trefaldiga nåden*, 4.

8. Åström, *Den trefaldiga nåden*, 5.

9. The size of farms varied greatly in Sweden during the nineteenth century. The normal size of a small farm was between five and ten hectares. Bygdeå kyrkoarkiv, *husförhörslängder (1874–1884)*, 630; Morell, *Jordbruket i industrisamhället*, 4:33–34.

10. Morell, *Jordbruket i industrisamhället*, 4:34.

11. The church records do not indicate how old Maria was when she died, but it is likely she died in infancy.

12. The church records show that the Åström family resided in Medelpad for quite a long time, but this does not mean they were fixed to one place. On the contrary, they moved another eight times in the area between 1887 and 1910. Jonsson correctly notes

coast of central and northern Sweden was dominated by the world's largest lumber industry.[13] The invention of steam-powered, rather than water-powered, sawmills made it possible to locate the sawmills closer to the coast, which facilitated shipping. Already by 1871, there were up to twenty steam-powered sawmills in the Sundsvall area alone.[14] The region became the lumber industry's "Klondike" because of the number of people that were attracted to it.[15]

In his landmark study of the ideas and ideals of the region from 1880 to 1930, Ronny Ambjörnsson boils them down to the value of being "well-behaved" (skötsam).[16] Being "well-behaved" was much more than conforming to a set of ethical rules. Ambjörnsson describes it as an "adaptation" to the capitalistic demands that followed in the wake of Sweden's rapid modernization and industrialization process of the late nineteenth and early twentieth centuries.[17] Combined with the influences of the temperance movement, it encapsulated a strong work ethic and a deep contempt for all kinds of unproductive activities such as gambling, drinking, and wild living.[18] On the other hand, being "well-behaved" instilled a virtue of acquiring knowledge through reading up on the latest inventions, and the famous works of philosophers, scholars, and poets like August Strindberg, Viktor Rydberg, and Sigmund Freud. Thus, a "well-behaved" person worked hard, did not engage in frivolous activities, and sought to develop an understanding of the great thinkers of the day—a set of values that Gerda also manifested.[19]

Lars-Evert Jonsson demonstrates that Vapelnäs and the Medelpad regions were not inhabited by blind conformists. Eight years before the Åström family arrived, the first labor strike in Swedish history took place there in 1879. The walk-out started when the owners of the lumber mills

---

that tracing Gerda's whereabouts is quite precarious. Gerda remained single her entire life, and it was not until 1921, at the age of 43, that she was recorded as having her own residency. Jonsson speculates that there could be several reasons for her absence in the church records, but it is unlikely that it had to do with prejudice from the authorities, but rather that single women were registered with their parents until they married. Jonsson, *Gerda Åström*, 12.

13. Högman, "Flottningens historia."
14. Åsa Blom, "Sågverksindustrins utveckling i Norrland," 41–42.
15. Högman, "Flottningens historia."
16. Ambjörnsson, *Den skötsamma arbetaren*.
17. Ambjörnsson, *Den skötsamma arbetaren*, 35–36.
18. Ambjörnsson, *Den skötsamma arbetaren*, 35–36.
19. Ambjörnsson, *Den skötsamma arbetaren*, 28.

decided to cut the workers' wages by 15–20 percent due to falling timber prices. The strike could probably have been avoided if the owners had spent the three million crowns they received in government aid on the workers, rather than using it to fund a lavish party.[20] It is important to note here, as Jonsson does, that the motivation to act against injustice coincided with the spiritual awakening that was sweeping the country in the middle of the nineteenth century. To show how religious convictions and political actions intertwined, Jonsson recounts an interesting exchange between Isak Boström, who was a key participant in the strike, as well as a member of the recently formed Mission Covenant Church of Sweden,[21] and the local governor: The governor purportedly told the young man, quoting the Apostle Paul: "You shall submit to the ruling authorities." Boström countered with another quote from Apostle Paul: "Carry each other's burdens and you will fulfill the law of Christ."[22] Gerda therefore grew up in an environment where the free church movement did not lack a voice.

It was during these turbulent years in Medelpad that her interest in Christianity began to grow. She allegedly discerned God's "small still voice" in her schoolteacher's Christianity lessons, her Sunday School classes and when she walked alone on the country roads. It was also at this time that she first sensed God's call to become an evangelist.[23] Although she was exposed to the message of Christ at an early age, her childhood faith was not enough to dispel her ignorance of sin.[24] However, when the movement of confirmation came on June 10, 1893, she was ready to be "adopted as a child of God."[25] Yet, her spiritual breakthrough only came a year later, at the age of fifteen, after having attended several unsatisfactory meetings at the Swedish Covenant Church at Vapelnäs.[26] After a dark night of the soul, she experienced that the Lord forgave her sins and filled her "whole being with blissful peace."[27]

---

20. Jonsson, *Gerda Åström*, 10–11.

21. The Mission Covenant Church of Sweden was established in 1878, after its leader Paul Petter Waldenström broke off from the Swedish Evangelical Mission, a pietistic, low-church, branch of the Lutheran Church of Sweden.

22. Jonsson, *Gerda Åström*, 11.

23. Åström, *Den trefaldiga nåden*, 10.

24. Åström, *Den trefaldiga nåden*, 4.

25. Åström, *Den trefaldiga nåden*, 5.

26. Jonsson, *Gerda Åström*, 14.

27. Åström, *Den trefaldiga nåden*, 7.

Gerda's conversion in 1894 was not the only formative experience during this time. Gerda did well in school, and the church records demonstrate that she had an aptitude for learning. Notes from catechetical meetings from 1892 to 1899 indicate that her ability to read was "good, with distinction."[28] Her thorough knowledge of the Bible also began at this time. Not only did a church member from her early years of ministry in Ånäset, like Axel Burman, testify to her "incredible Bible knowledge,"[29] but later records from house calls in 1921 and 1925 also show that her knowledge of the Bible was above the norm, receiving grades of A and A+ in "knowledge of Christianity."[30] She was also linguistically proficient and was able to read English literature from a young age.[31]

A common experience for young women in the nineteenth century was to move away from home and live as a housemaid for another family.[32] Since Gerda is listed as a housemaid ("*piga*") in the church record after the family moved to the small town of Timrå, a little north of Sundsvall, in September 1897, it is clear that she also had this experience.[33] The next step in her life, however, would be more unusual and set her on a path to become a Pentecostal pioneer.

FROM HOUSEMAID TO PENTECOSTAL PREACHER

Gerda was baptized by immersion at an outdoor baptismal service at Hallen, a small village on the outskirts of Östersund in Jämtland county, on July 23, 1899.[34] Jonsson states that Gerda's decision to be baptized by immersion in Östersund is shrouded in some mystery. Östersund is situated two hundred kilometers west of Timrå, in the central parts of Sweden, and there are no records that indicate that Gerda ever previously visited Östersund. The church protocol from July 16, only mentions that a "sister" from another town had voiced an interest in being baptized, but no explanation is given as to why.[35] That this unnamed "sister" was indeed Gerda Åström

---

28. *Församlingsbok Skön Westland Alla/2 1894–1911*, 859.
29. Burman, *Pingst-Väckelsens början*, 20.
30. *Församlingsbok Nysätra Ånäset A2 1912–1932*, 893.
31. Åström, *Den trefaldiga nåden*, 14.
32. Jonsson, *Gerda Åström*, 12.
33. *Inflyttningsboken till Timrå B/4 1895–1912*, 15.
34. She was baptized by Carl Hedeen. Nyberg Oskarsson, "I Lucy Farrows fotspår," 86; Jonsson, *Gerda Åström*, 14.
35. Jonsson, *Gerda Åström*, 14–15.

is evident from the fact that she is listed in the congregation's membership roll as having been baptized on July 23, 1899.[36] However, a few historical facts can help to unravel the mystery why she decided to get baptized as an adult in Östersund. First, her decision reveals that she must have had contact with Baptists in her home region. Based on Martin Gidlund's study, Roger Skoog notes that the Medelpad region had become a center for the spread of Baptist views towards the middle and end of the nineteenth century.[37] The Baptist Union had also just concluded their National Assembly in Sundsvall two weeks prior to Gerda's decision to be baptized. Thus, the Baptist movement was thriving in her home region, which explains why she was drawn to it. Secondly, Jonsson surmises that a vital clue can also be found in the ministry of Carl Hedeen (1863–1950), who was the pastor of the Bethel Baptist church in Östersund at the time.[38] Hedeen's openness to evangelical revivalism marked his ministry, and the congregation's significant growth in 1897 likely attracted her to this spiritually vibrant community.[39] The opening of a railroad connection in 1882 also made the commute between the two cities easy and enjoyable. A final clue is found in Gerda's comment that "the Lord had placed the biographies of two sanctified men in her hands" before deciding to be baptized.[40] This is an indication that she was also exposed to the teachings of the Holiness Movement. The identity of these "sanctified men" is unknown, but it could have been R. A. Torrey (1856–1928) and F. B. Meyer (1847–1929), whose Holiness writings were popular and had been translated to Swedish before the turn of the century. Other popular Anglo-Saxon Holiness authors who could have influenced her were Andrew Murray (1828–1917) and William Boardman (1810–1886).[41] It was therefore more to Gerda's decision to be baptized in Östersund than merely a newfound conviction of believer's baptism. Östersund was a place where a "higher spiritual life" was sought, which Gerda also desired.

36. Jonsson, *Gerda Åström*, 14.
37. Skoog, "Baptiströrelsen i Piteå," 5.
38. Carl Hedeen would later become a key leader of early Swedish Pentecostalism.
39. Jonsson mentions that the church grew from 88 members in 1884 to 260 members in 1900. Jonsson, *Gerda Åström*, 15.
40. Åström, *Den trefaldiga nåden*, 10.
41. Söderholm, *Den svenska pingstväckelsens historia 1907–1927*, 1:108. The fact that she also ascribes indebtedness to Jesse Penn-Lewis (1861–1927) shows that she was aware of the writings of both male and female Holiness leaders. For an overview of the influence of Anglo-Saxon Holiness preachers on the Swedish evangelical movement, see Halldorf, *Av denna världen?*, 56–60; Struble, *Den samfundsfria församlingen*, 10–11.

Gerda did not reside long in Östersund but was admitted to John Ongman's (1845–1931) Bible school in Örebro, a city located two hundred kilometers due west of Stockholm, in the autumn of 1899. John Ongman was an influential Baptist pastor and leader, and the founder of the Örebro Mission Society. Gerda's decision to seek admission at John Ongman's Bible school was logical for two reasons. Firstly, Ongman's Bible School admitted female students as opposed to the Baptist Bethel Seminary in Stockholm. Ongman was inspired by Fredrik Franson (1852–1908) and Catherine Booth (1829–1890), who both supported women's right to preach the Gospel.[42] Gunilla Nyberg Oskarsson notes that Ongman was not afraid to advocate for women's right to preach at the Baptists' annual conferences during the 1890s despite vocal opposition.[43] Although Swedish Baptists were primarily influenced by German/continental Baptist teachings that opposed women in ministry, Ongman's clear stance in favor of women preachers attracted women like Gerda Åström.

Secondly, Ongman's Bible school was part of a larger center for Holiness teaching in the Örebro region from the 1880s onward. The Swedish Holiness Movement (*Helgelseförbundet*) had been established at the midsummer, *Torp,* conference outside Kumla, not far from Örebro in 1887.[44] The conference grew from two thousand to six thousand attendees within just a few years, and the news of the Holiness movement spread far beyond the immediate vicinity.[45] It is likely that the news of what was going on in Örebro also reached Gerda. Ongman's Bible school therefore became the answer to her "burning question" of where she could receive teaching about "entire sanctification" that she had read about in the biographies of the Holiness preachers.[46]

John Ongman's road into the Holiness movement had come through his studies at the Baptist Union Theological Seminary in Chicago from 1876 to 1877, which was "permeated by reformed and holiness thinking."[47] Chicago was also a center for holiness advocates like D. L. Moody (1837–1899) and Ira Sankey (1840–1908). Ongman was not an original thinker

---

42. Alvarsson, "Pingstväckelsens etablering i Sverige," 1:27, 44.

43. Nyberg Oskarsson, "Kvinnorna marginaliserades när väckelsen etablerats," 2:268.

44. *Helgelseförbundet* was not established as a denomination but as a mission society. It was only when it was challenged by the emerging Pentecostal movement that it established a firmer structure.

45. Söderholm, *Den svenska pingstväckelsens historia 1907–1927,* 1:108.

46. Åström, *Den trefaldiga nåden,* 11.

47. Hermansson, "Vad är då en människa?"

or theologian, but he passed on the message he had heard in Chicago to his students in Örebro.[48] This is evident from Gerda's testimony that she encountered teachings about "a clean heart," "full salvation," and "entire sanctification" at the institution.[49] Gerda stayed at the Bible school for one month. Yet, she did not experience her much sought-after "heart-cleansing" during her time of study, even though she sought it with "prayers and tears." She apparently ministered for several years before God removed her pride, or "the feather from her hat" as a classmate called it, by drawing her into "the cleansing spring of the cross."[50]

Gerda's description of her sanctification experience resembles the typical sanctification narrative of Holiness women at the time. Susie C. Stanley observes that Wesleyan Holiness women were "lay theologians who, for the most part, lacked a college education. [. . .] They were not outlining a systematic theology. [. . .] Rather, they based their theological understanding on their personal experience as it was confirmed in the Bible and the experience of others."[51] Stanley further notes that the pattern was established by Phoebe Palmer (1807–1874) in her book *Way of Holiness*, and the "auto component" of their testimonies focused on "the spiritual self in all areas of life" and consisted of three parts: "the sinful self, the saved self, and the sanctified self."[52] Gerda's sanctification experience mimics this pattern and it contains no perspective beyond the "spiritual self," apart from a brief comment about the difficulty of living with her missionary colleague after having been used to living alone. The narrative is therefore devoid of any social, cultural, psychological, or political perspective that could have given a broader understanding of the experience and this formative period of her life. It only concentrates on her struggle with residual sin, her desperate longing for release, and her eventual victory through the knowledge of being "crucified with Christ" and "dead to sin."[53]

A further important point here is that Gerda wrote about her sanctification experience in 1913, which was before the "Finished Work of Calvary" doctrine reached most Pentecostals in Sweden. No records indicate that she changed her view of entire sanctification as a second work

48. Hermansson, *Vad är då en människa?*
49. Åström, *Den trefaldiga nåden*, 11.
50. Åström, *Den trefaldiga nåden*, 11.
51. Stanley, *Holy Boldness*, 61.
52. Stanley, *Holy Boldness*, 61–62.
53. Åström, *Den trefaldiga nåden*, 8–12.

of grace later in life. However, as a person who focused on experience rather than doctrine, it is fair to assume that she adjusted her views as "new revelation" came to light.[54]

Gerda testifies to a period of joy and courage after salvation but also a subsequent time of testing "to help her understand the awfulness of sin and its ability to pollute and drag down purified souls." This insight taught her about "her own propensity to sin." Even though saved and in constant prayer to God, the devil was still able to tell her that she was in his "net." She therefore asked the Lord to help her out of this predicament and to get a fully cleansed heart. When preparing to write to a friend about her temptations, she wanted to include a Bible verse, and her eyes fell on 2 Cor 6:2, "At an acceptable time I have listened to you, and on a day of salvation I have helped you." Paul's words led to a breakthrough and instead of writing to her friend about her temptations, she could now write that she was "*totally free*" [Italics in original].[55]

Gerda was commissioned as an evangelist, or as an "Ongman sister," after completing her studies. Alvarsson explains that "Ongman sisters" was a well-known concept and reflected Ongman's view that "women were to participate in evangelistic and church work."[56] The sisters were also commissioned two-by-two like Jesus's disciples in Luke 10, and received no permanent salary, relying solely on voluntary gifts.[57] Gerda's whereabouts are difficult to trace from the time she was commissioned as an evangelist for the Örebro Mission Society in 1899 until the outbreak of the Pentecostal Revival in 1906/1907. She ministered in the adjacent county of Västmanland, but she could have also served in other parts of Sweden.[58] That she kept in contact with Ongman's work in Örebro is evident from the fact that she moved her membership from the Bethel Baptist church in Östersund to the Filadelfia Baptist church in Örebro on October 19, 1903.[59]

---

54. Davidsson, "Between Multiple Worlds," 184–185, 204–205.

55. Åström, *Den trefaldiga nåden*, 7–10.

56. Alvarsson, "Pingstväckelsens etablering i Sverige," 24.

57. Söderholm, *Den svenska pingstväckelsens historia 1907-1927*, 1:120; *EH* (January 25, 1917) 16.

58. Åström, *Den trefaldiga nåden*, 14; Wendén, "Ett stort verk genom ett svagt redskap," 60.

59. Jonsson, *Gerda Åström*, 14. Ongman established the Filadelfia church after he, and 92 other members, split from the First Örebro Baptist Church in 1897. See, Struble, *Den samfundsfria församlingen*, 11.

The Pentecostal revival arrived in Sweden in the late fall of 1906 through the ministry of Andrew G. Johnson (1878–1965), who had been a first-hand witness of the Azusa Street Revival in Los Angeles. Johnson initially brought the Pentecostal message to Skövde, a small town between Lake Vänern and Lake Vättern in south-central Sweden, but after Ongman invited him to Örebro, the revival also gained a foothold at the Filadelfia church and other Baptist churches in the Örebro area.[60] As an "Ongman sister" and an evangelist in the region at the time, Gerda soon experienced the Pentecostal revival and adopted its teaching of salvation, entire sanctification, and Spirit baptism as a subsequent empowerment for service. Gerda's account of her Spirit baptism in the early spring of 1907 followed the same pattern of the "spiritual self" as outlined above but is extended to include a new element: the "Spirit-baptized self." The pattern is based on (1) a deep spiritual crisis with a solution that only God can provide, (2) periods of doubt and uncertainty, and finally, (3) a moment of divine intervention that overcomes the crisis. Although remarkable in its vividness, the story shares features of other famous accounts of the Baptism of the Holy Spirit, except for one glaring omission, namely, that the initial physical evidence of the experience is not ascribed to the gift of speaking in tongues but to a prophetic message.

The story begins with Gerda retelling her need for power as she ministered as a sanctified, but not yet Spirit-baptized, evangelist. She was convinced that she had received the power on several occasions, but it did not remain for long.[61] In the winter of 1906–1907, Gerda had reached a point of "bankruptcy so thorough that the power of the testimony was expunged."[62] Returning home that winter in despair and ready to quit the ministry, she stayed with some friends who had received "the promise of the Father" the previous year.[63] The first night with her friends the Spirit impressed on her "to grasp" the promise, but she pleaded with God that he would give her a "visible and tangible sign that the devil could not steal away through unbelief."[64] The second night God answered her prayer by allowing "nimble waves of light and fire" to appear and "walk around her bed." The waves of fire formed an "eye" that penetrated her body from the

---

60. Gäreskog, *Utanför lägret*, 264; Alvarsson, "Pingstväckelsens etablering i Sverige," 22–24.

61. Åström, *Den trefaldiga nåden*, 13–14.

62. Åström, *Den trefaldiga nåden*, 14.

63. Åström, *Den trefaldiga nåden*, 14.

64. Åström, *Den trefaldiga nåden*, 15.

head to the fingertips. The experience repeated itself until she could not bear it anymore. A voice from heaven then proclaimed that these were just "the initial drops" of what she was about to receive.[65] The fact that this experience was just the "initial drops" caused her later to doubt that it was the Baptism of the Holy Spirit she had experienced, but through a prophetic message, she was eventually assured that she had indeed received it.[66] The experience taught her two valuable lessons. First, it underlined the importance of believing, loving, and suffering "through" with "longing and anxious souls." Secondly, the drops underscored that the power was not given once and for all but was to be received repeatedly.[67]

Gerda's account of her Spirit baptism is a unique story but resembles and deviates from other contemporary accounts of the Baptism of the Holy Spirit. It shares, for instance, an experience of supernatural light and tongues of fire as described by Pentecostal leaders as T. B. Barratt (1862–1940), William Durham (1873–1912), and Gunnar Vingren (1879–1933).[68] The account is also interspersed with personal and/or "divine" interpretations of the experience, which was a frequent practice when describing supernatural encounters. It is written for general edification, but it is also meant to promote Pentecostal theology. She quotes, for instance, Pentecostal "proof texts" such as Acts 1:8, 2:4, 8:17, and 19:6, and includes comments like, "a cleansed heart is not sufficient" but the "power of heaven is also necessary" to make the Pentecostal claim explicit.[69] The account also stresses the preoccupation with "praying through" and not viewing Spirit baptism as a one-off experience. However, Gerda deviates from the accepted norm and does not ascribe her assurance of Spirit baptism to speaking in tongues but to a prophetic message. This could be an unintentional oversight since she cites all the key texts from the Book of Acts that Pentecostals used when defending the doctrine of initial evidence. However, it can also reflect Ongman's, Andrew Johnson's and especially William Seymour's understanding that did not restrict the evidence of Spirit baptism to merely speaking in tongues.[70]

---

65. Åström, *Den trefaldiga nåden*, 17–19.
66. Åström, *Den trefaldiga nåden*, 18.
67. Åström, *Den trefaldiga nåden*, 18.
68. Barratt, *Apostolic Faith* (December 1906) 3; Durham, *Brudgummens röst* (September 1911) 21–25; Holmgren, *Sanningens vittne* (May 1934) 5.
69. Åström, *Den trefaldiga nåden*, 14.
70. For an in-depth explanation, see Synan and Fox, *William J. Seymour*, 72–83.

PENTECOSTAL MISSIONARY IN VÄSTERBOTTEN

The information about Gerda's ministry is very limited from 1907 until she began publishing updates in the Pentecostal journal, *Evangelii Härold* (the Gospel Herald), in 1916. The only available information is an article in the Örebro-based and Pentecostal-friendly journal, *Närkesbladet*, on November 8, 1907. Gerda and her companion Berna Kristensson recount that they ministered in Örebro and the neighboring county of Västmanland before spending a few weeks in an unknown village in Jämtland county in the summer of 1907.[71] Although it could have been Östersund as Alvarsson claims, the report does not state it explicitly.[72] Gerda and Berna Kristensson were still the first evangelists to bring the Pentecostal message to this part of Sweden.[73]

The next time Gerda appears in the records, she is ministering at the Second Baptist church in Gränsfors, located ca. fifty kilometers south of Sundsvall in the winter of 1915.[74] The Second Baptist church in Gränsfors was a Pentecostal-friendly church that had been established on the Day of Epiphany, January 6, 1914. The church had grown from fourteen to forty-five members in only two years, partly due to Gerda's ministry.[75] Gerda transferred her church membership from Ongman's Filadelfia church to the new church plant on April 17, 1916. The church became her "base" as a missionary of the Örebro Mission Society until she left in 1921.[76]

71. Söderholm, *Den svenska pingstväckelsens historia 1907–1927*, 1:399–400.

72. Alvarsson, "Pingstväckelsens etablering i Sverige," 31.

73. Gerda left two accounts of the early meetings in Jämtland, one personal and one generic. The account in *Närkesbladet* is generic, describing Northern Sweden as a "hard place," but where a half-dozen people were "released [from sin]," "filled with the Spirit," "cried, laughed, and shouted of joy," "fell to the floor" and "received the gift of speaking and singing in foreign languages." These manifestations scared some of the attendees, but the fear subsided when a lady started to sing in tongues. Gerda also gave a personal account of the final meeting after most people had left. She recalls praying for a sick lady when "an invisible hand" removed her hands from the sick lady and "waves of power" started to flow through her body. The power was so overwhelming that she was physically unable to stand up for several hours and almost "drowned in an ocean of joy." Söderholm, *Den svenska pingstväckelsens historia 1907–1927*, 1:399; Åström, *Den trefaldiga nåden*, 19.

74. *EH* (February 10, 1916) 23.

75. *EH* (February 10, 1916) 23.

76. Jonsson states that Gerda left for the independent Pentecostal churches in 1918. This information is probably incorrect since she received aid from the Örebro Mission Society's "neglected fields" fund from 1917–1919 and from their "evangelist fund" from 1919–1921. The break more likely happened when she co-founded a "free biblical congregation" in Ånäset in 1921. Jonsson, *Gerda Åström*, 23; Gäreskog, *Utanför lägret*, 303 n.216.

Gerda was commissioned as a "missionary" to Northern Sweden in January 1916. Edgar Wendén writes that Gerda had a longing from the time she was Spirit baptized that God would send witnesses to her home region. When this did not happen, she accepted that she had to go alone.[77] Although it is impossible to verify Wendén's claim, this "realization" could have happened when she ministered in Gränsfors in the winter of 1915, since she was soon thereafter commissioned as one of the church's missionaries to Västerbotten together with Ernst Andersson and O. L. Lindsten.[78] Apart from a short period in the spring, Gerda ministered without the aid of a "sister" during her first year in Västerbotten, which supports Wenden's assertion.[79]

Jonsson and Wendén suggest that Gerda first started her ministry in Västerbotten in the summer of 1916. Jonsson, following Wendén and partly Burman, further claims that she held her first service on June 19, 1916 at the Swedish Covenant Church's building in Robertsfors, a small village seventeen kilometers south-east of her childhood home in Södra Stortjärn.[80] N. Söderström's report in *Evangelii Härold* shows, however, that Gerda began her ministry already at "New Year" and that the church received stories of "pretty good victories" from the mission field already in May 1916.[81] Gerda's article in *Evangelii Härold* in December 1916 also confirms that she ministered in Västerbotten for the entire year.[82] Furthermore, the church in Gränsfors appealed for funds to be sent to Gerda's home in Överklinten, situated between Södra Stortjärn and Robertsfors, on July 13, 1916, which is proof that she had settled there before the summer.[83] Thus, Gerda's ministry in Västerbotten in the spring of 1916 was more than a sporadic visit, or that she only came "to

77. Wendén, "Ett stort verk genom ett svagt redskap," 61.

78. EH (May 31, 1916) 91. Jonsson makes a point of the fact that Gerda is listed before the male missionaries, but it would be wrong to assume, on this basis alone, that she was more esteemed than the male missionaries. The report mentions two other female missionaries before Gerda, and there is nothing in the report that suggests that they were viewed more highly than Gerda. However, the glowing reviews she receives in the reports are evidence that she was held in high regard, but not beyond the others.

79. *EH* (December 7, 1916) 199.

80. Jonsson, *Gerda Åström*, 23; Burman, *Pingst-Väckelsens början*, 6; Wendén, "Ett stort verk genom ett svagt redskap," 62.

81. EH (May 31, 1916) 91.

82. Gerda rented a room in the house of Mr. and Mrs. Österlund and held services in their spacious kitchen. EH (December 7, 1916) 199; Burman, *Pingst-Väckelsens början*, 44.

83. EH (July 13, 1916) 114.

spy out the land" in 1916, as Wendén suggests.[84] The meeting in Robertsfors probably never happened.[85]

As a sought-after speaker, Gerda interrupted her ministry in Västerbotten for a meeting with the famous missionary to Brazil, Gunnar Vingren, in the town of Selånger near Sundsvall, on Pentecost Sunday, June 12, 1916.[86] She was accompanied by her former colleague, Berna Kristensson. This should not be viewed as a renewed partnership, but only as a temporary arrangement to assist with music, since Gerda could not sing or play herself.[87] Two weeks later, on June 24–26, she ministered at Gränsfors Second Baptist church's mid-summer conference, where she testified to God's work in Västerbotten. She reported about the region's spiritual darkness and the people's deep prejudice of free church missionaries, but also about some who accepted a "Full Gospel."[88]

Gerda wrote an annual report from her first year of ministry in Västerbotten in *Evangelii Härold* on December 7, 1916. The report contains the oft-repeated claim of "neglected fields" and "souls who dwell in the darkness of sin, ignorance, and delusion."[89] It also describes the challenge of not receiving any local financial support. The report also opens a brief but revealing window into her thought life as an unmarried and lonely female missionary in Northern Sweden. Gerda writes: "The Lord was stern, when he called me, a lonely weak woman, to prepare this way. Why did he not send a man to go ahead and open the doors? [. . .] It is difficult to contemplate the necessity of having to remain here alone for another winter."[90]

---

84. Wendén, "Ett stort verk genom ett svagt redskap," 62.

85. It is Wendén who proposes that Gerda's first meeting took place in the Mission Covenant church at Robertsfors in the summer of 1916. However, it is Jonsson who claims that it took place on June 19. This date is not supported by any sources and is only suggested because it corresponds with Gerda's thirty-eighth birthday. Although feasible in terms of public transportation, considering the cost and the difficulty of getting from Selånger on June 12, to Robertsfors on June 19, and back again for the mid-summer conference in Gränsfors on June 24 (a roundtrip of over 600 kilometers), it is unlikely the meeting took place. It is more likely she remained in the Sundsvall region the entire month. *EH* (July 13, 1916) 114; *EH* (May 31, 1916) 91; Burman, *Pingst-Väckelsens början*, 6.

86. *EH* (June 22, 1916) 103.

87. Nyberg Oskarsson states that it was Berna Kristensson who teamed up with Gerda in 1917 when it was, in fact, Gertrud Kristoffersson. Nyberg Oskarsson, "I Lucy Farrows fotspår," 87; *EH* (June 22, 1916) 103; Burman, *Pingst-Väckelsens början*, 6.

88. *EH* (July 13, 1916) 114.

89. *EH* (December 7, 1916) 199.

90. *EH* (December 7, 1916) 199.

She also mentions that occasionally, "the agony of her soul was so profound that she almost perished."[91]

These statements show that Gerda faced, not only the challenge of establishing a Pentecostal work alone in a hostile environment but also the additional difficulty of being an unmarried woman. Northern Sweden was dominated by the Swedish state church, which showed little acceptance for the Pentecostal movement or female preachers, despite having been the place of low-church pietistic revivals.[92] The Lutheran catechism placed the wife's role in the home, as well as in a subservient and dependent role to the husband. This understanding also prevailed in the free churches and society in general.[93] Based on Hirdman's theory of the gender contract, Swande further explains that women in the 1920s were perceived as weak and nurturing whereas men were viewed as strong and assertive.[94] Gerda seems to have accepted this socially constructed gender division, but the article also points to some of the reasons she managed to persevere. It speaks of a deep sense of gratitude for having been called by God, a duty to bring help to people in need, the comfort of seeing converts come to the Lord, and the prospect of receiving help for the coming year.[95] The last point probably being as vital as the other three.

Gerda's second year of ministry in Västerbotten is quiet in terms of reports in *Evangelii Härold*. She only appears once when she is back at her base in Gränsfors for a meeting at the building of the Good Templars, an order associated with the temperance movement, on July 1, 1917.[96] Yet, in her annual report in November 1917, she mentions that she did receive reinforcements in the form of sister Gertrud Kristoffersson in January 1917. The two worked primarily in the villages of Flarken and Ånäset, situated between the larger coastal towns of Skellefteå and Umeå, where they managed to rent a building for their meetings with the odd-sounding name "*Ol Pers-gården*" from farmer Karl Glaas.[97] Although

91. *EH* (December 7, 1916) 199.

92. "The fields in Västerbotten's coastal regions are difficult to till. Folk in general is high church, and consequently one is afraid of a full gospel since one does not understand the Scriptures or God's power." *EH* (March 24, 1921) 55. See also, *EH* (April 30, 1925) 220. Jonsson particularly highlights the influence of pietist, Carl-Olof Rosenius (1816–1868), who came from the same town as Gerda. Jonsson, *Gerda Åström*, 29–31.

93. Lindberg, *Förkunnarna och deras utbildning*, 188–89.

94. Swande, *Kvinnans roll i pingströrelsen*, 5.

95. *EH* (December 7, 1916) 199.

96. *EH* (June 21, 1917) 104.

97. Burman, *Pingst-Väckelsens början*, 6.

they succeeded in reaching villages fifty kilometers from Ånäset during the summer months, the work was more about "sowing" the Full Gospel than reaping its fruit. Wartime shortages also complicated the work.[98]

Gerda was busy establishing the work in Ånäset for the next three years. She recruited additional help from Örebro Mission Society and/or Filadelfia Bible School in Stockholm.[99] Burman states that it was during these years that the first adult baptismal services were held. The very first service was held on July 6, 1919, and the candidates were Karl Glass, Ruth Bergström, and Edgar Wendén. Otto Witt (1875–1923), a former missionary to South Africa, conducted the service.[100] Roland Gäreskog surmises that it was during this meeting that Gerda first met Otto Witt's wife, Eva Witt, with whom she later opened a healing home in Sävar, ca. twenty kilometers north of Umeå, in 1925.[101] On top of pouring all of her "soul, strength, and mind" into the work in Västerbotten during these years,[102] she also traveled to Central and Southern Sweden for mission- and edification conferences in places like Gränsfors, Nyköping, Smedby, and Alnön.[103]

By 1920 the work in Ånäset and the surrounding parishes had grown to the point that Gerda believed it was time to purchase a church building. On April 29, she wrote in *Evangelii Härold* of her desire to raise money for the purchase of an old cinema. Since the land on which the cinema stood was not for sale, the plan was to purchase the property for 2,500 crowns, move it to another piece of land that they had been given, and refurbish it for another 2,500 crowns.[104] Through volunteer efforts and numerous small donations,[105] the work on the chapel was finished in the fall of 1920 and joyfully inaugurated on January 2, 1921. Based on Gunnar Lindén's report of the festivities, it is clear whom the church

98. *EH* (November 8, 1917) 183.

99. There are unfortunately no extant enrollment records from the initial years of the Filadelfia Bible School. *EH* (August 29) 139; *EH* (September 2, 1920) 139; Burman, *Pingst-Väckelsens början*, 7.

100. Burman, *Pingst-Väckelsens början*, 6–8; Jonsson, *Gerda Åström*, 27.

101. Gäreskog, *Utanför lägret*, 303.

102. *EH* (February 12, 1931) 102.

103. *EH* (August 22, 1918) 135; *EH* (August 29, 1918) 139; *EH* (April 26, 1919) 66; *EH* (September 16, 1920) 146.

104. *EH* (April 29, 1920) 67. Burman writes that the land was not donated but bought for a small price of Otto Tjärnström. Burman's information is probably a more accurate description of the situation. Burman, *Pingst-Väckelsens början*, 11.

105. *EH* (September 2, 1920) 140; Burman, *Pingst-Väckelsens början*, 11.

credited for the achievement: "The friends here have, besides God, Gerda Åström to thank for her sacrificial work that the building now stands erected."[106] The church was formed as "a free biblical congregation" with thirteen initial members and was given the name "Elim."[107] Konrad Alexandersson was elected senior pastor and Gerda assumed the role as the church's secretary and treasurer.[108] Although Alexandersson was elected pastor, the protocol indicates that the church honored Gerda by unanimously voting that she would have exclusive rights to the rooms on the second floor as long as she remained in the area. Gerda also participated in the administration of the elements at the church's first communion service.[109] Even though a man was elected as the senior pastor of the church, Nyberg Oskarsson notes that Gerda continued to exercise indirect leadership. The church leadership sought her "advice and council" and it was she who wrote the reports of the work to *Evangelii Härold*.[110]

The church grew from thirteen to ninety members from 1921 to 1924.[111] The growth can be attributed to the successful recruitment of both male and female evangelists,[112] but also to the use of modern inventions such as an automobile in evangelistic outreaches.[113] Gerda also seems to have cooperated well with the congregation's two first pastors, Konrad Alexandersson and Arvid Persson.[114] Burman notes that pastor Persson was especially in favor of Gerda and proposed that she should become the church's first deaconess. Gerda was elected to the role on January 6, 1924.[115] Somewhat surprisingly, Burman adds the less flattering information that when the need for more deaconesses arose, Gerda opposed the idea on the basis that "the sisters were still willing to serve; wash and iron

---

106. *EH* (January 13, 1921) 7.

107. *EH* (January 13, 1921) 7. The term refers to a radical form of ecclesiology that the Swedish Pentecostal Movement adopted in 1919. The local church was to be free from organizational ties and solely responsible for the commissioning and support of local missionaries. For an in-depth discussion, see Davidsson, *Den svenska pingströrelsens församlingssyn*, 26–57.

108. *EH* (January 13, 1921) 7; Burman, *Pingst-Väckelsens början*, 12–13.

109. Burman, *Pingst-Väckelsens början*, 13; *EH* (January 13, 1921) 7.

110. Nyberg Oskarsson, "I Lucy Farrows fotspår," 88.

111. *EH* (October 30, 1924) 524.

112. *EH* (March 24, 1921) 55; *EH* (July 28, 1921) 138; *EH* (October 30, 1924) 524.

113. Gerda raised the funds for the car during her itinerary trips to southern Sweden in the Spring of 1924. *EH* (October 30, 1924) 524.

114. Persson succeeded Alexandersson in 1922. *EH* (October 30, 1924) 524.

115. Burman, *Pingst-Väckelsens början*, 32.

the preachers' clothes, cook, host visitors, etc." Only on January 6, 1929, several years after Gerda left Ånäset, did the church elect other deaconesses.[116] It is difficult to know why Gerda opposed the election of other deaconesses, but her elevated status could have created a sense of entitlement that she did not want to share with other sisters. Even if the reason for Gerda's stance remains unknown, the incident shows that not only men and complementarian theology stood against the advancement of women in the early Pentecostal movement but occasionally also other women.[117]

The services at Ånäset resembled typical Pentecostal church services with preaching, the singing of hymns, Sunday school, communion, and the occasional display of charismatic gifts.[118] By the 1920s the services in the Pentecostal movement were more structured and less spontaneous than when the Pentecostal revival first arrived. However, a Bible study week in June 1922 has attracted scholarly attention as an example of the lingering enthusiastic tendencies in early Swedish Pentecostalism, especially as it came to prophetic messages. Joel Halldorf explains that the Pentecostal movement had an ambivalent relationship to prophetic messages. On the one hand, Pentecostal leaders were adamant that prophetic messages had to be "tested," but on the other hand, there was a "radical wing" within the movement where these instructions were not always heeded.[119] Halldorf implies that a radical wing existed in Ånäset.

The immediate background to the controversy stemmed from a report by Einar Mellquist of the Bible study week in June 1922 that the recently appointed editor of *Evangelii Härold*, Sven Lidman (1882–1960), had carelessly let slip through his fingers.[120] Mellquist retells that the role of the prophetic gift in the church had just been discussed at the annual conference at Kölingared, and what transpired in Ånäset functioned as an "illustration in miniature" of what God was willing to do all over the country.[121] The meetings ran according to schedule until Friday when an unnamed "prophet" suddenly interrupted the service.[122] The prophet declared that the meeting was full of "unclean spirits," and participants were

116. Burman, *Pingst-Väckelsens början*, 32.
117. Nilsson, *Swedish Pentecostal Movement 1913–2000*, 380–90.
118. EH (August 10, 1922) 127; Burman, *Pingst-Väckelsens början*, 33.
119. Halldorf, *Biskop Lewi Pethrus*, 94–95.
120. Halldorf, *Lewis brev*, 53.
121. EH (August 10, 1922) 127.
122. Halldorf suggests several potential names, but only concludes that the person came from within the church's own ranks. Halldorf, *Lewis brev*, 56–57.

accused of various sins and forced to confess. Having appointed himself as a prophet, the man seized control of the meetings. He decided, for instance, that the same song should be sung repeatedly and that no leader but himself was allowed to select or give expositions on biblical texts.

Gerda is described as a passive and compliant bystander until she is dragged into the self-appointed prophet's most controversial activity. At one point in the meetings, the prophet received "a word from the Lord" that there was a man in the congregation who needed to be dismissed and "would not be saved."[123] The prophet approached a man in the congregation, but before ushering him out, he took the church's "standing witness," Gerda Åström, along for support. As Gerda and the prophet led the man outside, Gerda felt like "a darkness descended over the man." It was supposedly later found out that the man "had testified against God and mocked his Word."[124]

Halldorf writes that Mellquist's article led to a letter correspondence between Sven Lidman and Lewi Pethrus. Pethrus did not react harshly, either toward Mellquist or Lidman. Pethrus and Otto Witt did, however, write follow-up articles that addressed how to distinguish between true and false prophecy.[125] It is important to note here that nothing in the sources suggests that Gerda or the church in Ånäset belonged to a "radical wing" of the Pentecostal movement. The enthusiasm displayed at the Bible study week in June 1922 never happened before or after. It should rather be viewed as an isolated occurrence in a newly established church that lacked the proper checks and balances. Nevertheless, the account points to the informal authority Gerda had accumulated by 1922. Both the prophet's actions and Mellquist's epithet of her as the "standing witness" show that she possessed an informal authority above the other evangelists, and on par with, if not above, the senior pastor. Women were not allowed to baptize, administer the Lord's Supper, or assume the role of elder or senior pastor.[126] However, Gerda's ministry in Ånäset confirms Swande's observation that these rules were less rigidly applied in remote parts of the country.[127] Gerda performed most of these roles without official recognition.

123. *EH* (August 10, 1922) 127.
124. *EH* (August 10, 1922) 127.
125. Halldorf, *Biskop Lewi Pethrus*, 97–98; Halldorf, *Lewis brev*, 58.
126. Nilsson, *The Swedish Pentecostal Movement 1913–2000*, 385.
127. Swande, *Kvinnans roll i pingströrelsen*, 11.

THE FINAL YEARS

Gerda's pioneer work in Ånäset came to an end in 1925. *Evangelii Härold* explains that "through God's marvelous guidance," God had called Gerda Åström and Eva Witt to open a healing home in Sävar, located ca. fifty kilometers south of Ånäset, "to help those who wanted the Lord as their healer."[128] As we will see, the decision to open a healing home was not only for altruistic reasons but also to meet Gerda's own need for rest and physical recovery after many years of intense labor. Another reason could have been the loss of support she experienced when Arvid Persson left for a new pastoral position in Lycksele.[129] It is also conceivable that she realized that her "apostolic" ministry was no longer needed when new evangelists were recruited.[130] Yet, the transition does not seem to have been a result of deep-seated frictions, since a large and enthusiastic contingent from Ånäset attended the opening of the healing home on November 8, 1925.[131]

Gerda dedicated significant time and effort to the healing home in Sävar, and just as in previous years, she continued to work as an itinerate evangelist and conducted services in neighboring communities like Lögdeå and Nordmaling.[132] She also managed to recruit additional help from Maja Nerman, who possibly replaced Eva Witt in 1927.[133]

Gerda decided for unknown reasons to break up from Sävar and open a new healing home on the island of Gotland in the Baltic Sea in 1929. Through the help of Lovisa Svensson, Tora Westerström, and J. Lindblad, she managed to buy a big house strategically located seven kilometers south of Visby. It had a kitchen and seven rooms and was prepared for harsh winter conditions.[134] Her time in Gotland lasted only one year because of increasingly deteriorating health. Gerda was never described as physically strong, but rather as "a petite, weak, and simple woman."[135] Signs of her deteriorating health started in 1924 when she

---

128. *EH* (December 3, 1925) 613.
129. *EH* (April 30, 1925) 221.
130. *EH* (December 3, 1925) 613.
131. *EH* (December 3, 1925) 613.
132. *EH* (April 21, 1927) 203; *EH* (October 20, 1927) 540.
133. *EH* (May 19, 1927) 260.
134. *EH* (July 18, 1929) 459.
135. *EH* (February 27, 1941) 191.

developed an ulcer because of her heavy workload.[136] By the time Gerda participated in the Elim church's tenth anniversary in 1931, Gunnar Eriksson described her appearance as someone who had "burned out in the work of the Lord."[137]

Gerda moved her residency to Burträsk parish in Västerbotten county on October 21, 1930 and asked for readmission to the Elim church in Ånäset the same year.[138] She managed to open another healing home in her new hometown of Burträsk,[139] located ca. thirty-five kilometers north of Ånäset, but the total absence of information about her work there suggests it was minimal. She made her last recorded appearance in January 1936 when she attended the fifteenth anniversary of the Elim church. Since Lewi Pethrus was in attendance, the celebration was moved to a more spacious sanctuary in Robertsfors. The informal leader of the Swedish Pentecostal movement was thus present when Gerda last told the story of "the grace and hardships she experienced before the church was founded."[140]

Gerda passed away on December 28, 1940, sixty-two years of age. The funeral service was held on January 19, 1941 at the chapel of the Mission Covenant Church in Robertsfors and was officiated by A. Lundkvist, the current pastor of her home church in Ånäset. The white casket was richly decorated with flowers as Gerda had wished.[141] The numerous eulogies from church members and other acquaintances during the memorial service testified to the fruit of her life and ministry, and what God could do through a weak vessel that had dedicated themselves to his service.[142]

CONCLUSION

Gerda Åström's life story is an account of a woman with an "above the norm" set of personal abilities that allowed her to become a pioneer for the Pentecostal movement in Northern Sweden. She had an aptitude for

---

136. *EH* (October 30, 1924) 524.

137. *EH* (February 12, 1931) 102.

138. Burman, *Pingst-Väckelsens början*, 44; *Församlingsbok Burträsk Gamla skolan Gammelbyn 1925–43*, 923.

139. *EH* (February 12, 1931) 102.

140. *EH* (Mar 26, 1936) 271.

141. *EH* (February 27, 1941) 191.

142. *EH* (February 27, 1941) 191.

learning, and she combined it with personal determination and perseverance to overcome numerous obstacles. She possessed great communication and relationship skills that made her a natural leader and a sought-after public speaker. It is no wonder therefore that she was given honorary epithets like "apostle" and "standing witness" from her inner circle of admirers. Coming from a meager working-class background that set limits to the potential for upward social mobility, her upbringing in the last decades of the nineteenth century still exposed her to a vibrant cultural and religious environment that marked her future journey. Gerda never "rocked" the religious or cultural "boat" she belonged to but was rather driven by a desire to experience and manifest its values and teachings. Thus, despite having a great mind, she never used it to criticize but to establish and promote the free church tradition she was part of. She never ascribed the motivation for her dedication to any external factor, but solely to the sovereign work of God.

Yet, Gerda's story is no fairy tale but demonstrates the pain and suffering that often accompanied early female Pentecostal pioneers. It also speaks of her human limitations and weaknesses. She experienced family loss firsthand. Although infant mortality rates were high among working-class families at the end of the nineteenth century, she still had to accompany four of her siblings to their final rest. Even if Gerda received much appreciation and esteem for her labor, and could exercise significant indirect influence in ministry, she never received full credit for her efforts. The fact that a man became the senior pastor of the church she helped to plant in Ånäset underscores Tackett's observation that "Women could plough the hard, fallow ground and plant the seed, but they were expected to give over the role of harvesting the grain to men."[143] She was also overlooked after her death. In his doctoral dissertation about the Pentecostal movement's early expansion in Northern Sweden, Lars Samuelsson mentions thirteen key local evangelists. The list is comprised of eleven men and only two women—none of whom is Gerda Åström. Her absence from the list is remarkable considering that she was the first to bring the Pentecostal message to the region.[144] Although partially overlooked herself, she committed the same error by opposing the promotion

---

143. Tackett, *Callings, Giftings, and Empowerment*, 79.

144. The names Samuelsson includes in his list of key native evangelists are Napoleon Bjuhr, Rickard Israelsson, Oskar Johansson, Gurli Danielsson, Ida Hägglund, Vilhelm Eclundh, Viktor Sjöberg, Abraham Holmgren, Fridolf Karlsson, Gottfrid Alenius, and E. J. Lyxell. Samuelsson, *Väckelsens vägar*, 71–72, 129–30.

of other "sisters" to leadership positions in the church. She cannot therefore serve as an example of a woman who facilitated the elevation of women in the church. Finally, Gerda's incredible efforts and hard-fought victories came at a steep price. Already at the age of forty-six, her health had deteriorated to the point that she could not continue in apostolic ministry. Her story thus serves as a warning example of somebody who "burned her candle at both ends."

The story of Gerda Åström is one of resilience in hardships, spirituality as a driving force for ministry, and the importance of community and companionship in missionary work. But it is also one of human frailty and the dangers of neglecting personal needs over time. Even if her story could have had a greater ending, nothing can take away her legacy of being the "standing witness" and the introducer of Pentecostalism in Northern Sweden.

BIBLIOGRAPHY

Alvarsson, Jan-Åke. "Pingstväckelsens etablering i Sverige: Från Azusa Street till Skövde på sju månader." In *Pingströrelsen: händelser och utveckling under 1900-talet*, 1:11–43. Örebro: Libris, 2007.

Ambjörnsson, Ronny. *Den skötsamma arbetaren: Idéer och ideal i ett norrländskt sågverkssamhälle 1880–1930*. Stockholm: Carlsson, 2017.

Åström, Gerda. *Den trefaldiga nåden*. N.d.: Ånäset, 1913.

Blom, Åsa. "Sågverksindustrins utveckling i Norrland: 1850 till andra världskriget." Umeå: Sveriges lantbruksuniversitet. Institutionen för skoglig vegetationsekologi, 1995.

Burman, Axel. *Pingst-Väckelsens början i Västerbottens kustland*. Rev. ed. Ånäset: Filadelfiaförsamlingen, 1978.

Davidsson, Tommy. "Between Multiple Worlds: Emerging Scandinavian-American Pentecostal Theology, 1907–1919." In *Revising Pentecostal History: Scandinavian-American Contributions to the Development of Pentecostalism*. Eugene, OR: Pickwick, 2024.

———. "Den svenska pingströrelsens församlingssyn: samfundsfri församling, riksförening, trossamfund." In *Pingströrelsens ecklesiologi i förändring*, 26–57. Forskningsrapporter från Institutet för Pentekostala Studier 11. Skillingaryd: Skilltryck, 2023.

Gäreskog, Roland. *Utanför lägret: En berättelse om missionären och evangelisten Otto Witt*. Forserum: Stema, 2017.

Halldorf, Joel. *Av denna världen? Emil Gustafson, moderniteten och den evangelikala väckelsen*. Skellefteå: Artos & Norma, 2012.

———. *Biskop Lewi Pethrus*. Skellefteå: Artos & Norma, 2017.

———. *Lewis brev*. Örebro: Libris, 2007.

Hermansson, Kenneth. "Vad är då en människa? John Ongmans gudsbild och människosyn." Linköpings universitet, 1999. http://www.kennethhermansson.se/ongman.pdf.
Högman, Hans. "Flottningens historia i Sverige." September 9, 2022. https://www.hhogman.se/flottningen-kartor.htm.
Jonsson, Lars-Evert. *Gerda Åström, "Västerbottens apostel": "Just för en tid som denna."* Skillingaryd: Skilltryck, 2016.
Lindberg, Alf. *Förkunnarna och deras utbildning: Lewi Pethrus ideologiska roll och de kvinnliga förkunnarnas situation*. Lund: Lund University Press, 1991.
Morell, Mats. *Jordbruket i industrisamhället: 1870–1945*. Vol. 4. Det svenska jordbrukets historia. Stockholm: Lagersberg, 2001.
Nilsson, Nils-Olov. "The Swedish Pentecostal Movement 1913–2000: The Tension Between Radical Congregationalism, Restorationism, and Denominationalism." Skillingaryd: Insamlingsstiftelsen för pingstforskning, 2024.
Nyberg Oskarsson, Gunilla. "I Lucy Farrows fotspår—svenska kvinnor möter den tidiga pentekostala rörelsen." In *Azusa Street i Örebro: Pingstväckelsens intåg i Sverige*, 26:78–89. Örebro: Örebro teologiska högskola, 2008.
———. "Kvinnorna marginaliserades när väckelsen etablerats: 'Systrarna' länge utanför församlingsledningarna." In *Pingströrelsen: Verksamheter och särdrag under 1900-talet*, 2:267–86. Örebro: Libris, 2007.
Samuelsson, Lars. *Väckelsens vägar: Pingströrelsens framväxt i Lycksele och Arvidsjaur socknar fram till ca. 1940*. Klippan: Ljungbergs, 1983.
Skoog, Roger. "Baptiströrelsen i Piteå: En studie av baptismens framväxt och utveckling mellan 1850 och 1910." Högskolan Dalarna, 2011.
Söderholm, G. E. *Den svenska pingstväckelsens historia 1907–1927*. Vol. 1. Stockholm: Filadelfia, 1927.
Stanley, Susie C. *Holy Boldness: Women Preachers' Autobiographies and the Sanctified Self*. Knoxville, TN: University of Tennessee Press, 2004.
Struble, Rhode. *Den samfundsfria församlingen och de karismatiska gåvorna och tjänsterna: Den svenska pingströrelsens församlingssyn 1907–1947*. Stockholm: Almqvist & Wiksell International, 1982.
Swande, Rebecka. "Kvinnans roll i pingströrelsen, utifrån ett genuskontrakt." N.d.: Örebro teologiska högskola, 2010.
Synan, Vinson, and Charles Fox. *William J. Seymour: Pioneer of the Azusa Street Revival*. Alachua, FL: Bridge Logos, 2012.
Tackett, Zachary Michael. "Callings, Giftings, and Empowerment: Preaching Women and American Pentecostalism in Historical and Theological Perspective." In *Women in Pentecostal and Charismatic Ministry*, 73–98. Leiden: Brill, 2017.
Wendén, Edgar. "Ett stort verk genom ett svagt redskap. Några ord om evangelisten Gärda Åströms livsverk." In *Julens härold*, 26:59–66. Stockholm: Filadelfia, 1941.

Image #8. Frida Vingren.

7

Frida Vingren
Hitting the Glass Ceiling[1]

Jan-Åke Alvarsson

Swedish Frida Vingren (1891–1940) was a woman who caused a battle for the right of women to exercise all services in the church, especially in the *Assambleia de Deus* in Brazil, the largest national Pentecostal church in the world—a battle that is still going on! She was also an extremely talented preacher, hymn composer, and writer that many people liked to listen to or read. With time, she became a role model in the fight for women's rights in Brazil.

BACKGROUND

Frida Maria Strandberg, married Vingren, was born on June 9, 1891, in Själevad, just west of the city Örnsköldsvik in northern Sweden.[2] She grew up in an environment marked by the pious, Lutheran, low-church movement *Evangeliska Fosterlandsstiftelsen* (EFS)[3] and became a member of that movement at a young age. Furthermore, her diary from her

---

1. All translations in this chapter are the author's own.
2. From the main periodical of the Swedish Pentecostal Movement, *EH* (October 17, 1940) 791; *Svenskt Frikyrkolexikon*, 494.
3. *EH* (May 31, 1917) 89.

early years reveals an interest in blood and bride mysticism,[4] which also indicates influences from the Moravian movement.

In her youth, she felt a calling to become a missionary. Thus, in 1914, at the age of 23, she registered as a student at *Svenska Bibelinstitutet* (the Swedish Bible Institute) in Södertälje and attended an eight-month-long Bible course.[5] After that, she moved to Vänersborg and attended medical training at the infirmary there, a training that ended with a three-month course at the Children's Hospital on Planterhagsvägen in Stockholm.[6] After that, she planned to register as a missionary for EFS.

MOVE TO STOCKHOLM

But the plans were changed. When she returned to Stockholm in 1916, she got in touch with some Pentecostal friends in the Filadelfia church at Uppsalagatan 11. Their spirituality,[7] combined with a large investment in social activities in the form of, for example, "The Rescue Mission," "the Visiting the Sick Committee" and a children's home,[8] seem to have captured Frida and on January 24, 1917, she was baptized in Filadelfia and thus became a member of the congregation.

To "rebaptize," i.e., to be baptized as an adult, when one had already been baptized as a child, was a big step for a faithful Lutheran. Not long after the water baptism, Frida had the transcendent experience that the Pentecostals called "Spirit baptism." She describes it very vividly: "Shortly afterwards, God baptized me in the Holy Spirit," and "The Lord is able to

---

4. See Norell, *Halleluja, Brasilien!*, 140.

5. *Svenska Bibelinstitutet* was founded in 1910 in Östertälje, nowadays a suburb of the city of Södertälje, just south of Stockholm, by the *Evangeliska Fosterlandsstiftelsen* (EFS) to increase "the knowledge of the Bible in EFS," and to create a way of preparing students for the *Johannelunds teologiska institutut*, founded in 1862 in Stockholm. *Svenska Bibelinstitutet* later was transformed into *Hagabergs folkhögskola* in Södertälje. (In *Svenskt Frikyrkolexikon*, it is claimed that Frida attended a Bible course at Götabro, but in her own account it is clearly stated that she attended *"Svenska Bibelinstitutet"* which is more logical, given her EFS background.)

6. *EH* (May 31, 1917) 89.

7. The Moravian (Herrnhut) movement has often been mentioned as a precursor of the Pentecostal movement when it comes to spirituality: the ecstatic elements, the emphasis on Jesus, the redemption in his blood, the congregation as the bride of Christ, as well as mysticism. All these phenomena have been predominant in both movements.

8. See, Sundstedt, *Pingstväckelsen och dess vidare utveckling*, 72–86.

release a bound soul and give it wings, through which it can ascend to the living God in jubilation and thanksgiving."⁹

Frida Strandberg became a member of a congregation which at that time was strongly marked by mission and especially mission in Brazil. First pastor Lewi Pethrus's childhood friend from the province of Västergötland, Daniel Berg, had in 1910 on his own initiative traveled from the USA to Pará in Brazil and started missionary work there together with his good friend Gunnar Vingren, who had also emigrated to the USA in 1903. Over time, because of Pethrus's and Berg's friendship, the two missionaries made contact with the small "seventh Baptist congregation" at Uppsalagatan 11 in Stockholm, which was started also in 1910. The venue was called "Filadelfia" after John Ongman's Baptist congregation in Örebro.¹⁰

After Filadelfia's exclusion from the Swedish Baptist denomination in 1913, the interest in organizing missionary work on their own steadily grew. A "missionary account" was established and in the minutes from November 24, 1913, it was stated that actions should be taken to "encourage us to more faithful work and prayer for these millions, who still grope in the darkness of paganism."¹¹ Because of the contact with Berg and Vingren, fomented by their visits to Stockholm, it was natural that Brazil became one of the focal points.

On June 5, 1916, it was time for the congregation to separate and send out their first missionaries, Lina Berggren and Samuel Nyström. This was a young couple, still not married, which led to the separation ceremony being supplemented with a wedding feast. Gunnar Vingren was one of the guests. It is unclear whether Frida Strandberg participated, since she did not become a member until six months later, but she knew about this engagement in Brazil.

When Frida was no longer thinking about EFS mission work in Eritrea, Ethiopia or India, Brazil therefore became a natural choice. Which came first, the interest in Brazil or her future husband Gunnar is unclear, but one reason could, of course, have been that she met Gunnar in different contexts and became fond of him. When she became a member of Filadelfia, he was back in Sweden for some time, and he was regularly advertised as a preacher at various gatherings in the Stockholm

---

9. See, Sundstedt, *Pingstväckelsen och dess vidare utveckling*, 72–86.

10. See the introductory chapter for the history of John Ongman and the "Örebro Baptists."

11. Reproduced in Sundstedt, *Pingstväckelsen och dess genombrott*, 55.

area. Another reason could be that their interest in Brazil brought them together. At the time, Frida was twenty-six years old, and Gunnar was thirty-eight, high time for both to think about marriage, according to the expectations of the time.

However, the relationship between Frida and Gunnar was preceded by strange events. Gunnar had had a "betrothed" in the US who planned to travel with him to India. But when Gunnar changed his mind and opted for Brazil instead, she broke up by letter. Gunnar's laconic reaction was: "May the Lord's will be done!"[12]

Later, in 1910, when Gunnar was a Baptist pastor in South Bend, Indiana, a Swedish American, Adolf Ulldin, received a prophetic message directed to Gunnar. In his diary Gunnar writes that "The Spirit" said that he should go to Pará (a place he did not know existed) as a missionary, but also predicted his future spouse: "The Spirit also said that I would marry a person called Strandberg."[13] In a letter after her husband's death, Frida herself claims that "already before they became a couple, she had seen him in a vision, and that he had asked her if she wanted to help him in God's work."[14] In practice, the Spirit seems to have "arranged" Frida's and Gunnar's relationship. What they *felt* was thus subordinate.

Both belonged to the fast-growing Pentecostal movement and were subsequently regulated by a fairly strict set of rules. To reveal any type of relationship before you were engaged was therefore impossible. But as everything in connection with their wedding happened so fast, this implies that everything must have been well prepared and that the relationship probably had been going on for a long time, probably since Gunnar's time in Stockholm. We know that they had met at prayer meetings in the home of a family called Väster, and even in the home of the first pastor Lewi Pethrus. In these prayer meetings, among other things, they had prayed for "Frida and the calling she has had from the Lord."[15]

Even though Frida had been a member of Filadelfia for just a few months, she had her first article published in the magazine of the Filadelfia church, *Evangelii Härold* (The Gospel Herald, henceforth abbreviated *EH*), already in April 1917. The title was challenging: "Congregation of God—are you betraying your ideals?" Departing from Jeremiah 18:14

12. Vingren, *Pionjärens dagbok*, 22.
13. Vingren, *Pionjärens dagbok*, 25.
14. See Norell, *Halleluja, Brasilien!*, 140.
15. Araujo, *Frida Vingren*, 31. The original text reads: "*por Frida e pela chamada que ela havia recebido do Senhor.*"

she produced an essay about the responsibility of the congregation to missionize in the "heathen lands." At the end, the reader was provided with a poem written by Frida herself:

> *Roses are growing on the path of thorns,*
> *The sowing will be watered by the dew of tears,*
> *The crowned warrior, consecrated at the cross*
> *From all slag will be cleansed.*[16]

The very same month she was also announced as a speaker in the outpost of the congregation, "Filadelfia Aspudden."[17]

MISSIONARY TO BRAZIL

Only a month later, there is a headline in *EH*: "New worker for Brazil" with a photograph of a serious "Miss Frida Strandberg" in a nurse's uniform. Even though she had been a member for just half-a-year, she had been accepted as a missionary, an almost incomprehensible happening in the Pentecostal movement at the time. In the text about her departure one can also sense a certain triumphalism:

> On the evening of the second day of Pentecost, a new worker departed for the field of the free mission in Brazil. Sister Strandberg had originally planned to work for a missionary society, but then the issue of baptism became revealed to her. When she had experienced the baptism in water, she opted for, and received the baptism in the Spirit. It cost her quite some struggle to sacrifice the relationship with the circles she previously had belonged to, to head for the path of the despised faith, but God gave her grace to obey.[18]

It is obvious that the Pentecostal movement was proud of recruiting a potential EFS missionary with medical training! And she had experienced the "grace to obey" [the truth]. It is conceivable that the "recruitment" helped to speed up the process, and that Gunnar Vingren also recommended Frida to the board of the congregation.

In the report there is also an article by Frida incorporated, based on John 12:24, "If the grain of wheat does not fall into the soil and dies, it will

---

16. *EH* (April 26, 1917) 71.

17. *EH* (April 12, 1917) 64: The original text reads: "*Filadelfia Aspudden Jarlagatan 35, Söndag kl 7 em Frida Strandberg.*"

18. *EH* (May 31,1917) 89.

remain alone, but if it dies it will bear much fruit," a parable that indicates that Frida had given up her life in Sweden and dedicated it to Brazil instead. She also mentioned her former plans to work for the EFS—and was not afraid to declare the name of the denomination. If the introduction had a tone of sacrifice, the conclusion was a kind of praise: "The Lord has called me to Brazil, and now he has opened the way for me, and I can go there to proclaim the glory of Jesus Christ. Glory to God!"

On May 28, 1917, Frida Strandberg left Stockholm to travel to Brazil via Norway and the USA. On June 12, she arrived in New York. And who met her there, if not Gunnar Vingren. This must be seen as more than a coincidence. In a later travel report, she also specifically mentions this event.[19] The couple had eight days together, and then Frida traveled alone to Brazil and the city of Pará (now Belém), the Swedish missionaries' first stop in the country. Gunnar had not received the necessary visa.[20] However, leaving Gunnar behind was not that easy. After all, he was the only one who tied her to Brazil. Now everything else was unknown: "Oh, how small and lonely I felt! As soon as the friends on the dock were out of sight, I had to have a good cry. And I did that for two days. So probably it was properly done. But the Lord, the Lord helps and comforts."[21]

The boat trip down to Brazil was also anything but pleasant—and the experience was marked by Frida's mood: "The boat was Brazilian, so was the food. I was sick from hunger, sometimes even seasick."[22]

She arrived in Pará on July 7 and was met by an acquaintance, Samuel Nyström from the Filadelfia congregation in Stockholm. They took the tram together—in second class, of course—to the "whitewashed mud house" where Frida was to settle. There she also finally got "a Swedish meal." Already that evening it was time for Frida's first Pentecostal service in Brazil.[23]

19. "In New York, where we arrived on June 12, bro. Vingren met up. He had just arrived from a trip out 'West.'" *EH* (September 6, 1917) 145.

20. At the time, Gunnar Vingren was an American citizen. Thus, he had to comply with different conditions than Frida. In Vingren, *Pionjärens dagbok*, 89, Gunnar stated that, "I felt sad that I had not yet received a passport so that I too could travel to Brazil [with Frida]." The reason was thus probably a question of passport renewal or a passport submitted to the Brazilian embassy for a visa.

21. From a letter "to Sweden" from Frida, reproduced in Vingren, *Pionjärens dagbok*, 97.

22. From a letter "to Sweden" from Frida, reproduced in Vingren, *Pionjärens dagbok*, 97.

23. From a letter "to Sweden" from Frida, reproduced in Vingren, *Pionjärens dagbok*, 97.

Once settled in Pará, living with Lina and Samuel Nyström—decency had not tolerated anything else—she immediately began studying Portuguese.[24] Even though she was now past twenty-six years old, her studies progressed quickly. She had a gift for languages and could soon talk to people and find her way around the city. After some time, she was also able to give her first testimony in the Pentecostal church in Portuguese.[25] The first task outside the church that she took on was to, together with Lina Nyström, work among the prostitutes in Pará.[26] This, dedicating oneself to society's most marginalized groups, was something that characterized the Swedish Pentecostal mission in general—and Frida in particular.

MARRIAGE TO GUNNAR VINGREN

In October 1917, Gunnar Vingren finally came back to Brazil from the USA. He returned to Pará and he and Frida could meet again. That they were in some way a couple already before is shown by the fact that they were married already on October 18.[27] The wedding officiant was missionary colleague Samuel Nyström.[28] However, the friends back home in Sweden did not find out about the marriage until March of the following year when an announcement was published in *EH*.[29] Now Frida Strandberg suddenly became Frida Vingren—the pioneer's wife.

Around the time of the wedding, Lina and Samuel Nyström left Pará to move to the state of Amazonas. But Gunnar and Frida would not be alone in the house for long. Gunnar's pioneer colleague, Daniel Berg, was ill with tropical fever and moved in with the Vingrens.[30]

Parallel to all these activities, Frida continued as a writer. During the trip, an article was published in *EH*'s "*Appendix*" entitled "Transforming Tears."[31] Then follows the report from her first time in Brazil in Septem-

---

24. *EH* (October 18, 1917) 170.

25. *Brudgummens röst* (The Voice of the Bridegroom, an early Swedish Pentecostal journal), January 1918, 150.

26. *EH* (November 29, 1917) 195.

27. From *Matteus dödbok*, Riksarkivet (The National Archives), Stockholm.

28. Bundy, *Visions of Apostolic Mission*, 401.

29. *EH* (March 21, 1918) 47.

30. *Brudgummens röst* (April 1918) 63.

31. *Bilaga till EH* (1917) 2.

ber 1917.³² It is placed on the front page of the journal and illustrated with a street shot from Pará—the only photo in the entire magazine! Both the placement and the illustration were something very unusual for a missionary report—unless it was written by Lewi Pethrus or another of the "leading brethren." Both articles were of course published under the name Frida Strandberg.

The year after she was married, the first article was published in *EH* under the name Frida Vingren. It is not a theologically oriented article but more of a social analysis: "The woman and the home in Brazil." She gave a depiction of Brazilian everyday life at the beginning of the century with interiors mainly from poor homes, even a report "from a mud hut." She showed strong sympathy for the poor but was critical of those who bowed "the knee before the idols." Only in the last sentence did she turn to the Swedish reader: "What are you doing to make that name known?"³³ The name referred to was of course "Jesus."

In March 1919 another report was published under the title "Letter from Brazil" in which Frida first gave an insight into the work of Daniel Berg and Otto Nelson, and then depicted the effects of the Spanish flu which was ravaging the country at that time. She was strongly critical of the Catholic Church's attempts to protect the population from the plague with fairs and made-up miracles. The most interesting thing in the article, however, is the small glimpses from Frida's own life: how she confronted a Catholic priest and how she hinted at certain homesickness: "Sometimes a thought goes to my dear Norrland. But more often the thoughts go to the right motherland, from where we await the Savior. Hallelujah! Soon Jesus will come, may we be ready then."³⁴

FIRST EDITORIAL WORK

In 1919, the Vingren couple started the magazine *Boa Semente* to support the growing Pentecostal movement *Assembléia de Deus*. The first

---

32. *EH* (September 6, 1917) 145. Incidentally, this is the second time that Frida has ended up on the front page of *EH*. Also, the report on her departure, "New worker for Brazil," was placed on the front page of *EH* illustrated with a photo of Frida. *EH* (May 31, 1917) 89. To be placed on the front page of *EH* as a missionary twice in the same year has probably never happened either before or after this. Frida must have been in good confidence with the editor Alfred Gustafsson.

33. *EH* (October 17, 1918) 165–66.

34. *EH* (March 27, 1919) 51.

issue contained articles by Gunnar and his closest colleagues Daniel Berg and Otto Nelson, and were mainly theological expositions. Over time, however, this magazine also became a springboard for Brazilian writers.[35] And in the background we can sense Frida's editorial efforts, something she came to practice more and more in the following years.

The year after they were married, in 1918, the first child was born, a boy named Ivar. Two years later, another boy, Ruben, was born.[36] Being the parents of young children takes time, and that is perhaps why we hear nothing from Frida and Gunnar during 1920. The most important reason, however, was probably that the most skilled writer in the family was seriously ill and close to death. Her son Ivar wrote in retrospect, with a note from his father's diary:

> Frida became seriously ill with malaria with terrible bouts of fever. At one point her pulse stopped completely. It was a life and death struggle, which lasted no less than two and a half months. [Gunnar] Vingren writes about this [in his diary] on April 3 [1920]: "Today I asked the Lord to either heal her or take her home. She then got a little better. Glory be to Jesus who hears prayer!"—One day when she was very weak and exhausted, in the middle of a fever she had a vision. She saw Jesus on the cross, and the cross itself shone like silver.[37]

Despite the temporary improvement and the transcendent experience, the illness continued—and Frida "suffered badly." Not until June 3, 1920, did she fully recover. The whole congregation had prayed for healing and the members were now convinced that God had intervened.[38] Frida quickly returned to her chores.

Her spiritual authority was shown again already in the same month. She prophesied over her husband who was thinking of going south and starting work in Rio de Janeiro. Gunnar wrote in his diary on June 24, 1920: "Frida, my wife, had a message for me today where the Lord said: 'The harvest is ripe. Fear not. I am with you. It is I who am sending you!'" Bolstered by this, Gunnar traveled to Rio. He was there for the first time on July 7.

---

35. Bundy, *Visions of Apostolic Mission*, 401–2.
36. See *EH* (June 9, 1921) 106.
37. Vingren, *Pionjärens dagbok*, 104–5.
38. Vingren, *Pionjärens dagbok*, 105. Gunnar wrote in his diary that: "Now she is well again. Jesus has healed her!"

The following year, 1921, there was a report showing that the spouses were both seriously ill again and that the missionary colleagues now feared that Gunnar would die, or as his friends put it: "that he would be allowed to move to a better homeland than the earthly one." The decision among the missionaries was quite natural that the Vingren family needed to travel home to Sweden to recover and rest from "the murderous climate."[39] The dramatic journey home was described as follows:

> On May 8 [1921], the brethren therefore took Brother Wingren out of bed and helped him down to the boat. At that time, a ship went directly from Pará to England. It was an arduous and difficult journey. Broken to the point of health for their own part, they had to care for their little boys Ivar and Rubin [sic], who are both under three years old. However, the Lord had wonderfully helped and accompanied them, so that now at the appearance they feel very grateful to God for his glorious help. From England, the trip had gone by boat directly to Bergen in Norway, with a short stopover. Likewise, they made a stop in Kristiania, where our friends attended a meeting at Myllerg. 38, at brother Barrat's.[sic][40]

The report is illustrated with three photos, one of Gunnar, one of Frida and one of Ivar and Ruben. As for the activities in Brazil, the reporter sums them up triumphantly: "The brethren work in the sign of victory."[41] And despite Gunnar's state of health, he was announced at a "missionary meeting" as early as June 26, 1921![42]

VISIT TO SWEDEN

In the Filadelfia congregation in Stockholm, the increase in the number of members had led to the fact that the first premises on Uppsalagatan was now far too small. Under great pressure, a building committee had therefore seen to it that new premises, with the same name, "Filadefia," would be established at Sveavägen 45.[43] When the premises were finished, there was an inauguration ceremony from September 2 to 6,

39. *EH* (June 9, 1921) 106.
40. *EH* (June 9, 1921) 106.
41. *EH* (June 9, 1921) 106.
42. *EH* (June 23, 1921) 120.
43. These premises were later transformed into the "Grand" cinema house at Sveavägen, Stockholm.

1921. On Monday evening, September 5, the "missionary meeting" was announced with "offerings for Brazil." Both Frida and Gunnar were then advertised together with Adina and Otto Nelson.[44] In the long report after the inauguration ceremony, written by the reporter Edvin Tallbacka, the participation of both spouses was confirmed: "The friends Vingrens and Nelsons gave all four warm-hearted testimonies about the revealed deeds of Jesus among the people of Brazil."[45] Thus Frida was part of representing the Pentecostal missionary work at the most important event of the Pentecostal movement that year!

During 1921, Frida's husband Gunnar was the one who was in the spotlight the most. He was the one who wrote several articles and despite his weakness, he was also widely advertised as a speaker. But on some occasions "missionary Vingren with wife" is advertised, for example in Trollhättan, the Tabor parish in Stockholm, Nyköping, and Ekeby (Sköllersta). And in the penultimate issue of *EH* there was also finally an article by Frida: "Faith to Victory"—a theological exposition on belief and unbelief based on the Book of Numbers, chapters 13, 14 and 15, about the Israelites' exodus from Egypt. Her conclusion was, as usual, a call to other believers: "That we really enter into his rest from our own works, the adherence of faith to the promises of the Lord in all conditions of life."[46] A reader of our days, however, wonders if she was also processing her own belief and unbelief here, as well as the fact that she now clearly stands in her husband's shadow and was often reduced to a mere "with wife."

During 1922, Gunnar was in full activity in Sweden. He was advertised about ten times, but it was quieter about Frida. One of the reasons may be that she was heavily pregnant and on May 24 gave birth to her third child, a girl who was named Margit.[47] They then lived in Rönninge where Frida stayed most of the time while Gunnar was out on trips to different places. In June, however, the silence was broken when Frida published yet another article in *EH*.

The title is "Sowing and Reaping" and is unusually personal. A bit into the article, she says, "I sat on the forest hill and listened to the song of spring in nature, and my whole soul agreed with this wonderful song. But there is a note in this song that is so poignant. It is a note of sadness.

44. *EH* (September 1, 1921) 160.
45. *EH* (September 8, 1921) 165.
46. *EH* (December 22, 1921) 235.
47. *EH* (June 1, 1922) 88.

Why?" We get the explanation when she talks about her sister's untimely death. The sister had grown up in a pious home but was attracted by "the world." Out in this worldly environment, she had been broken down by her "chasing for wind." She managed to be "saved" before she died, but then regretted that she had "done nothing for Jesus." Frida balances out the melancholy tone by showing another side: "But there is also a joyful tone of hope in the song of spring. Have you heard it?" This jubilant tone is based on the conviction that "everything that is done through the Holy Spirit in love for Jesus, will receive its reward, even if in our eyes it is so small and insignificant that we do not even give a fleeting thought to it."[48]

During 1922 something also happened in the relationship between Frida and Gunnar. In the past, they had usually published their articles under their own names. Gunnar had written reports and a great deal about the financial support of the mission. Frida had written reports and theological expositions. From the middle of that year, they changed that. Now they published the articles in *both* names. An educated guess is that it is the last-mentioned person who wrote the article. If it says, "Gunnar and Frida Vingren," Frida probably wrote it.

In the same year, Frida, as the first woman ever, got to write in *Evangelii Härolds Månadshäfte* (a monthly, mostly theological appendix to *EH*). It was a periodical publication with articles on doctrinal matters only, usually reserved for male preachers and Bible teachers.[49] This shows the status that Frida Vingren had already achieved in the young Pentecostal movement. Perhaps it was also at this time that Frida achieved her greatest success in Sweden. Ten years later, the attitude was completely different.

BACK IN BRAZIL

In August 1922, it was time for the Vingren family to return to Brazil. They had recovered and were now in "full health." They traveled as before via the United States and indicated a temporary address in New York where letters could be sent, as well as a permanent address: "Caixa 672, Pará, Brazil." The greeting was signed "Frida and Gunnar Vingren."[50]

---

48. *EH* (June 22, 1922) 98.
49. Gunilla Nyberg-Oskarsson p.c. 2020.
50. *EH* (August 31, 1922) 138.

In Brazil, the Vingrens resumed the duties they left a year earlier. Gunnar reported home about heat, febrile illnesses, home visits with prayers for the sick, but also about meetings and successes around the country—also in the south. He also sent grateful greetings to the friends in Sweden who invested funds for needy Brazilian evangelists and asked them to continue to pray for the missionaries in "the fierce battle."[51]

In December 1923, another report by Frida Vingren was published in Sweden. As an exception, she signed the article with only her own name. The report was entitled "Golden wooden figures" and was illustrated with *two* large photographs—something very unusual at the time— apparently taken by herself. Based on Isaiah 46, which depicts idolatry, Frida talked about the *Nazaré* feast, perhaps the biggest Catholic event in the state of Pará and compared the two. One of the pictures showed the procession in which a bull pulls the chariot with the saint's image, while the other depicted the huge crowd, mainly dressed in white. Frida wrote that this reminded her of her childhood painting "The Great Wide Flock" (with motifs from the Book of Revelation). But here it was a question of "thousands and thousands, blinded, bound in darkness and sin, going to eternal destruction." The article gracefully ended with a call to think of "Brazil's 25 million people"[52] and implicitly to contribute economically to the mission's work there.

TOWARDS THE CAPITAL

In January 1924, we find out for the first time that "Vingren is in Rio de Janeiro."[53] The address is still Pará, but the eyes are increasingly directed towards the capital. In Pará, Frida received yet another supernatural greeting. In a later letter we learn that: "When we were going to travel here to Rio de Janeiro, there was a sister in Pará who had a vision one day. She saw Gunnar picking down ripe fruit in a very large garden, she saw me in a corner of the garden. There I operated a large water sprayer, which irrigated the entire garden."[54] Does the prophecy apply to Frida's important work with the magazines—that she was going to "sprinkle"

---

51. *EH* (August 23, 1923) 285.
52. *EH* (December 27, 1923) 618–19.
53. *EH* (January 17, 1924) 31.
54. Letter from Frida Vingren "to Sweden" on May 27, 1932, published in Vingren, *Pionjärens dagbok*, 218–19.

holy water over the whole Brazilian Pentecostal revival, so that it could grow?

On June 3, 1924, Frida and the rest of the family arrived in Rio. Now the venture was to evangelize Brazil's capital at the time, Rio de Janeiro. Simultaneously, in Pará, Samuel Nyström took over the work from Gunnar and Frida.[55]

In a private letter to the first pastor in Filadelfia Stockholm, Lewi Pethrus, Gunnar requested funds for "a bigger hall" for the spiritual activity. In this letter we also get a brief insight into the family's situation:

> When I went to Brazil 14 years ago, I had faith only for myself, now the Lord provides for me, my wife and four small children. Of course it is a little cramped and awkward when it comes to housing. We have expensive rent to pay here, which we didn't have in Para, because we lived in the mission home. Here we live so cramped, that we have to pack the children together just in any way, because we don't even have room to put up the beds we need; but everything works, glory be to Jesus![56]

Indirectly, we now see that the fourth child, a girl named Astrid, has now been born and that the family has become very cramped for space due to the move to Rio.

During the year 1925, several reports came from the Vingren couple, several signed with both names. It seems that Gunnar's letters were more factual and descriptive, while Frida's were, as before, more literary, filled with similes and Bible references. Therefore, it is relatively easy to guess which articles were written by Frida.

Frida's husband, Gunnar, was often out on trips and his almost repetitive accounts were almost always about how many people have "been saved" or "baptized in the Spirit" at a certain location. However, there were some exceptions. In the report published in August 1925, we get a small glimpse of the hardships that characterized many of the journeys:

> During this journey we had to live in small huts with mud walls and endure the bites of the many kinds of insects, which troubled us night and day both outside and inside, so that one of my legs swelled, also one of my hands, so that I had to return

---

55. Vingren, *Pionjärens dagbok*, 130; cf. Söderholm, *Den svenska pingstväckelsens historia 1907–1933, Del II*, 228.

56. The letter was published by A. P. Franklin in "Rop från missionsfälten," *EH* (December 4, 1924) 583.

home yesterday. My bed during this trip was usually a few hard boards.[57]

While her husband was away, Frida mostly remained in Rio de Janeiro with responsibility for the four children—but also for the activities of the growing congregation. She also continued to write Bible expositions for *EH* which were well received.[58] In a couple of cases, she even got positive reader reactions published in the same magazine,[59] something very unusual at this time.

In November 1927, she got an article published with the title "A Vision."[60] Considering what later happened to her in life, this description feels almost prophetic. It depicted a battle between "the heavenly" and "the forces of darkness." The heavenly, the eagerly struggling reapers with "short sharp scythes," belonged to the former category. They were "extremely few, small, and inconspicuous," and "simple, grave, and silent, with countenances marked with heavenly peace, holy courage, and resolution"—presumably the missionaries in the field. But who were the "well-dressed, magnificent men with large, fine scythes in their hands," that she also describes, Is it possibly they were the ones in power in the missionary organization? Anyway, they were described as very powerful.

Frida's description comes close to satire when she describes the powerful men in more detail: "They looked very contented, where they stood and looked at the beautiful scythes, which flashed in the sun's light, all the while they spoke animatedly to each other. But—they only cut into the air, not a single ear fell." When the "black cloud" approached and a storm "broke loose" they "looked at each other in horror, while the scythes fell from their hands."[61] In retrospect, it is surprising that this

---

57. *EH* (August 6, 1925) 398.

58. One example is Frida's Bible exposition "Färjställena i öknen" (The Ferry Berths in the Desert), based on 2 Sam 15:28, published on the second page of *EH* (March 18, 1926) 130–31. Another example is an exposition, based on an unknown English original, entitled "Underkastelse" (Submission). *EH* (September 15, 1927) 467.

59. In *EH* (June 3, 1926) 278, Frida is thanked cordially for her exposition by a person who so far "never had understood or been able to live a life under the guidance of the Spirit" [. . .] "your testimony has strengthened my mind to be steadfast to the Lord's word." In *EH* (October 13, 1927) 526, there is another recognition: "I recently read sister Frida Vingren's translation from English in our dear journal E. H. And I was deeply affected anew by the truth that we constantly need to remain broken down, not only in our and other's eyes but in God's eyes [. . .] Sara Eklund."

60. *EH* (November 10, 1927) 570–71.

61. *EH* (November 10, 1927) 570–71.

depiction was published, but here Frida was able to use Pentecostalism's "freedom in the Spirit" to describe in spiritual terms something as an address directly from the divine, which meant that it could hardly be questioned if one shared the same respect for the sacred.

Another spiritual reading could, in retrospect, indicate the crisis that would erupt in Frida's own life just a few years later. In that case, the "black cloud" would be her own personal concern. But that interpretation can hardly have been Frida's when she wrote it down.

Frida continued with her articles in Swedish during these years.[62] Among other things, she got to write an essay about "The Lord's wonderful deeds in the capital of Brazil" in the Christmas newspaper *Morgonstjärnan* (The Morning Star) in 1928,[63] an assignment that was given to more prominent missionaries. Around the same time as that article was published, a greeting from Frida was also printed in *EH*, which is unusually personal:

> As for ourselves, we are fine. The children are healthy. Three go to school. The little crowd has been extended by another little girl, called Gunvor. A new proof of the Lord's goodness. We ask for the intercession of friends. The work is large and demanding, the tasks are many, and you feel it as a heavy burden at times. But Jesus can! He knows that we are weak and small. We hope, by God's grace, if Jesus lingers, to stay here for a few more years, or maybe even until Jesus comes.[64]

In retrospect, we get the children's experiences of Frida and Gunnar as parents. Ivar writes, e.g., about her mother Frida that she was "a passionate, faithful, and persistent missionary, who understood that in addition to caring for the children and the family, she also participated in and supported her husband's work. Countless are the souls she won for God during all the years she fought by her husband's side, first up in Pará during the difficult and struggling pioneer years in the oppressive climate there and then in Rio de Janeiro during the pioneer years there."

Earlier the same year, Otto Nelson wrote an overview article about the work in Brazil and mentioned, among other things, Vingren's work in Rio de Janeiro and the surrounding area:

---

62. See, e.g., *EH* (November 10, 1927) 577; *EH* (March 15, 1928) 166; *EH* (December 6, 1928) 775–76.

63. Advertisement in *EH* (November 8, 1928) 717.

64. *EH* (December 6, 1928) 775–76.

> In the state of Rio we now have thirteen larger and smaller congregations with a membership of around 600. Four evangelists work with these congregations. The Lord has performed true miracles among these believers. Those who have been bitten by deadly snakes, the Lord has healed through the prayer of faith. Even those who were dying, the Lord has healed and revealed his power on, so that real enemies have fallen at the feet of Jesus and confessed that God is among his people.[65]

In January 1929, Gunnar wrote a letter home to Stockholm where he, as so often, thanks for the quarterly maintenance and talked about how "God's work is progressing wonderfully in all places." But he also had a more serious message: "My wife especially asks for intercession. Her heart and nerves are overworked by much prayer struggle and work."[66] This is the first sign that Frida is not feeling well. Journalist Kajsa Norell, who did extensive research on Frida Vingren for her book *Halleluja Brasilien!* (2011), believes that she finds evidence in later medical journals for the fact that Frida suffered from hyperthyroidism or goiter for many years,[67] which would explain a great deal of what later happens in Frida's life.

In a letter, written on April 12 of the same year, 1929, Frida lays bare one of the reasons for the stress: the family's finances were so bad that they had had to go into debt to survive. When she goes on to tell us about the constant successes in the spiritual work and how many have been baptized recently, we also get a small personal glimpse: "One of these was our own son Ruben. Even our oldest boy, Ivar, is baptized in water and knows the power of God but has not come through to the baptism of the Spirit yet."[68]

In a rather sharp theological essay, entitled "Lost occasions—lost values," published in August 1929, Frida once again becomes very personal. After an exposition based on John 4:35 she lays bare her own despair over "lost opportunities":

> Well, what more can I say—a humble servant of the Lord? Still, I've cried and battled until I have become dead tired many

---

65. The article is based on a letter from Gunnar Vingren, *EH* (May 24, 1928) 328.
66. The letter was published in *EH* (March 14, 1929) 165–66.
67. Norell, *Halleluja, Brasilien!*, 159. An internet source states, among other things, the following possible side effects: "Nervousness, anxiety, depression and easy to cry" (www.skoldkortelforbundet.se). Another source states "miscarriage, irritability, anxiety, and anemia"—unfortunately all of these fit Frida's problems.
68. The letter was published in *EH* (May 16, 1929) 310.

times out here. Why? The Lord knows. A fire burns in my soul. Don't say I am overstrung. Do we understand what was in Jesus' words: "I thirst"? It was probably more than a natural thirst.[69]

ON THE BATTLEFIELD IN RIO

On August 5–11, 1929, the first Bible study week was held in Rio de Janeiro with about twenty-five participants. The teachers were Gunnar and Frida Vingren. In the "official" photograph from the week, Frida and Gunnar were the only foreign adults—the Brazilian-born sons Ivar and Ruben are, however, also in the picture.[70]

At the end of 1929, the Vingren family was joined by Helge Fällström, who later conveyed his impressions of Frida and Gunnar Vingren's extensive work in Rio de Janeiro. His report provides us with a snapshot of the activities going on:

> I arrived here on 21 Dec. 1929 and took in with brother Vingren, who is witnessing to Jesus in this big city—it has about 1 1/2–2 million inhabitants. Brother Vingren lives in a workers' quarter, where the main [missionary] work is also located. The congregation rents a hall here, accommodating around 350 people, for which they pay approximately SEK 5,000 in rent per year. There are meetings every day, public and prayer meetings. The friends have a prayer night once a week. Street meetings are held three times each week. Work is also carried out in the suburbs. Besides brother Vingren and his wife, there are 7 native evangelists who work wholly or partly for Jesus, more or less supported by the congregation.
>
> Considering the short time that the work has been conducted here, about 5 1/2 years, one must say to the glory of Jesus, that the result is brilliant. The congregation consists of around 400 members. One is surprised at the multitude of young men who have trodden the narrow road.[71]

In the spring of 1930, Gunnar traveled alone to Sweden, probably to sort out the consequences of the so-called "Franklin Battle" (see below) and asked the leaders of the Pentecostal movement to come to Brazil to mediate between the missionaries and the national pastors, but also between

69. *EH* (August 8, 1929) 505–6.
70. Sundstedt, *Pingstväckelsen och dess genombrott*, 94–95.
71. *EH* (March 13, 1930) 188.

the missionaries themselves. It was a short visit, and already in July he was on his way back, now together with Lewi Pethrus. Meanwhile, Frida was more or less solely responsible for the missionary work in Rio. During this period, she was visited by Signora Dragland, who was on her way to Argentina but stopped for a few days with Frida in Rio. In an excerpt from her travelogue, we sense Frida's importance:

> It was a great joy for me to see sister Vingren and her six children. Brother Vingren himself was on a trip to Sweden, but the work did not stand still because of that, but advanced, and souls were saved at the meetings. Mrs Vingren was in charge of the work. I must thank God in my heart for all the faithful brothers and sisters, whom God has placed as beacons to shine among the people of other nations.
>
> The boat was there for several days, so I had the opportunity to be part of several glorious meetings, and I got to see souls come and surrender themselves to God. During a Sunday evening meeting the room was full, and people stood far out into the street listening attentively to the word of God, and the result was not lacking. Glory be to Jesus! We could see sinners kneeling at the cross. I got to give my testimony, and Sister Vingren interpreted for me, and we were both blessed. It was truly a wonderful meeting. God has done great things in Rio de Janeiro, and it is a glorious work that is being done there.[72]

Through the work of the Berg and Vingren families in Pará and in many other places, Brazil had become the Swedish Pentecostal movement's most successful mission work. The movement, with the help of several missionaries and a large number of national evangelists and pastors, had grown and spread from Pará out across northern Brazil. In 1930, it included several tens of thousands of members. Now, in addition, evangelists, missionaries and "ordinary" members had begun to work in the southern part of Brazil, in the capital Rio and the largest industrial cities.

THE CONFERENCE IN NATAL 1930

In Sweden, the "Franklin battle" raged, where Anders Petter Franklin, the leader of the Swedish Free Mission, and Lewi Pethrus, first pastor of the increasingly powerful Filadelfia congregation in Stockholm, and unofficial leader of the Pentecostal movement, measured their strengths.

72. *EH* (August 28, 1930) 596–97.

Pethrus won the battle and Franklin was excluded from the Pentecostal movement and the Swedish Free Mission was officially disbanded. For the Brazilian missionaries this was a shock. No one had cared as much about the mission in Brazil as Franklin—even if the relationship with the Vingrens had not always been without problems.

Pethrus was therefore concerned about his relationship with the Swedish missionaries in Brazil. Now he needed to consolidate his regained central role in the missionary work. That's why he accepted, when he was invited to a conference between missionaries and national pastors on September 5–10, 1930, in Natal—even though he was right in the middle of a huge church construction in Stockholm.[73] The main issue was officially a discussion about handing over the work to the national pastors.

Pethrus was obviously also aware that the view of women preaching was loaded in Brazil, but it was still surprising once he was there that the question of women's participation and positions in the spiritual work was given such a large role. In Sweden, after all, this was in practice a "minor issue." The Baptist community, from which many of the Pentecostal leaders came, was divided on the issue. The "Örebro Baptists," with their leader John Ongman, were open to women as preachers and from 1908 let them attend the three-year theological training in Örebro, Örebro Missionsskola. The "Stockholm Baptists," on the other hand, were fierce opponents of women as church leaders. Only men were allowed to attend their theological education at *Betelseminariet* (Bethel Seminary) in Stockholm.

Lewi Pethrus had attended Bethel Seminary and acquired a rather large skepticism towards women as preachers and church leaders. When he was called to the small Filadelfia congregation in Stockholm in 1910, two of the board members were women. When he had been in the congregation for a few months, none of them were left. Gunnar Vingren had instead attended Götabro Bible School, where prominent female preachers, such as Nelly Hall, oversaw the community. Samuel Nyström had attended Örebro Mission School. They both therefore had a completely different basic view of the issue than Pethrus.

In the heat of the battle that ensued (where Frida's work was at the center), however, the basic view did not always apply. Gunnar Vingren held his line fully, but Samuel Nyström swerved, somewhat inexplicably,

---

73. Lundgren, *Lewi Pethrus i närbild*, 136.

completely. Possibly under the strong influence of his Brazilian colleagues, he briefly became an "anti-women preachers," and in particular "anti-Frida."

Lewi Pethrus was clearly more of a pragmatist than an ideologue, which became evident in many other phases of his life. Despite his skeptical attitude towards women as church leaders, it still seems that he had a special heart for Gunnar and Frida for a long time. Partly he had "recruited" Frida from EFS, and partly he realized early on that she had a talent for speaking and writing. She was therefore given the opportunity to both preach at outposts to Filadelfia and write in *EH*, although she was at the time completely unknown in the rest of the movement.

Adina Nelson, wife of Otto Nelson was the other woman who received criticism. Both she and Frida were good preachers. They taught in their respective congregations, but they were also out on mission trips around the district. When their respective husbands were first pastors, it also happened that they took over the leadership of the congregation during their absence. Interestingly, the battle hardly touched Ester Andersson and Beda Palm. They engaged in pioneering work and founded congregations. Other women also contributed to the spiritual work alongside social activities such as orphanage work.[74] But it was Adina and Frida who ended up in the porthole.

Women standing in the pulpit teaching men was very controversial at the time. Here, Gunnar and Frida Vingren's view of the role of women, characterized by Fredrik Franson's and John Ongman's teachings, collided with a Latin American, patriarchal view of women in official contexts. Gunnar wrote in a letter to colleague Samuel Nyström on April 1, 1930:

> God is my witness, that the Holy Spirit should have his way—his own way—in this land, and may God's glorious work continue as it has begun. I cannot deny my conviction that God *has called and still calls both men and women* to devote themselves entirely to the service of the gospel, to win souls for Jesus and testify to his love and wonderful salvation, and that together in heaven we shall one day rejoice over the sheaves we won for Jesus and during our stay on earth. I myself was saved through an evangelist sister, who came to Björka, Småland over thirty years ago and had meetings. Later, a sister came from the United States and taught about the Holy Spirit. Even those who prayed me through to the baptism of the Spirit were sisters. I believe that

---

74. Alvarsson, *Om Pingströrelsen*, 341.

God wants to do a wonderful work in this country. Shall we then hinder God? Or should we give full freedom to the Holy Spirit to work as he wants?

But Samuel Nyström and some of the other male missionaries drifted to the opposite opinion. Missionary Ingrid Andersson wrote home to the new mission secretary in Filadelfia Stockholm, Paul Ongman, that:

> We sisters have found ourselves forced to withdraw from almost all activities outside the home. It has been difficult, but the Lord has sustained us and in the meantime let us go about His work in many ways.[75]

The matter was first discussed informally at the missionaries' pre-conference and opinions were probably divided. In the "official" picture from the pre-conference, nine male missionaries and one female—Frida Vingren—were depicted. She also sat next to her husband Gunnar in the middle, in a place of honor. Lewi Pethrus, who was the only non-missionary, stood in the middle of the back row![76]

The discussion then continued formally at the big conference where opinions were divided. One of the concrete results was a statement, formulated by the Brazilian secretary in the following, typically "Pentecostal" way:

> Proposals were launched that a statement should be made regarding the work that women are permitted to do in the church of God. The participants believed that the sisters should be given the right to participate in evangelical work by bearing witness to Jesus and His salvation and also to bear witness, which includes teaching, and to lead meetings, where needed. On the other hand, it was considered that the woman's task is not to hold the office of teacher in the congregation, or pastor, however, it was emphasized that exceptions can be made quite naturally as other rules in the Bible show examples of (Matthew 12:3–8). This is

---

75. Letter from Ingrid Andersson to Paul Ongman in Filadelfia Stockholm, July 29, 1930, quoted in Vingren, *Det började i Pará*, 79. This section of Vingren's work is largely the merit of Gunilla Nyberg-Oskarsson's editing.

76. Sundstedt, *Pingstväckelsen och dess utbredning*, 289. The caption says: "In September 1930 there was a big conference in Natal, Brazil. In the front row, from the left: Daniel Berg, Otto Nelson, Gunnar and Frida Vingren, and Samuel Nyström. In the back row from the left: Algot Svensson, Nils Kastberg, Lewi Pethrus, Joel Carlson, Nels J. Nelson and Anders Johansson."

especially possible when it comes to places where there is a lack of suitable brothers as leaders and teachers.[77]

The most important question at the Natal conference, however, was who would have the main responsibility for the evangelistic work. From the very beginning, a great responsibility had rested on Brazilian evangelists and workers. It was also mainly these who had contributed to the spread and growth of the movement. Nevertheless, it was ultimately the missionaries who made the decisive decisions. Wasn't it time to hand over the northern field to the nationals? Then the missionaries could "leave these areas and go south to those of the states of Brazil, where Pentecostal activities do not yet exist."[78]

The conference decided unanimously in accordance with the proposal and the work was also formally "handed over." Thereby a great threat of division was removed and the attitude towards the missionaries changed in an instant. The result was, instead of a power struggle, a desire for extended cooperation. In 1930 there were 14,000 Pentecostals in this area. Ten years later, the work had almost quintupled. In Brazil as a whole, there were already as many as 60,000 Pentecostals in 1940—only in the movement that originated from the work of Berg and Vingren—almost as many as there were altogether in Sweden at that time. However, it would not be long before the Brazilian movement overtook the Swedish one in numbers.

A side effect was that the two Pentecostal magazines *O Som Alegre* and *Boa Semente* were merged and given a new name, *Mensageiro da Paz*.[79] Beginning in 1930, it was edited and printed in Rio de Janeiro. Frida Vingren, who had been with *Boa Semente* since its inception, became a key person even during the first years with the new magazine. The men Gunnar Vingren and Samuel Nyström stood as official editors while the woman Frida Vingren did the work.

Lewi Pethrus reports extensively, and on several occasions, back home to Sweden from his trip to Brazil and the conference in Natal. Of course, his reports were published in a prominent place in *EH*. But even though Frida Vingren, and several of the other female missionaries, played an important role during the conference and the pre-conference,

---

77. *EH* (October 23, 1930) 722–23. The "Pentecostal" in this statement is a sensitivity for "the guidance of the Holy Spirit," which means that an address from the Holy Spirit can change an established interpretation of a passage in the Bible!

78. Lewi Pethrus, reproduced in Sundstedt, *Pingstväckelsen och dess utbredning*, 287.

79. *EH* (October 23, 1930) 722.

Frida is only mentioned once, when she started a meeting before Pethrus got there.[80] Otherwise, only men are mentioned. In a private *letter* to Sweden, however, Pethrus admitted that when he needed a good interpreter of Portuguese for his Bible studies, Frida was the best. Gunnar interpreted for him in the first meeting, then it was Frida who had to take over, the rest of the time for Pethrus's visit, from August 13 to 24, 1930—and not only in Rio but also in São Paulo and Santos.

However, this disclosure of Frida's name does not seem to have affected *EH*'s readers. They followed the success in Brazil with great excitement. This is reflected, e.g., by the fact that the readers now spontaneously set up a special whip-round to collect funds "For Gunnar and Frida Vingren, Rio de Janeiro, Brazil."[81] Anyone could now deposit money into this account to support their work. A small Sunday school in Björka, e.g., sent in SEK 10. Others gave larger gifts. There was great variation between individual donors and institutions. In 1930 alone, reports about the results of this fund appeared three times in *EH*. However, when the Vingrens eventually received these gifts, they immediately distributed them to Brazilian employees who were worse off than they.

In April 1931, we get a new insight into the daily operations. Frida writes a report about an outdoor meeting at the Central Station at Plaça da República in Rio de Janeiro. A Brazilian associate, probably Sylvio Brito, and herself were proclaiming to a curious audience. At one point, she dealt with a man who tried to disrupt the gathering. Frida succeeded.

DECLINE

After that, all we meet is silence from the Vingren family in the Swedish media. Both spouses were severely burned out. Their dedicated and intensive work had taken its toll. Gunnar fell ill with something that would eventually turn out to be cancer, but which manifested itself in weakness and thus a tendency to contract diseases, e.g., pneumonia, which was close to taking his life already at that stage. Frida suffered from something completely different.

In Frida's life, transcendent experiences had been central. "God's guidance" is what had mattered. This had shaped her life direction, her choice of husband, and much else. It is therefore highly possible that she

---

80. *EH* (October 2, 1930) 675.
81. *EH* (July 17, 1930) 502.

was never affected by something as human as infatuation or falling in love. She had also worked so intensively, almost night and day, in "God's work" that she had never had the opportunity to even think about falling in love with any man other than her husband.

But then things happened that, in Frida's own imagination, could not happen to a person who was so committed to God's work. She worked closely with a young man, probably the co-editor of *Mensageiro da Paz*, Sylvio Brito. They understood each other. They worked closely together. For practical reasons, he even moved into Vingren's house. Then they could work several hours in a row on the editing of the journal. They also managed to translate hymns together. Sylvio admired Frida for her sense of language, drive, and enterprise.[82]

The missionary colleagues considered the close collaboration as most inappropriate. Presumably, Gunnar received provocations earlier, but in September 1931 the gossip reached the Swedish Pentecostal leadership. Joel Carlson wrote to Lewi Pethrus and claimed that "sister Frida is in the company of a young man."[83] After a few months, Samuel Nyström claimed to the same authority that "the young man [. . .] should not be allowed to live (at home) with the Vingrens."[84] The mere fact that a man and a woman were alone in the same room was at this time—and still is in some parts of the world—tantamount to sexual intercourse even if there was no other evidence. It was even more compromising that a man lived at a woman's house, even though there was quite a big age difference between them. Carlson and Nyström were thus concerned about the reputation of the missionaries—and thus the entire Pentecostal movement—in Brazilian society.

Frida did not care. For her, God's work was the most important. She and Silvio were an effective team. They accomplished a great deal together. During 1930 alone, Frida produced twenty-one articles and three hymns, and in 1931 she wrote twenty-three articles and wrote or translated eight poems and hymns—two of them together with Silvio. In addition, they held successful public outdoor meetings together.[85]

---

82. He is not the only one. In 1932, Samuel Nyström wrote to Lewi Pethrus that there was "a domination of young boys (in the Rio congregation) that looked up to Frida." Norell, *Halleluja, Brasilien!*, 309.

83. Norell, *Halleluja, Brasilien!*, 307.

84. Norell, *Halleluja, Brasilien!*, 307–8.

85. Araujo, *Frida Vingren*, 131. Here Silvio Brito is mentioned by name. Cf. *EH* (April 9, 1931) 270.

Thus, initially, this was not a problem for Frida, then she would probably never have agreed to the arrangement. But somewhere along the way, it happened. Frida seems to have become infatuated with the much younger Silvio. Perhaps it was the only time in her life she experienced this passion. And she could no longer control either her feelings or her actions. She became more and more intimate with Silvio and once they were found in the same room in night clothes.[86] From what follows, we can assume with reasonable probability that Frida never allowed any sexual relationship, but that she was in his bed, giving in to intimacy—something that came to torment her for the rest of her life.

In the early fall of 1932, little Gunvor, Frida's and Gunnar's youngest child, died, only four years old. This was another hard blow for the worn-out Frida. It is also far from impossible that she blamed herself for the child's death. She knew her Bible and the story of King David and the prophet Nathan. In 2 Sam 12:14–18 Nathan judged David for taking Uriah's wife. The punishment was that the son he had with Bathsheba died. Was Gunvor's death caused by the same kind of punishment? Was there a double meaning in Gunnar's claim during the journey home that "Frida cried a lot last night, when she thought of our little daughter Gunvor, who remained there, buried in the Brazilian soil."[87]

The battle for women's rights continued in the missionary corps. The eldest son, Ivar, wrote long afterwards about what happened in 1932: "At this time there were some difficulties among the missionaries and the native brothers due to the publication of the Pentecostal newspaper Mensageiro da Paz." He did not mention that his mother Frida was at the center of the accusations.

As early as November 12, 1931, a telegram arrived from Stockholm ordering Gunnar to hand over the newspaper *Mensageiro da Paz* to Samuel Nyström. Gunnar obediently replied that they would transfer it as soon as possible but that they preferred to work with it until they traveled to Sweden. However, Samuel Nyström could not hold back. On January 6, 1932, Gunnar wrote in the diary: "I received a nasty letter from brother Samuel Nyström. God have mercy on him!"

Why couldn't Samuel Nyström calm down on this issue? Kajsa Norell has examined the correspondence between Samuel and Lewi Pethrus

---

86. Norell, *Halleluja, Brasilien!*, 309. The information comes from an interrogation that Samuel Nyström had with the young man who stepped into the room, Paulo Leivas Macalão.

87. Vingren, *Pionjärens dagbok*, 223.

where the former claimed that "his honor was at stake." According to Norell, Samuel "was part of Lewi Pethrus's inner circle, the small group of men who protected the leader and were unfailingly loyal to him!" and now he demanded countermoves from Pethrus as compensation.

Theologically or ideologically, it is difficult to grasp Samuel's position. He was brought up at Örebro Missionsskola, the earliest theological education for women and where female preachers were taken very seriously. Of course, you don't have to accept all the views of a school just because you attend there, but Samuel should have had many reasons to accept that women could be teachers. The passages in the New Testament that were used as arguments can also be interpreted in several ways.

Perhaps we must therefore see Samuel's actions in this matter as a personal battle. It was Frida Vingren that mattered. Had she kept a lower profile, perhaps all this would never have happened. Perhaps, in the short time she was a member of Filadelfia in Stockholm, she had not had time to learn how to avoid conflict by following the subtle cultural rules about how to behave and express yourself? Maybe Lewi Pethrus had sent her out too soon before she learned all the codes because he was so admiring of her?

If we go even deeper, the fault may have been in Samuel's eyes. Frida was a woman, she was too strong, she was too straightforward—and far too skilled in so many areas. The son Ivar said of his mother that "she had a gift to teach and preach like no other, and for this reason she suffered much persecution." What he implies here is that others must have been jealous of Frida's gifts. As for Samuel, he had every reason to be jealous of Frida because he was neither a great preacher nor a "skilled writer" according to Norell. It thus became a question of Samuel's "honor."

Early in 1932, Gunnar wrote in his diary: "Today we have fasted and prayed and surrendered everything to the Lord." This should probably be understood as the spouses reasoned together, prayed over the issue, and then gave up in the face of massive opposition. From January 1932, Frida no longer wrote in *Mensageiro da Paz*. She probably then also made sure that her employee Silvio left the house, and they stopped hanging out.

In January, Gunnar sent out a circular letter to the movement's pastors' conference, which was held on the twentieth to the twenty-fourth of the same month, that he was handing over the newspaper and all work to Samuel Nyström. The letter was also published in *Mensageiro da Paz*. On March 5, the capitulation was a fact. A broken Gunnar Vingren agreed to "peace" with Samuel Nyström. He even offered him the most successful congregation in Brazil, Vingrens' own congregation in Rio de Janeiro.

It would take a while before Nyström could take over in Rio. In the meantime, activities in the parish continued. Both spouses were devastated, but it still seems that Frida had to take the biggest responsibility. In a letter from Frida to Sweden on May 27, 1932, she wrote that: "Gunnar has for quite a long time, due to illness and travel, not taken any further part in the work until now." She continued later in the letter to reflect on her seven years in Rio:

> During this time I have several times been broken down to the nerves and suffered from a bad heart, but have been strengthened and healed again [. . .]. Now that we have handed over the publication of the Pentecostal magazine out here, I immediately thought that now either our work in Brazil ends or does the Lord have another task for us.
>
> For a week I prayed to the Lord for a sign of this. Gunnar was then out on a trip. On the following Thursday's meeting, God's power fell wonderfully. The believers came to the platform and we laid hands on them. In ten minutes, Jesus baptized four in the Holy Spirit. This has since continued meeting after meeting . . .——[leaving Brazil:] For me, it's like tearing my heart out of my chest when I think about leaving Brazil to maybe never return. However, the will of the Lord be done!"[88]

Frida and Gunnar had sacrificed a great deal. They had invested ten years without a furlough in missionary work in Brazil. But unlike many other missionaries, they had seen obvious results. When they moved to Rio de Janeiro, they started with a small group of about ten people. As they were now forced to leave, their life's work was "one of the largest Pentecostal congregations in the world," at the time, "with over 2,000 members."[89]

In his diary for Sunday, August 14, 1932, Gunnar wrote: "Today I officially handed over the congregation to brother Samuel Nyström." [. . .] (I) "also got to lay my hands on the brothers Nyström and Sörheim." Gunnar had thus been forced to hand over the work he and Frida had built up to Frida's main opponent.

---

88 Vingren, *Pionjärens dagbok*, 219.

89. Aronson "De tog elden till Brasilien." Cf. *EH* (November 17, 1932) 774: "Over 2,000 saved in 20 congregations."

GUNNAR'S ILLNESS AND DEMISE

In August 1932, they prepared their farewell of the congregation and friends in Rio de Janeiro. A few days into September, Frida, Gunnar and the five children arrived in Stockholm. On September 10-14, Filadelfia held a "mission and edification conference," and despite his weak condition, Gunnar was persuaded to participate briefly:

> Brother Vingren and his family also came home from Brazil during the conference and participated in the last days of it. During the trip he had been seriously ill with pneumonia, but God had raised him up, and God met with him further during the conference. However, both he and his wife are still in need of the intercession of friends. Just before the journey home, they suffered the severe grief of losing one of their children.[90]

In November, Frida felt strong enough to write an overview article about the work in Rio with surroundings; a sort of financial statement and report to all the Pentecostal friends who followed their mission and contributed funds to the work. She wrote about spiritual activities, open-air meetings, and tract distribution. Then she dropped a piece of news: The Vingrens had started a mission in Rio's prisons. "Thus, every Saturday morning a group of saved and interested prisoners gathered for Bible study. Those were wonderful moments. Several of them bore glorious testimonies of salvation. One of these prisoners was freed and now belongs to the congregation in Rio. Yes, we believe in a glorious harvest for this work."[91]

At the same time as Frida wrote this overview, she and Gunnar were struck by yet another grief. Helge Fällström, who was their coworker in Rio de Janeiro, hastily passed away. Frida wrote a beautiful eulogy. She began it without the bloated glory words that were common in *EH* at the time. Instead, she noted, very unconventionally in the Pentecostal movement, that: "again a young life has been harvested by the layman." Then she reproduced some memories of Helge. The strongest was: "I especially remember Helge in a big 'campaign' among the soldiers in Rio. In a few days, we distributed 1,000 New Testaments among the soldiers and had open-air meetings at the barracks." In the end, she stated that

---

90. *EH* (September 22, 1932) 644.

91. *EH* (November 17, 1932) 774. The article is called "A Greeting to the Friends of the Mission." In connection with the article, there is a large photograph of Frida, surrounded by male prisoners.

"His working day was short."[92] Did she even then sense that this would also apply to her own life?

The Vingren family now lived in one of the two "missionary homes" in Stockholm that Filadelfia had prepared for missionaries who were on furlough in Sweden.[93] Through meeting ads, we can see that they made occasional appearances at meetings, but probably they were both too weak to do much more. The sons, Ivar and Ruben, were admitted to schools in Stockholm while the other children were allowed to stay at home.

At the beginning of 1933, Gunnar got worse and worse and the family was offered to move to Sjöarp, a retirement home that Filadelfia had bought, located in the beautiful areas outside Vetlanda in Småland. There, Gunnar could receive more care as the intercessions had not produced any lasting results. "Ever since he came home from Brazil last September, he has been very feeble, and though much intercession has been offered for his recovery, time after time only temporary improvement has occurred."[94]

It was now established by the doctors that Gunnar suffered from an "internal cancer," i.e., a cancer that had spread in his body and that nothing could be done. He died on June 29. Frida, who had been his life partner for sixteen years, who bore him six children and who had now been his personal health care provider for a long time, was suddenly all alone with her five children. In the funeral announcement, Frida wrote: "We hereby have the extremely painful duty to announce that my beloved husband and our dear father, the missionary Gunnar Adolf Vingren, went home to Jesus on Thursday, June 29, blessed and happy, at the age of 54 years. Sjöarp on July 1, 1933. Frida Vingren. Ivar, Ruben, Margit, Astrid, Bertil." In conclusion, 2 Tim 4:7 was quoted.

Gunnar received a full biography from the then-mission secretary in Filadelfia Stockholm, Paul Ongman.[95] His last days were furthermore described by one of the employees at Sjöarp in a form reminiscent of saint legends.[96] A few days later, an appreciative obituary by Lewi Pethrus was published. He ended it with an exhortation: "May we remember his loved ones, who remain at the opened grave, sister Frida Vingren and their five children. God does not forget them! He is the father of the fatherless and

92. *EH* (November 17, 1932) 776.
93. *EH* (January 19, 1933) 38.
94. *EH* (July 6, 1933) 483.
95. *EH* (July 6, 1933) 483.
96. *EH* (July 13, 1933) 498.

the defender of widows. But may we, Gunnar Vingren's friends, not forget these tested siblings of ours either."⁹⁷

HEADING FOR DISASTER

Ironically, that is exactly what happened. At least in public, Frida Vingren's name was now taboo. Apart from a change of address, from Sjöarp back to Stockholm, which was published in October, Frida was never mentioned again in *EH*. She was not welcome at any meetings. She did not get the opportunity to publish any more articles. She was officially no more.

When Frida had reasonably recovered from Gunnar's death, she wanted to travel back to Brazil. But she soon realized that this was not possible. The gossip and her fight with Samuel made it impossible. Perhaps she also realized that the relationship she had with Silvio would turn into a disaster if she returned. She gave up on the plan.

But missionary zeal burned in her heart. Now she wanted to go to another Portuguese-speaking country, Portugal. She talked to Lewi Pethrus who surely brought up Filadelfia's strained finances and her situation: single with five children. But she managed to persuade Dagen's financial savior K. G. Ottosson to guarantee her maintenance. And this time she was close to succeeding. Filadelfia's board gave a cautiously affirmative message.

But then something happened that we do not know. Perhaps it was Samuel who was on the move again. He had felt a calling to go to Portugal. Thus, when Frida and the children were going to get on the train in Stockholm, Lewi Pethrus himself came and prevented them from getting on. And now all roads seemed closed for good.

Frida did not want to give up. She pressed the mission secretary Paul Ongman to let her go, but he then only got irritated and now he also turned on Frida. In an undated letter to Lewi Pethrus (!), Frida rightly complained that Paul "told me that I was haughty and proud, wanted to be big and remarkable and rejected all my work in Brazil [. . .]. Have suffered tremendously from this!"⁹⁸ That she turned to Lewi Pethrus was not so strange because he sat on the real power—and he was also the one who knew Frida's strengths—and weaknesses best! Somewhere around

---

97. *EH* (July 20, 1933) 506.
98. Quoted in Norell, *Halleluja, Brasilien!*, 305.

here, however, he also got tired of Frida and, as so many times with other people who no longer helped the business forward, and he closed the door. Kajsa Norell concludes that it was "precisely her personality that was the real problem."[99]

In September 1934, Frida's trip to Portugal was brought up as a matter in a parish meeting. For many of her supporters, not least among the women majority in Filadelfia, this must have come as a shock. But the case was well prepared in the male board and the arguments for denying her to go to Portugal were irrefutable—because no one outside the board was told what it was based on. In the minutes from the "ordinary parish meeting in Filadelfia" on September 10, 1934, it only says: "Sister Vingren's work in Brazil had been of such a nature that it was detrimental to the work there, nor had her conduct there been blameless." Therefore, there was a danger "that the work begun in Portugal would be destroyed."[100]

That Frida got irritated by such a statement—and Lewi Pethrus's sudden rejection—is not particularly surprising. With the aptitude for "irritability" and "fierceness" that her supposed goiter brought, the reaction was fierce. Somewhere she went too far in her criticism of Pastor Pethrus and his board. Only three weeks later, she received the sentence. She was, shockingly, expelled from the congregation she had belonged to for seventeen years.

In the minutes of November 5, it only says: "Missionary Frida Vingren—had, especially in recent times, gone about with slander and shown in every way that she did not want to bow to the ideas or decisions of neither the brethren nor the congregation. The congregation unanimously decided to immediately exclude her from the congregational community."

The decision was of course a disaster for Frida. Her entire identity was associated with the congregation and its activities. It was within the congregation and the Pentecostal movement that she lived and worked throughout her adult life. Now she was excluded, outside and devastated. The children later talked about when she came home after the news: "she was crying and completely beside herself."

Now her life elixir ran out in the sand—to be allowed to "go out on the mission field again." Now the shame, the guilt, the sadness returned after what happened to Gunvor, Gunnar, Helge—and the repressed, lost

---

99. Norell, *Halleluja, Brasilien!*, 304.
100. Norell, *Halleluja, Brasilien!*, 280.

passion. The zest for life was waning and not even the children could lift her out of the ever-deepening well of despondency she sank into.

She stayed in a nursing home, but nothing helped. One day, Ivar, who was now sixteen years old, came home and found his mother "tottering back and forth in the stocking outside the gate, despairing and worried. She screamed straight out." What did he do? He went to the "brethren in the church" to get them to do something. In retrospect, he has told his children that "the brothers then forced him and Ruben to take the mother to the Psychiatric Hospital."[101]

Even though close friends, such as Sara Berg, claimed that "Frida was not mentally ill," she was admitted to a psychiatric clinic. She did not like it, did not want to be there, and asked to get out of there. She was excommunicated from the Filadelfia congregation in November 1934 and yet, a couple of months later, the first pastor of the congregation personally came to the hospital, visited the chief physician, and announced that "the leadership of the Filadelfia congregation fully believes that the patient is mentally ill and in need of care."[102]

While Frida struggled to first return to Brazil, and later to go to Portugal, with the leading brethren—without any success whatsoever—some missionary friends did not give up. They collected money for her, and sometimes for "Frida and Ruben Vingren." But nevertheless, it took seven long years before the readers finally got to see her name again—and then in a moving short announcement. Frida passed away, only forty-nine years old:

> Our dear little mother, Frida Maria Vingren, born on 9/6 1891, has today, after much suffering, gone to be with the Lord forever. Deeply mourned and missed by us, father, siblings, other relatives, and brothers and sisters in the faith. Stockholm, 30 Sept 1940. IVAR. RUBEN. MARGIT. ASTRID. BERTIL. "For those who sow with tears shall reap with joy. They go forth weeping and bearing their seed, they return with rejoicing and bearing their sheaves." (Ps 126:5, 6.)[103]

But even after her death, she did not receive any official recognition. She did not even get an obituary in *EH*. Her entire important contribution to Brazil was passed over in silence. Officially, she never existed in the

---

101. Norell, *Halleluja, Brasilien!*, 324.
102. Norell, *Halleluja, Brasilien!*, 327.
103. *EH* (October 17, 1940) 791.

Pentecostal movement. But her loyal supporters knew nothing of the power game behind the silence. They remembered a strong and inspiring woman and writer. They cherished her memory.

In Brazil, she was not forgotten either. In 2016, the Assambleia de Deus publishing house published a biography of Frida's life, written by Isael de Araujo: "Frida Vingren—a Biography of a Woman of God."[104] The fascination with Frida's short but intense life's work is not, however, limited to the Pentecostal movement she co-founded. In one of the universities in Sao Paulo, an essay on "Frida Strandberg" was written by a women's researcher who elevates her to one of the important fighters for women's causes in Brazil!

In Sweden, she gained new attention in 2011 when journalist Kajsa Norell "discovered" Frida and her fate and wrote about her in her book *Hallelujah Brazil!* Kajsa was not satisfied with the seven-year silence at the end of her life but did everything to talk about these painful years as well. Today, even in Sweden, Frida stands out as one of the women who, despite time and time again hitting her head against the "glass ceiling," managed to come back in her fight for her own and other women's rights.[105] Perhaps it was her seemingly unwavering faith that carried her through the unimaginable hardships?

BIBLIOGRAPHY

Alvarsson Jan-Åke. *Om Pingströrelsen: Essäer, översikter och analyser*. Skellefteå: Artos, 2014.
Alvarsson, Jan-Åke, ed. *Svenskt Frikyrkolexikon*. Stockholm: Atlantis, 2014.
Araujo, Isael de. *Frida Vingren: Uma biografia da mulher de Deus, esposa de Gunnar Vingren, pioneiro das Assambleias de Deus no Brasil*. Rio de Janeiro: CPAD, 2016.
Aronson, Torbjörn. "De tog elden till Brasilien." *Arvet glöder—Vinterbilagan* n.d. (2015) n.d. https://www.academia.edu/12859932/De_tog_elden_till_Brasilien._I_Brasilien_finns_världens_största_pentekostala_rörelser_och_svenska_missionärer_lade_grunden.
Bundy, David D. *Visions of Apostolic Mission: Scandinavian Pentecostal Mission to 1935*. Studia Historico-Ecclesiastica Upsaliensia 45. Uppsala: Uppsala University Library, 2009.
Lundgren, Ivar. *Lewi Pethrus i närbild*. Stockholm: Den kristna bokringen, 1973.
Norell, Kajsa. *Halleluja, Brasilien!* Stockholm: Bladh by Bladh, 2011.
Söderholm, Gustaf Emil. *Den svenska pingstväckelsens historia 1907–1933, Del II*. Andra omarbetade upplagan. Stockholm: Filadelfia, 1933.

104. Araujo, *Frida Vingren*.
105. In 2020, Frida was awarded an entry in *Svenskt Kvinnobiografiskt Lexikon* (Biographical Dictionary of Swedish Women).

Sundstedt, Arthur. *Pingstväckelsen och dess vidare utveckling, Band 2.* Stockholm: Normans, 1971.

———. *Pingstväckelsen och dess genombrott, Band 3.* Stockholm: Normans, 1971.

———. *Pingstväckelsen och dess utbredning, Band 4.* Stockholm: Normans, 1972.

Vingren, Ivar. *Det började i Pará: Svensk Pingstmission i Brasilien.* Ekerö: MissionsInstitutet PMU, 1994.

———. *O diario do pioneiro Gunnar Vingren.* 4th ed. Rio de Janeiro: CPAD, 1991.

———. *Pionjärens dagbok. Brasilienmissionären Gunnar Vingrens dagboksanteckningar.* Stockholm: Lewi Pethrus, 1969.

Image #9. Hilda Backlund.

8

Hilda Backlund and Linnea Halldorf
Early Pentecostal Missionaries to Congo and Burundi[1]

GUNILLA NYBERG OSKARSSON

INTRODUCTION

Early in 1921, the young Swedish Pentecostal Movement began to send missionaries to what was then Belgian Congo, to the Kivu province, in the eastern part of the country. They were also to found Pentecostal churches in the neighboring Ruanda-Urundi [Rwanda and Burundi]. To the Swedish Pentecostal missionaries, these three countries were considered as one mission field. Most of the time, two-thirds of the missionary corps were women. In this chapter, I will follow two of these women, Hilda Backlund (1895-1983) and Linnea Halldorf (1896-1996), who both arrived in eastern Congo in 1925. After a short introduction, I will describe their youth, their ministry in Sweden, and their ministries as Pentecostal missionaries. I will analyze their priorities in ministry and in what areas they had a significant and lasting influence on the Pentecostal churches mentioned above. I have primarily used sources such as Swedish Pentecostal periodicals and interviews. It has been easier to find materials about Hilda Backlund than about Linnea Halldorf, as the latter

---

1. All translations in this chapter are the author's own.

did not like to be interviewed and did not write as much in the periodical *Evangelii Härold* as the former did.

In 1921, the Swedish Pentecostal missionary, Axel B. Lindgren, came to the Kivu province together with three Norwegian Pentecostal missionaries, Gunnerius and Oddbjørg Tollefsen, and Hanna Veum. The three of them first went to the English Pentecostal center Kalembe-Lembe, where among others, Arthur and Mary Richardson were working.[2] The Swedes and the Norwegians explored different parts of Kivu province and realized that many different groups of people were living there, each one with their own language. They found it more practical to split up and divide the areas between them instead of continuing a common work.[3] The following year more missionaries were to come. They founded a missionary station in Uvira, near Lake Tanganyika.

The application to get permission for mission work was sent in by *Mission Libre Suèdoise* (Swedish Free Mission, SFM), an association created by local Pentecostal congregations to be able to address the Belgian government. The latter was skeptical towards the Pentecostal mission and its teaching about healing and speaking in tongues. The authorities feared that those phenomena would create prophetic movements, which might cause problems for the Belgian state, as they thought had happened in the early twenties with the movement called Kimbanguism.[4] The Pentecostal missionaries had to declare that they took kinin and provided health care for the population. It was not until 1930 that SFM was granted *personnalité civile,* which was the official authorization to work in the Belgian Congo. The SFM sought authorization to work in Burundi in 1935 and Rwanda in 1940. As said above, these three countries were looked upon as one common mission field, to which the Swedish Pentecostal movement sent a total of 614 missionaries in years to come.

Despite the delayed permission, the missionaries started missionary work already in the 1920s. The Swedes emphasized personal salvation in Christ as a transformative experience wrought by the Holy Spirit. They also stressed that pneumatic phenomena such as speaking in tongues, prophecies, healing, and miracles should be sought, accepted, and consciously encouraged among members. They were

2. The center belonged to the Assemblies of God in Great Britain.

3. Davidsson and Alegre, *Development of Scandinavian Pentecostal Medical Mission,* 4–5.

4. To learn more about Kimbanguism, see for example, Sundkler and Steel, *History of Christianity in Africa.*

characterized by eschatological urgency and a passion for souls. Meeting social needs, they soon realized they also had to start schools and address medical needs.

Letters and reports from Pentecostal missionaries show that there were important conceptions in common between the Swedish Pentecostal Movement and the traditional religions in Congo and Burundi: (1) The belief in a spiritual reality; (2) the view that existence was, first and foremost, a struggle between good and evil spiritual forces; (3) the view that people might be spirit-possessed; and (4) the habit of referring to a spiritual power in cases of sickness, barrenness, drought, or other important issues of life.[5]

HILDA BACKLUND

Hilda Backlund was born in Sunnanås, Indal, in the countryside in the northern part of Sweden, not very far (40 km) from Timrå, in the county of Medelpad. Her father worked as a log-driver and her mother took care of their home and helped people in need in the village. Hilda described the situation in her home with the words: "We did not live in luxury but we did not lack the necessities of life. We could pick wild strawberries and sell them to buy shoes."[6] She learned how to read and write at home and began second grade of primary school directly. She finished school toward the end of the sixth grade. After her schooling, she first worked at local farms and then as a housekeeper to her elder brother. She read a great deal and tried to gain different kinds of knowledge on her own.[7]

The family belonged to the local Baptist church at Liden. In 1904 there was a revival in the area and Hilda decided that she wanted to become a Christian. She then felt a calling to become a missionary. She had learned a great deal about missionary work in her home. It often happened that evangelists stayed at their home. One of them, who belonged to *Örebromissionen, ÖM,* [The Örebro Mission Society] a pentecostalized missionary association within the Baptist Union, told her about the Baptism in the Holy Spirit in 1908. Hilda experienced it shortly before she was baptized in the local Baptist church, nearly 13 years old.

---

5. Oskarsson, *Le mouvement pentecôtiste,* 297.
6. Hilda Backlund, interview by Stig Robertsson, October 1, 1981.
7. Hilda Backlund, interview by Stig Robertsson, October 1, 1981.

In 1918 she went to a Bible school for a month and then worked as an evangelist in Medelpad within the Baptist Union from 1919 to 1920. Convinced as she was of having a missionary calling, she studied at Örebro Missionsskola from 1920 to 1923, a theological educational program, open both to women preachers and charismatic manifestations.[8] What she learned there would be of great importance for her work as a missionary. According to my sources, she was the only woman among the Swedish Pentecostal missionaries in these countries to have a three-year theological training.[9] She was then accepted as a missionary for ÖM. Having finished her studies there, she went to Paris to study French. She was consecrated as a missionary to Congo within ÖM at the Baptist church at Timrå the same year. John Ongman, the founder of Örebro Missionsskola, participated in the ceremony.[10] First, she continued as an evangelist, in the Baptist church at Timrå. In an article in the Pentecostal journal *Evangelii Härold* in 1925 she describes how, for some years, the Spirit had been poured out in the local Baptist church. During that time, she and other members had been influenced by the ecclesiology of the Pentecostal movement, the idea of the independence of the local church, with no outside interference or denominational organization. In February of that year, she and fifteen other members left the Baptist church and founded a "free biblical congregation," an epithet for a Pentecostal one. They decided on the name *Sionförsamlingen*, Timrå.[11]

Hilda continued to work together with another young woman as Pentecostal "witnesses" in the countryside around Timrå. During that time, in the advertisements in *Evangelii Härold*, words such as "pastor" or "evangelists" were not used. Everyone, man or woman, was called a "witness" or a "speaker." It is obvious from another article in that periodical that people were ready to listen to them—as women preaching the word of God. In that article we are told: "Jesus has called two sisters, Jenny Nilsson and Hilda Backlund, to do the work of God among us, which they do with success."[12]

Hilda was now told that she had to send a letter to give up the position as a missionary within *Örebromissionen*, which she did. She then

---

8. *EH* (1974) 3.

9. There were other female Pentecostal missionaries studying there for one or two years.

10. *Missionsbaneret* (1924) 1.

11. *EH* (1925) 173.

12. *EH* (1925) 434.

got a letter from the pastor in the Elim church in Malmö, a Pentecostal congregation, telling her that they were to send a missionary, Linnea Halldorf, to Congo, and asked if Hilda wanted to go with her to the Pentecostal mission field in Congo. She had gotten to know that particular pastor at *Örebro Missionsskola*. She answered she was ready to go. In July she participated at a missionary conference in Malmö. During the journey to Malmö, she visited the Pentecostal church at Rydaholm in Småland, which also decided to support her as a missionary.[13] Their support was important since her sending church at Timrå was very small. In addition, she was told by ÖM that she could use the money that had been collected when she was consecrated as a missionary to pay for her journey to the Pentecostal mission field. After her farewell service in Timrå, she took the boat to Stockholm where she packed her trunks and continued by train to Belgium, where she was met by Linnea Halldorf.[14]

They left Marseille in August 1925 to go by boat to Congo together with three other Swedish Pentecostal missionaries. They arrived at the Swedish Pentecostal mission station, Nia Magira, in the Kivu province, on October 21. Nia Magira was the only missionary station of the Swedish Pentecostals in Congo at that time. This mission center was recently established, since the missionaries had been forced to change places, from Uvira to Nia Magira.[15] Nia Magira was later called Lemera.

Four Swedish missionaries died in 1923. Three of them at Uvira, after having been struck by relapsing fever, and two others had returned to Sweden for a furlough the following year. The spouses Ruth and Julius Aspenlind and Lars Johansson, who had arrived half a year earlier, were the only missionaries who were working there when Linna and Hilda arrived.[16] All newcomers had to learn Swahili, and Lars Johansson who had a gift for languages, shared what he had learned.

A little less than six months later, in April 1926, Hilda was sent to Machumbi in Masisi in the northern part of the Kivu province,[17] together with Linus and Agnes Blomkvist. SFM had gotten permission to start work there already in 1922, but as it was far from Uvira, they left it to American missionaries belonging to the Assemblies of God. In 1925, SFM was asked to take it back, because the American missionaries Anna

13. *EH* (1925) 367; Hilda Backlund, interview by Stig Robertsson, October 1, 1981.
14. Hilda Backlund, interview by Stig Robertsson, October 8, 1981.
15. *EH* (1925) 471; (1974) 3.
16. Söderlund, *Pingstmission i Kongo och Ruanda-Urundi*, 23–25, 27, 29.
17. In early reports Machumbi is called Masisi, which was the name of the area.

and Arthur Berg needed to leave Congo for a furlough in their home country. Thus, there was already a small congregation and a school with both children and grown-ups when Hilda arrived.[18] It was a great joy for Hilda to listen to the Africans giving their testimonies, praying, and singing Christian songs during the first church worship. On the day of Pentecost, they baptized eleven men and celebrated the Holy Communion together. Hilda described the occasion with the words: "All day the Lord was wonderfully near [. . . .] We were greatly delighted to see a small God's assembly of black people around us."[19] The male missionary, Linus Blomkvist, suggested that he and Hilda take turns to preach every other Sunday.[20] They also taught the evangelists and, later on, the elders and the pastors. When there were only women missionaries at a missionary center during the first decade, they were the ones doing the preaching and the teaching. To begin with, the local evangelists were teachers in the village schools. Later on, they also taught and preached at the centers and became elders, working as pastors.

Hilda was responsible for the school and performed simple medical treatment, especially wounds. Sometimes the medical needs were more serious. She expressed in her diary her sorrow of not being able to help a woman who was trying to give birth and the child died. Later on, other missionaries were to be trained as nurses and midwives.

A little more than two years after they came to Machumbi, they reported about the first Congolese being baptized in the Holy Spirit: "We heard them speaking in tongues, praising God. [. . .] A young black man conveyed an encouraging message to us white people and many serious exhortations to the black brothers."[21] Two years later, Hilda declared: "It is both interesting and wonderful to see when the Spirit of God falls upon the blacks. Although they have never been to a Pentecostal meeting and seen how it is done, you recognize the expressions from glorious Pentecostal days at home in Sweden."[22]

In January 1930 the first Bible school for evangelists was started. Among the evangelists were Petro Shematsi and Samuel Kyahi, who were going to be close coworkers with Hilda for many years. They were sent out to villages to preach the Gospel and to teach children how to read

18. Söderlund, *Pingstmission i Kongo och Ruanda-Urundi*, 17.
19. *EH* (1926) 482–83.
20. Hilda Backlund, interview by Stig Robertsson, February 11, 1982.
21. *EH* (1929) 25.
22. *EH* (1930) 517.

and write.[23] Previously, Samuel Kyahi had been going with Hilda on her walking safaris to the neighboring villages. In interviews, she was keen to underline the good work he did. Upon arriving in the village, he declared that they first had to give the Word of God to the inhabitants before getting food.[24]

Some years later, in 1931, the Swedes were asked to take over another American missionary station, Walikale, a six-day walk from Machumbi.[25] The American missionaries had been working there for ten years, so there was a rather established community work with about two hundred Christians and twenty-five evangelists. When the Swedes were asked to take over, missionary Alvar Lindskog wrote in *Evangelii Härold*: "They look upon themselves as a faith mission, even claiming to be Pentecostals, but according to our opinion some of their doctrines are not biblical." The Swedes could not accept the Americans' way of doing missionary work.[26] First Alvar Lindskog and Linus Blomkvist, and later Hilda Backlund, visited the place. They were heartily welcomed by the local people and decided to take over the center. Hilda, together with Agnes Liljedahl who had recently arrived, were responsible for Walikale from September of that year. Hilda left for her first furlough in February 1932. The Swedes soon found out that at both these places they were not satisfied with the lives of the Christians. Thus, quite a number were excluded from the congregations.

Although Hilda had no formal education as a teacher, she spent much of her time during the first decades teaching at primary schools— in the beginning very simple lessons; teaching reading, writing, and Christian beliefs. After some time, she added geography and science. In her younger days, she had learned how to sew and for many years she made clothes as Christmas gifts to schoolchildren and evangelists. She had formed the impression that children were the most important tools when it came to spreading the Gospel among the inhabitants and she encouraged the readers of *Evangelii Härold* to pray especially for the children.[27] Statistics later showed that most of the early Pentecostals were gained among the pupils. In 1957, the missionary secretary at

23. *EH* (1930) 312.
24. Hägglund, *Hilda Backlund*.
25. It has not been possible to find the name of the missionary society in question.
26. *EH* (1931) 456; Hägglund, *Hilda Backlund* (subtitles), 13.
27. *EH* (1928) 829, *EH* (1929) 632; Hilda Backlund, interview by Stig Robertsson, February 11, 1982.

Filadelfiaförsamlingen (Philadelphia church) in Stockholm, Samuel Nyström, declared that around 70 percent of the members in the Pentecostal churches founded by Swedes in this region, were seen as a fruit of the schools.[28]

During school holidays, Hilda made long journeys together with her Congolese coworkers and schoolboys to places away from the missionary station. She explained that they had two reasons for doing this: to get to know the villages and to reach them with the Gospel. The meetings could extend for hours, but people stayed and listened. The missionaries made these visits in the company of African Christians. Hilda explains: "We rejoiced to see them so willingly witness, pray and sing."[29] She established good relations with the chiefs she met. One of them told her already in 1927 that it was not enough for them to come and stay just for a couple of days—he wanted her to send them teachers, "so that we can listen to the Word of God daily and our children can learn how to read."[30] Probably, the chief had realized that a new time was about to dawn, a time when it was necessary to know how to read and write. In her diary, she expresses more than once her wish to be able to visit people in the villages much more often.[31]

Hilda had a gift for languages. There were several local languages in the Kivu province. Quite early, however, most of the Swedish missionaries concentrated on using Swahili, which served as the *lingua franca* in Eastern Congo and commercial centers in Burundi and Rwanda. There were exceptions though, and Hilda belonged to them. During the six months at Lemera, she learnt to speak Swahili so well that after some months she could use that language during the worship services. After coming to Machumbi, she began to study the local language, Kihunde. An American missionary had started to write a grammar of that language, a work that Hilda finalized. During her first working period from 1926 to 1932, she and her coworkers also translated one hundred songs and the Gospel of Mark. The latter was printed in London in 1930. During the second period, they finished the translation to Kihunde of the Gospel of Luke, which was also printed in London.

That Hilda also got to know the inhabitants and their way of thinking early on is shown in the book, *Från Kongos berg och Tanganyikasjöns*

28. EH (1957) 6–7.
29. EH (1927) 186.
30. EH (1927) 186.
31. For example, PA/KA/64/H. Backlund diary, June 19, 1937.

stränder (From the Mountains of Congo and the Shores of Lake Tanganyika) published in 1932. In that book, she wrote a chapter entitled, *Innan de visste något om Gud* (Before they knew anything about God). To her, the Congolese were living in darkness. They prayed and gave offerings to different spirits, of whom they sometimes were afraid. She also described different ceremonies and traditions in detail, such as the ones relating to the coming of age.[32] In a letter written in July 1929, she described how very sad she was when a group of young boys were taken from school to be initiated. That meant that they should pass three to four months of isolation in the rain forest, and according to Hilda, were taught "a lot of heathen superstitions [. . .] although everything is kept secret." She found it difficult to let them go, but hoped they would return later and "once more learn what is better."[33]

Unlike missionaries from more established missionary societies, she did not try to explain away the spiritual experiences of the Congolese by giving them scientific explications of what they met in life. She finished the chapter in the book mentioned above with the following words: "We cannot tell them that what they believe is only rubbish and imagination. They know better than that. [. . .] They need to get something to counteract the power of Satan. Praise the Lord, that we can tell these poor people about Jesus, the blood and the victory, that is gained at Calvary!" The non-converted Congolese would not call all spirits bad spirits, but that was how the missionaries in general regarded them. That was also true when it came to the veneration of the ancestors, whose spirits were thought to be responsible for illness or other problems if they were not satisfied with how they were venerated.[34]

At the same time as Hilda was very eager to see the Congolese becoming Christians, she could show a certain understanding of how difficult that could be. Many of the pupils at the school at the missionary station lived at the station during the school year. After a visit to a village together with some of these schoolboys, on a ritual occasion that upset Hilda, she asked the boys if they would have preferred to stay behind in the village where their families lived. They answered unanimously "No." She then added:

---

32. *Från Kongos berg och Tanganyikasjöns stränder*, 54–65.
33. *EH* (1929) 632.
34. *Från Kongos berg och Tanganyikasjöns* stränder, 54–65.

> However, it made me feel so sorry for them, when I thought how desperately difficult it must be to be uprooted from all this heathenism to be planted in a completely new and for them foreign soil. In addition, they also have to bear insults from those closest to them, which for the blacks is something terrible.[35]

During the 1930s, SFM and their Congolese coworkers established two more missionary stations in northern Kivu: Ntoto and Pinga. Pinga was the first place where she and her coworkers Oscar and Märta Lagerström, and Samuel Kyahi started a work from scratch in 1935. The aim of trying to get pupils to attend school and establish good relationships with Congolese parents was very much the same at these centers. Hilda continued the same kind of work as before and she continued her translation work. Together with Märta Lagerström, she worked on the translation of hymns. Already in 1937, she was obliged to leave Pinga as she was needed at another center in Ntoto.

The distance between the different centers was at that time considerable. To walk from Machumbi to Walikale took five to six days, to Ntoto two days, and to Pinga four to five days.[36] To get from Lemera to Machumbi, they first had to walk to Bukavu, then take a boat across Lake Kivu, which took two days, and continue to walk for another four days.[37] With time, they could use bicycles more and more. From the late 1940s, ordinary roads were being built. It happened rather often that single women missionaries were transferred to another missionary station when a couple who was responsible for it left for furlough. In 1937–1938, Hilda spent almost a year as the only missionary at Ntoto. And she enjoyed it. In her diary she confesses: "Finally alone! I can't help loving being alone more than anything else," meaning that she enjoyed being the only missionary there.[38] Despite this, she does not seem to have had any problems cooperating with other missionaries, when working together at the same missionary station. She also seems to have had good relations with her Congolese colleagues. In a filmed interview, she mentions several of her Congolese colleagues with great respect. After her first farewell service, one of her missionary colleagues described her as follows: "She is very dearly loved and highly respected by the Congolese.

---

35. *EH* (1928) 410.
36. *EH* (1937) 696.
37. *EH* (1931) 456.
38. PA/KA/64/H. Backlund diary, June 4, 1938.

They call her one of their own."³⁹ During the service, the evangelists left farewell words for her. They and her former schoolboys, then grown up, thanked her for having shown them the way to salvation. She was to be called *Mama Mpenda* (loving mother).⁴⁰ In October 1948, when she was ready to go to Congo for the third time, Hilda wrote:

> God has been marvelously good towards me during the years I have served him in Congo, and I know He does not change. My only wish is to stay faithful and hereafter serve Him better than before. With God's help and grace, I will try to gain more people for heaven before Jesus comes."⁴¹

This quotation shows what her priorities were at that time. She intended to "gain more people for heaven" before Jesus's second coming. She was convinced of being sent and led by God. However, she soon began to question some decisions taken by the SFM at a conference in Congo. In August 1948, SFM decided to accept grants from the Belgian government for their schoolwork at the centers. The decisive factor behind the affirmative answer was the presence of Lewi Pethrus, the leader of the Pentecostal movement in Sweden, who for the first time visited this mission field. Before the conference, he had visited the different mission centers. The African leaders had told him how important it was that also the Pentecostals had their own primary schools so that their children did not have to go to schools run by Catholic missionaries.⁴² Lewi Pethrus therefore advised the missionaries to accept the government grants.

The decision to raise the school standard was not welcomed by all the missionaries. The female missionaries were supposed to be responsible for the new primary schools. Hilda was accepted as a teacher candidate by the Belgian authorities, a fact that she, to begin with, did not welcome. She expressed her reaction with the following words:

> I have loved the school as long as it has been a means to gain the souls for God and to train evangelists . . . If this /the new direction/ is to be the goal of our work here, I will not be able to continue and . . . there will be very few real servants of the Lord to be found this way.⁴³

39. *EH* (1932) 233.
40. *EH* (1932) 342; Hilda Backlund, interview by Stig Robertsson, February 11, 1982.
41. *EH* (1949) 2, 20.
42. At that time primary schools were run missionary societies.
43. PA/KA/35/H. Backlund September 28, 1949.

She had been awake several nights asking God if this was really His will. She hoped that there would soon come new missionary teachers so "we, the old ones, can devote our time to evangelism."[44] Despite that, she continued doing schoolwork and she did it well. She was headmaster of the secondary school at Kashebere during the 1960s and at the beginning of the 1970s.

This change in SFM's activities nevertheless resulted in the female missionaries getting more involved in the decision-making processes than had been the case before. Now school and literature committees were created, with both men and women as members. Hilda was a member of the literature committee, and in 1959, she was a member of the school committee for the northern field, together with the missionary John Österberg and two Congolese men, Marko Mungimba och Enoc Tambi.[45]

Hilda Backlund took a special interest in the situation of the women. She taught women how to read and write and to become familiar with the Christian message. She learned more about the local culture and expressed a much more positive view of the Congolese women and their situation than most of her missionary colleagues at that time. For instance, the latter looked at what they called "bride price" and said that a woman was a "commodity," obliged to do what the husband said. They did not understand that what a man gave to his bride's family functioned as an assurance. If he treated her badly, she could leave him and return home without returning the down payment, often paid in goats. Hilda Backlund understood how it worked:

> I've noticed that the women, especially around Machumbi, do pretty much what they want to do. If they want to leave their husband, they do that without being afraid. They are also rather strong towards their husbands. In the congregation, we have strong and God-fearing women. They are the ones who want something when it comes to work and thoughts and suggestions."[46]

When the center at Machumbi was moved to Kashebere at the end of the 1950s, it was the women who carried the bricks, taken from the old

---

44. PA/KA/35/H. Backlund September 28, 1949.

45. PA/KA/23/Minutes from the "Meeting of the Brethren," August 1950; from the SFM conference, July 20–23, 1959.

46. Hilda Backlund, interview by Stig Robertsson, February 11, 1982.

church at Machumbi, and walked for four hours to the new center.[47] Once a Swedish pastor was there to give courses to the evangelists. He expressed his surprise at seeing so many women coming to listen. Hilda calmly responded that they did not exclude the women because they were the most God-fearing in the congregation. During the course, she also noticed that the women were as interested and as attentive as the men.[48]

Throughout the years she also translated the rest of the New Testament, Bible study books, and other Christian literature to Kihunde together with her coworkers Samuel Kyahi and Petro Shematsi. In 1961, they had translated all the four gospels. Towards the end of the 1970s, Samuel Kyahi finished the work with the New Testament and translated most of the Apocalypse himself. It was ready to be printed in 1981.[49] Hilda then explained:

> I'm telling the elderly people that their children and their grandchildren will appreciate that the Bible exists in their own language when they want to get to know their own culture. I usually say that the people are the language and the language is the people.[50]

In an interview made in 1974, she regretted that she did not have more time for translation work.[51]

Hilda Backlund continued to work in the northern part of the Kivu province until she retired in July 1981, almost eighty-six years old. She was very active in the local church, participated in elders' meetings, and influenced decisions. According to one of her missionary colleagues, Hilda had taught the first generation of elders and pastors well. They had, in their part, molded the following generations.[52] She also continued to spend time with the small congregations in the villages.

Hilda spent most of her life in Congo. She did long mission periods, the first one lasted for six and a half years. The longest one was during the Second World War. She then left Sweden in the autumn of 1934 and did not return until the summer of 1946. That stint was only interrupted by

47. Hägglund, *Hilda Backlund*, 1980.
48. *EH* (1974) 16, 31.
49. *EH* (1930) 422; *EH* (1932) 223; *EH* (1961) 35: 16. Hilda Backlund, interview by Stig Robertsson, July 27, 1982.
50. Hilda Backlund, interview by Stig Robertsson, July 27, 1982.
51. *EH* (1974) 13:8.
52. Hilda Backlund and Inga-Lisa Turehagen, interview by Stig Robertsson, July 27, 1982.

a six-month furlough in South Africa in 1943. When working as headmaster during the second half of the 1960s and parts of the 1970s, she only went for a shorter furlough during the holidays every second year. Because of her position as a teacher and headmaster, the Congolese government paid for her ticket. She fled the country twice, once in 1961 and a second time in 1964, because of civil wars.

When looking back, she underlined, in an interview in 1980, how Pentecostals from the northern part of Kivu played an important role when it came to the spreading of the Gospel in other important centers, like Bukavu, the capital of the Kivu province, and Cyangugu in Rwanda.[53]

LINNEA HALLDORF

Image #10. Linnea Halldorf.

Linnea Halldorf was the first Swedish Pentecostal missionary in either Congo, Burundi, or Rwanda to have a teacher's education. She was born in 1896 into a teacher's family in Kronobäck, just south of Mönsterås, in the county of Småland in the southern part of Sweden. She was number seven of twelve siblings, of which three others also became missionaries, two in China and one in Portugal. The parents were highly engaged in a Lutheran "Mission house" situated nearby. They also now and then

---

53. Hägglund, *Hilda Backlund*, 1980.

frequented a chapel. Her father became a new-born Christian in 1885, when a revival touched the area. Her elder brother Einar Halldorf listened to T. B. Barratt preaching in Gothenburg in 1907. Einar experienced the Baptism in the Holy Spirit and became a pastor after having studied at *Örebro Missionskola*. He told his siblings about his experiences and his new conviction that they should be baptized in water with a "believer's baptism."[54]

Already as a child, Linnea felt a calling to missionary work among a people "living in darkness and in the land of the shadow of death,"[55] but she was not ready to accept the calling for many years. In 1916, she graduated as a primary school teacher and worked as such for seven years to come. In 1917, she was baptized in water in Karlstad. She longed for the Baptism in the Holy Spirit but did not experience it until May 1921, when she accepted a call to mission. In 1924, she spent one year at *Missionsskolan i Högsby*.[56] The missionary school opened in February 1922 and was run by Rickard Fris, who had been a teacher at *Örebro Missionsskola*, and his wife Rakel. They intended to form Pentecostal missionaries before they were sent to the mission field. Two more teachers taught at the school, Maria Lindquist, a language teacher, who had also previously worked at *Örebro Missionsskola*, and Osmin Halldorf, Linnea's younger brother. Osmin had just graduated from the University of Lund. They studied biblical knowledge, homiletics, church and mission history, English, French for future Congo missionaries, and mathematics. The education was the same for men and women. The Fris couple talked about women as "good preachers" and encouraged their ministry. During the school's first year, there were only female students mainly due to accommodation facilities. Many of them had been waiting for an opportunity to get educated or trained for the missionary task.[57] Several others of the early Pentecostal missionaries sent to Congo studied at that school during the 1920s. It was closed down towards the end of that decade because of a schism within the Swedish Pentecostal movement.[58]

People who were sent to the mission field usually worked as evangelists in Sweden before being sent. Most future Congo missionaries also spent two years at Högsby. Linnea was an exception in both cases

54. Ståhlberg, *Skollärarhemmet i Kronobäck*.
55. *EH* (1925) 120.
56. *EH* (1925) 120, *EH* (1966) 33:16.
57. Nyberg Oskarsson, *Le mouvement pentecôtiste*. 28
58. For more details, see Oskarsson, *Pingströrelsen*, 1:69–80.

because the missionary Rut Aspenlind had urgently asked her sending church, the Elim church in Malmö, for a teacher to help her at Nia Magira (Lemera). The same church then became the sending church of Linnea. She was known to the church because her brother, Einar Halldorf, had previously been a pastor there. After having written about her calling in *Evangelii Härold*, she explained: "Convinced to be in the complete will of God, I am happy to leave my beloved home. My prayer and my wish are to be faithful to Jesus among the Black people."[59] As mentioned earlier, she then spent some months in Belgium to study French before taking the boat from Marseille. When she first saw African people, she felt in her heart, "From now on, these people are going to be my people."[60]

Her first two periods were spent at Lemera. First, she had to learn Swahili. Then her task was to teach at the primary school and also, step by step, build up schools in the villages, with teachers whom she had taught how to read and write. She was eager to explain that it was necessary to teach them to read, so they could read the Bible. But it is important to note that she only said this early, when questioned why she, as a missionary, spent so much time teaching in school.[61] For most of the first period, she worked with an English Pentecostal missionary, Mary Richardson, from the Assemblies of God in Great Britain.[62]

It was rather difficult to get children to come to school in the beginning. The children were afraid of the strangers, but with the help of the locals who translated from Swahili to Kifulero, the local language, and gifts of small portions of salt that were very much appreciated, the children began to come in small numbers. The parents, however, thought the children should spend time helping them and taking care of younger siblings. After some time, Linnea found out that it was rather easy to get in touch with the women and convince them of the positive effects of schooling. Her efforts had good results. Already in 1927, they had 120 to 130 pupils at the center, and at a village, one hour's walk away, thirty to forty children were taught two hours daily.[63] As mentioned above, the teaching included reading, writing, and Christian beliefs in

---

59. *EH* (1925) 120.

60. Linnea Halldorf, interview by Jack-Tommy Ardenfors, May 10, 1985.

61. Halldorf, *EH* (1980) 12–13; Linnea Halldorf, interview by Jack-Tommy Ardenfors, May 10, 1985.

62. As mentioned earlier she had been working at Kalembe Lembe. Her husband had died early in 1925. Emmett, *W.F.P. Burton*, 5.

63. *EH* (1928) 200.

the beginning. Linnea usually worked together with another woman missionary. They also had courses for adult women. A report from 1935 tells us that "the sisters Halldorf and Palmgren are doing a wonderful work among women and children." The children were said to be very clever at reading, writing, and mathematics.[64] At the same time, Linnea was also preaching and proclaiming the Gospel. Like Hilda, she was all her life a very good walker and she could be away for fourteen days during school holidays, visiting villages, and sharing the Gospel.[65] The Congolese gave her the name Kanyabuyange, which means an African mountain herb.

When Linnea returned to the missionary field in 1939, she became responsible for the schoolwork at the missionary center at Kiremba in Burundi. There, she was also a teacher to the missionaries Winbergs' five children. She worked there in the same way as she had done at Lemera, including walks to preach and proclaim the Gospel in the surrounding hills during the holidays. She was the first Swedish missionary who tried to learn Kirundi, which is a difficult language to learn, as it is a language with a tonic accent. She always used Swahili when preaching. She could be away for two to three weeks, never spending more than one night at every place. She walked together with pupils who carried a safari bed for her, which she put in the out-school or lent to the house of the evangelist. At every out-school, there was an evangelist who also taught at the school. The number of lessons was much less than at the center. Together with the evangelist she then had evangelization meetings in the school or at a nearby market. At the markets, she played a disc on her phonograph. The small group sang some songs and someone gave a testimony. On Sundays, she preached during the worship service and the evangelist gave the invitation to conversion.[66]

We have the story from Elia Bamporeye, a future reverend, who got converted when Linnea preached at his out-school. His intention was not to convert but he had come to school just to learn how to read and write:

> Every word Kanyabuyange said went directly into my heart. [. . .] She finished and sat down. The evangelist who should invite people to come forward for repentance stood up. Then she said: "Excuse me, but I hear a voice telling me that I should give the invitation"

---

64. *EH* (1935) 26.

65. See, for example, *EH* (1929) 664–65; Linnea Halldorf, interview by Jack-Tommy Ardenfors, May 10, 1985.

66. Winberg, *Minnen ur familjen Winbergs liv,* 16; Nyberg Oskarsson, *Le Mouvement Pentecôtiste,* 178–79.

[. . .] And then she said: "you there, God is calling you and if you do not answer 'yes,' you will have problems."[67]

Bamporeye felt as though he had no strength, but he managed to get up. He went forward and bent his knees. Then Linnea said: "That's enough, here he comes." She put her hand on him and prayed, whereafter she closed the meeting.[68]

During the school week, it also happened that she walked into the neighborhood after the lessons were over at one o'clock. She was often translated by Manasse Mafefere, a future leader in the Burundian Pentecostal Movement.[69]

Early in the 1940s the Burundian Pentecostals started to meet at conferences. In 1944, Linnea was one of the speakers, together with three other missionaries, two women and one man, and one Tanganyikan Pentecostal preacher. The women preached from biblical texts talking about courageous and independent women. Linnea talked about queen Esther.[70]

Linnea stayed in Burundi until 1948. In the first months of 1946, she was together with the elders Abed Nego Madengo and Filipo Bwanike, who were responsible for the congregation at Kiremba after Thomas Winberg and his family had left for furlough.[71]

When SFM decided to accept governmental grants in 1948, and the new demands that followed, it was necessary to raise the standard of education at the primary schools at the centers. They realized that they had to train African primary school teachers, and to meet this need, SFM started a cooperation with the Norwegian Pentecostal Mission about a teacher training college at Lemera in 1950. The only missionary with formal teacher training was Linnea who was appointed headmaster. She had then spent some additional months in Belgium to follow what was known as the "colonial course." The Belgian authorities had decided that the course was compulsory for missionaries working in the state-subsidized schools. Linnea was the first of the Swedish and Norwegian Pentecostal missionaries to follow that course.[72] Linnea worked as a

67. Bamporeye, Elia, interview by Gunilla Nyberg Oskarsson, March 7, 2000.
68. Bamporeye, Elia, interview by Gunilla Nyberg Oskarsson. March 7, 2000.
69. Winberg, *Minnen ur familjen Winbergs liv*, 16.
70. Nyberg Oskarsson, *Le Mouvement* Pentecôtiste, 197–98.
71. Linnea Halldorf, interview by Jack-Tommy Ardenfors, May 10, 1985; Mahemeri, Yusefu, interview by Gunilla Nyberg Oskarsson, March 21, 2000.
72. Mail to author from Daniel Halldorf, March 1, 2024.

headmaster until December 1953, when the first group of twenty-eight schoolteachers finished their training. She expressed in an interview that she did not like that position. When more missionaries with a teacher education arrived from Sweden, others took over as headmasters. Linnea continued as a teacher.[73] One of her students declared, many years later, that she explained the Bible to him and gave him a foundation that he had not had before. Most important to him was the fact that she taught them how to pray.[74] She continued to visit the villages. One of her missionary coworkers wrote that Linnea left the missionary center early on Sunday mornings to walk to surrounding villages to preach the Gospel, although she had been preparing lessons and correcting students' work until late at night during the week.[75]

Even though women missionaries were now members of different committees, it was not obvious that a female missionary would get such a leading position. One of the male missionaries wrote: "It will of course be necessary later on to get a brother leading the school, but for the first year it will certainly function well with sister Halldorf."[76]

Back in Burundi in 1960, Linnea started another school at Mugara, a two-year program for evangelists, elders, and pastors who did not have much formal education. At the annual conference the year before, the African delegates had requested that such schools should be opened. The Burundian Pentecostal churches promised to take economic responsibility for the one in their country.[77] Linnea had a special concern for "the servants of God." She preferred teaching in a non-governmental school because she would then be free from governmental supervision, as she explains in a letter.[78] There were about fifty students in 1964. That year the missionary Viola Lindgren became her colleague. They both taught biblical and general subjects. In 1967, Viola Lindgren moved to the old capital Gitega, where ADEEP, the Burundian Pentecostal Movement, was responsible for the teaching of Protestant religion at the governmental secondary school. She was replaced at Mugara by Burundian Joel Bigirabagabu. Linnea underlined the very good cooperation she had with

73. Bengt Hägglund, dir. *Linnea Halldorf*, 1981.
74. *EH* (1980) 12–13.
75. Molin, *EH* (1957) 22.
76. Oskarsson, *Le Mouvement* Pentecôtiste, 224.
77. PA/KA/23/ Minutes from the annual SFM conference, July 20–23.
78. Halldorf, *EH* (April 12) 1964.

the latter.[79] For the school year of 1968/1969 she, in turn, replaced Viola Lindgren in Gitega. After that, she went to Sweden for a furlough during which she collected money at conferences for a church construction in Gitega. She added an inheritance she had received in Sweden to the sum she managed to collect, and persuaded relatives in the USA to provide further help. In this way, she managed to raise funds for half of the cost of the church building.[80] When she returned to the mission field in 1970, she was asked by Pentecostal leaders in Rwanda to open a secondary school there as well, which she did in Gihundwe. The first year she assumed the role of headmaster. She continued to teach there until July 1974 when she once more returned to Lemera in Congo.[81] There she became responsible for the two-year-long education for evangelists. She was still in that position in 1984, at the age of 88.[82] When she was close to her seventieth anniversary, the Elim church in Malmö invited her to celebrate the day in Sweden—an offer she did not accept. The church noted that "she preferred to celebrate it with her African friends and missionary co-workers."[83] In 1985, however, she participated in the sixtieth anniversary of the missionary work in Congo at the Elim church in Malmö. She spent some weeks in Sweden and then returned to Lemera. In 1988, at the age of ninety-one, she had to return to Sweden because of bad health and she spent the remainder of her life in Malmö, until she passed away in 1996, shortly after her hundredth birthday. She had never been ill up to that point, except for attacks of malaria during her first term.[84]

Today the Pentecostal church CEPAC in Congo/RDC, planted by Swedish Pentecostal missionaries, counts more than one million members and the same is true for the Pentecostal church, CEPBu in Burundi, planted by Swedish and Congolese missionaries. Linnea and Hilda were members of teams spreading the Pentecostal message in these areas. They worked together with other Scandinavian missionaries but the vast majority of those spreading the Gospel were Congolese and Burundians.

---

79. Oskarsson, *Pingstkyrkan i Burundi*, 198–99, 322; *EH* (1966) 16.

80. Oskarsson, *Pingstkyrkan i Burundi*, 250–51.

81. Hägglund, *Linnea Halldorf*; Axelsson, *Mitt liv i Afrika*, 91–93, 119.

82. Halldorf, letter to D. Möller February 2, 1981; Björklund, *Berättelsen om Joel— kongomissionär*, 108.

83. *EH* (1966) 16.

84. Linnea Halldorf, interview by Jack-Tommy Ardenfors, May 10, 1985.

CONCLUSION

Pentecostalism has always had a strong emphasis on mission, motivated by the belief that it was part of the preparation for the soon return of Christ. This was also true of the Pentecostal churches in Scandinavia. In this chapter, we have followed two Swedish women missionaries, Hilda Backlund and Linnea Halldorf, who worked in Congo and the neighboring countries of Burundi and Rwanda. There were great similarities between these two missionaries but also differences. They were both independent women, convinced of being sent and led by God and their respective missions. They spent most of their lives as missionaries. The most important thing for both of them was to spread the Gospel. They both felt more at home on the mission field than in Sweden. They were both doing ordinary schoolwork as well as teaching women, evangelists, and elders. To them, ordinary schoolwork had primarily been an instrument for preaching the Gospel. Hilda was more engaged in the question of educating women and encouraging them to serve the Lord in many different ways. Linnea was the one who spent most time teaching evangelists, especially after 1960.

They were both highly involved in the local congregations, although their approaches diverged over time. Hilda seems to have participated more at elders' meetings and planning the work of the local church. Linnea seems to have prioritized visitations and the evangelization of villages.

Their civil status was very important for what they were able to do. As single women they were free to choose whatever they wanted to do during the holidays—spending weeks walking and visiting villages to fulfill their task to preach the Gospel. The fact that both had grown up in the countryside had probably prepared them for that habit. In this way, they managed to combine what missiologist Donald McGavran called "the 'people movement' approach to mission with the traditional 'mission station' approach." According to McGavran, these two approaches were not compatible.[85] Not having responsibilities towards husband and children also meant that they could spend most of their lifetime in African countries since they didn't need to stay in Sweden for the educational needs of possible children. They also often had more responsibilities than married women missionaries. Hilda, with her theological training and her gift for languages, devoted as much time as possible together with her Congolese coworkers, to translating biblical texts, songs, and theological

---

85. MacClung, "Try to Get People Saved," 43.

literature. They both made significant and lasting impacts on the Pentecostal churches in the two countries, which were planted by Swedes, Congolese and Burundians.

BIBLIOGRAPHY

Axelsson, Iris. *Mitt liv i Afrika*. Aneby: SWH Layout, 2012.
Backlund, Hilda. Interview by Stig Robertsson. 1981–1982.
Bamporeye, Elia. Interview by Gunilla Nyberg Oskarsson. March 7, 2000.
Björklund, Lena. *Berättelsen om Joel—kongomissionär*. Pingst—arkiv och forskning, 2013.
Davidsson, Tommy H., and Rakel Ystebø Alegre. "From Medical Kits to the Fight against Rape as a Weapon of War: The Development of Scandinavian Pentecostal Medical Mission in the Democratic Republic of Congo." In *Sisters, Mothers, Daughters: Pentecostal Perspectives on Violence Against Women*, 154–84. Leiden: Brill, 2022.
Emmett, David. *W.F.P. Burton (1886–1971): A Pentecostal Pioneer's Missional Vision for Congo*. Leiden: Brill, 2021.
Halldorf, Linnea. Interview by Jack-Tommy Ardenfors. May 10, 1985.
———. Letter to D. Möller February 2, 1981.
Hägglund, Bengt, director, *Hilda Backlund*. Kungliga biblioteket avd. Svenska audiovisuella medier, 1980.
———. *Hilda Backlund*. Kungliga biblioteket avd. Svenska audiovisuella medier, 1980.
———. *Linnea Halldorf*. Kungliga biblioteket avd. Svenska audiovisuella medier, 1981.
MacClung, Grant L. Jr. "Try to Get People Saved." In *The Globalization of Pentecostalism*, edited by Murray W. Dempster et al., 31–51; Oxford: Regnum, 1999.
Mahemeri, Yusefu. Interview by Gunilla Nyberg Oskarsson. March 21, 2000.
Ngongo, Fatuma Kilongo. *Les héroïnes sans couronne, Leadership des femmes dans les Églises de Pentecôte en Afrique Centrale*. Theses No. 15, Genève 2015.
Nyberg Oskarsson, Gunilla. "1920-talet—Fortsatt tillväxt och inre strider—rörelsen sluter leden." In *Pingströrelsen: verksamheter och särdrag under 1900-talet*, edited by Jan-Åke Alvarsson et al., 69–80. Örebro: Libris, 2007.
———. *Le mouvement pentecôtiste—une communauté alternative au sud du Burundi 1935–1960*. Studio Missionalia Svecana XCV, Uppsala: Swedish Institute for Mission Research, 2004.
———. *Pingstkyrkan i Burundi och svensk pingstmission i landet 1935–1985*. Insamlingsstiftelsen för pingstforskning. Nr 2, 2020.
Sundkler, Bengt, and Christopher Steed. *History of Christianity in Africa*. Cambridge University Press, 2000.
Svenska pingstmissionärer. *Från Kongos berg och Tanganyikasjöns stränder*. Stockholm: Förlaget Filadelfia, 1932.
Stålberg, Tage. *Skollärarhemmet i Kronobäck*. N.p, 1960.
Swedish Pentecostal archives. Files from the following series: KA/23/KA/34/, KA/64/. Minutes from conference, 1959.
Winberg, P.-A. *Minnen ur familjen Winbergs liv*. Unpublished manuscript, 2002.

Image #11. Ingrid and Austin Chawner.

9

Ingrid Løkken Chawner
"The Missionary on the Steel Horse"[1]

LIV TORIL RINDING SKJEGGESTAD AND RAKEL YSTEBØ ALEGRE

INTRODUCTION

Ingrid Løkken Chawner was a Norwegian Pentecostal who as a young single missionary became the founder of Assemblies of God in Mozambique. In 1927 she started her work in the country and for several years she was the only Pentecostal missionary there. Ingrid established a main mission in the capital and evangelized town after town together with an increasing number of native evangelists. In the beginning, Ingrid went on foot to the villages, since the conditions were unsuitable for horses, but after some years she acquired a motorbike. She then became known as "the woman on the steel horse."[2] Ingrid Løkken endured many hardships while evangelizing in Mozambique, but she was convinced that this was her life's work and divine calling. She suffered from severe diseases, financial difficulties, loneliness, and a very difficult climate. In addition, she faced many discomforts and dangers, and efforts from the government and the Catholic church to restrict their work. In 1934 Ingrid married the

---

1. All translations in this chapter are the authors' own.
2. "Pinsevennenes ukjente heltinne," *KS* (April 23, 2017) 23.

Canadian missionary Austin Chawner and they became effective partners and continued the mission in Mozambique together.

The denomination Ingrid started *Assambleia de Deus de Moçambique* today has an estimated 1,4 million adherents.[3] She stands out as one of the most impactful Scandinavian pioneers, but she is also quite unknown. Very little has been written about Ingrid's mission work, especially before her marriage. In this chapter, we will give an overview of her life and ministry with a special emphasis on the pioneer years as a single missionary in Mozambique from 1927 to 1934. Thereafter we will discuss reasons why her story is rarely told and how she is an example of many female Scandinavian missionaries who had a strong impact but whose contributions have been "lost" in the historical narrative. Our sources for the pioneer years are primarily Scandinavian-language periodicals, and an important aim of this chapter is to make the information they contain available to a wider readership.

EARLY LIFE AND CALLING TO MISSIONS IN AFRICA

Ingrid Marie Løkken was born in the small town of Vestfossen in eastern Norway on the fourteenth of April 1899. Her parents were Thorvald and Helene Løkken, and her father worked as a train conductor for the Norwegian Railway Company. She seems to have spent most of her early years in the Drammen area, but by 1910 the family was living in the town of Horten in southeast Norway.[4] There is scarce information about Ingrid's life until she went to Mozambique but according to the author George Upton Ingrid was converted at the age of sixteen in Horten.[5] Shortly after this she felt God called her to go to Africa as a missionary, and when she was seventeen, she was baptized in the Spirit.[6] The latter indicates that she was part of the Pentecostal revival in Norway.

The Pentecostal revival started in Norway in 1907, around nine years before Ingrid's Spirit baptism. The revival spread to cities and towns in southeastern Norway, where she was from, and early leaders like T. B.

---

3. https://ieadmconvencao.weebly.com/introduccedilatildeo.html.

4. *Folketelling 1910 for 0703 Horten Kjøpstad*, https://www.digitalarkivet.no/source/36486.

5. Upton, *Miracle of Mozambique*, 92–93. George Upton's book has some factual errors, so the years may not be correct.

6. Upton, *Miracle of Mozambique*, 92–93.

Barratt and Carl Magnus traveled and preached in the region.[7] Communities of Pentecostals were formed in several places and it is highly likely that she was influenced by the Pentecostal revivals in nearby areas and was part of a Pentecostal community as a teenager.[8] Oscar Halvorsen was a Pentecostal leader who became especially important to Ingrid and her future mission work. Halvorsen was originally from Nøtterøy, near Tønsberg, which was only twenty kilometers from Ingrid's home in Horten. When he was a young man, he immigrated to America, and in 1907 he was baptized in the Spirit in New York and became a Pentecostal evangelist.[9] In 1908 Halvorsen returned to Norway where he continued his work as a traveling evangelist, especially in the region where Ingrid Løkken lived. Revival scenes broke out in several places and under his influence, many young people were baptized in the Spirit and several felt called to become evangelists and missionaries.[10] Ingrid was around ten years old when Halvorsen first started preaching in Horten. In 1916 he settled in Christiania (Oslo) to work among the poor and destitute, and this ministry led to the establishment of the church *Evangeliesalen*. Around 1917/1918 Ingrid went to Christiania where she joined Oscar Halvorsen's church and became active in Sunday school and youth work. Laura and T. B. Barratt did not know her at this time, but she was well-known in "Halvorsen's circles."[11] Ingrid was engaged in evangelistic ministry in different parts of Norway and became the first missionary that *Evangeliesalen* sent out.[12]

In July 1920, Ingrid Løkken traveled to the US where she joined other Scandinavian Pentecostals in Brooklyn.[13] Her contact in the US was Tom Christensen, pastor of the Norwegian Pentecostal church in

---

7. Ski et al., *Fram til urkristendommen*, 1:144.

8. Ski et al., *Fram til urkristendommen*, 3:122.

9. Halvorsen was born in 1876. He was instrumental in the emergence of the first Norwegian Pentecostal communities in Brooklyn and the Northeast of the US. He ministered in these regions with the Norwegian evangelist and missionaries Dagmar Gregersen and Agnes Thelle. See chapter 3 on Dagmar and Agnes and Alegre, "Trans-Atlantic Influences."

10. Ski et al., *Fram til urkristendommen*, 1:144.

11. "Fra Afrika," *KS* (May 10, 1930) 5–6. She may also have attended T. B. Barratt's Bible school at the Filadelfia church in 1919. See Upton, *Miracle of Mozambique*, 93.

12. Evangeliesalen, *Evangeliesalen 80 år*, 6; Bratlie, *Pinsevekkelsen gjennom 30 år*, 20–21.

13. Upton, *Miracle of Mozambique*, 93.

Brooklyn called *Eben-Ezer*.[14] It is unclear why Ingrid decided to go to the US and her occupation is listed as "missionary" in the immigration documents.[15] One source says that she was an evangelist while in the US, while another source says that she went to America to go to missions school.[16] Both of these things may be true. Some Norwegian missionaries went to the US for a period to learn English well, so this could also have been a motive for Ingrid. She stayed in the US for about two years and she developed a close connection to the Norwegian Pentecostals in Brooklyn.[17]

GOING TO SWAZILAND

In August 1922, Ingrid sailed for Africa, where she first worked as a missionary in Swaziland for about four years.[18] *Evangeliesalen* in Oslo supported her financially and counted her as their first missionary.[19] Swaziland was a British colony in South Africa and the Norwegian Pentecostals had supported missionaries there since 1910. It was one of four major 'fields' that Norwegian Pentecostals focused on in their early foreign mission organization *Norges Frie Evangeliske Hedningemisjon* (NFEH).[20] By 1922 there were five missionaries supported by the organization in Swaziland: Laura Strand, Anna Østreng, Julie Høgebøl, Hilma Hermansen, and Borghild Eriksen. The women established three mission stations

---

14. He is listed as "Friend" in the immigration papers (ship list). Teodor (Tom) Christensen was a friend of Oscar Halvorsen, and this may have been her connection to Brooklyn. See Alegre, "Trans-Atlantic Influences."

15. Passenger and Crew Lists of Vessels Arriving at New York, 1897–1957 (National Archives Microfilm Publication T715, roll 2805); Records of the Immigration and Naturalization Service, Record Group 85.

16. Upton, *Miracle of Mozambique*, 92–93; "Pinsevennenes ukjente heltinne," KS (April 23, 2017) 20–21. According to her friend Evangelina in Mozambique, Ingrid went to a mission school in the US.

17. *NT* (December 23 1926) 9; *NT* (December 26 1935) 12; *NT* (May 21, 1936) 12; *NT* (October 7, 1948) 11.

18. Upton, *Miracle of Mozambique*, 92–93. This is what we are told from George R. Upton's book. It has not been possible to trace from first-hand sources in Norway anything about her early years.

19. Evangeliesalen, *Evangeliesalen 80 år*, 6; Nilsen, *Modne marker*, 13, 49. She may also have received some support from friends in the US.

20. The other three were India, China, and Congo. When T. B. Barratt, Laura Barratt, and other Pentecostal leaders decided to form the NFEH in 1915, several of the missionaries in Swaziland became part of it.

in the country and named them New Haven, Betany, and Eben-Ezer.[21] Ingrid Løkken was in contact with these women, and it is likely she spent some time at their mission stations to assist them and to learn from their work. These were experienced missionaries and Løkken was only twenty-three years old when she arrived.

There is very little information about Ingrid Løkken's stay in Swaziland and as far as we can tell she was not mentioned in the Norwegian missionaries' reports in important periodicals such as *Korsets Seier*. She is also very rarely mentioned in histories of the Norwegian Pentecostal foreign missions in Swaziland.[22] However, evidence suggests that she knew the missionaries and their mission stations well,[23] and her later work in Mozambique seems modeled on their work there. In Swaziland the Norwegian Pentecostals established missions with a missionary in charge and from there they evangelized in the region and established outstations led by local ("native") evangelists. Many of the native evangelists received some sort of salary from the mission and attended yearly Bible courses or conferences.[24] Some evangelists also traveled with the missionary to preach in new places and to establish new outstations. At the main mission stations, the missionaries established schools for children, Bible courses for the evangelists, and in some instances also orphanages.[25] They itinerated to the outstations to encourage the evangelists and new believers, and to evangelize the unconverted. For Ingrid, the Norwegian Pentecostal work in Swaziland was also an example of how women could lead missions and travel with native preachers to minister in new places.[26]

21. Witzøe, *De aapne døre*, 134–60; Tollefsen, *Men Gud gav vekst*, 203; Nilsen, *Og Herren virket med*, 37. The three first were Anna Østreng, Laura Strand and Julie Høgebøl. Several of them had first been missionaries for the *Scandinavian Alliance Mission of North America* established by Fredrik Franson. The two last mentioned were supported by *The Scandinavian Alliance Mission of North America* until 1920.

22. Juul, *Til jordens ender*, 130–33. There is little information concerning Ingrid's ministry in Swaziland, and it is surprising that she is not mentioned among the pioneer missionaries referred to in the book, *Til jordens ender*, [To the Ends of the Earth] published in 1960. Neither is she mentioned in Tollefsen et al., *En såmann gikk ut til Swaziland* [A Sower Went Out to Swaziland]. In the last chapter of the said book (76–82), mission secretary Gunnerius Tollefsen gives a summary of all the missionaries who had served in Swaziland from 1910 until 1956. We do not find Ingrid Marie Løkken's name among those mentioned.

23. "Fra Afrika," *KS* (May 10, 1930) 5.

24. Witzøe, *De aapne døre*, 134–60; "Aarsrapport for N.F.E.H.," *KS* (August 20, 1926) 6.

25. Witzøe, *De aapne døre*, 134–60; "Aarsrapport for N.F.E.H.," *KS* (August 20, 1926) 6.

26. Witzøe, *De aapne døre*, 134–60; "Aarsrapport for N.F.E.H.," *KS* (August 20, 1926) 6.

While Ingrid was in Swaziland, she started to feel a special concern for the Thonga (Tsonga) people in Mozambique.[27] Mozambique was a Portuguese colony at the time, and the Catholic Church was the only permitted Christian Church. Ingrid needed a special approval from the government, which they rarely, if ever, granted to establish a mission there. She believed that Portuguese East Africa (Mozambique) was "Africa's most neglected mission field," and her goal was to enter the country to evangelize and establish a mission.[28] Ingrid then moved to the Province of Transvaal in northern South Africa to work with the Thonga people and to be close to the border of Mozambique. In Transvaal, she studied Portuguese and Thonga and started evangelizing along the border. She was also able to travel to Mozambique for periods and preach, even though she could not establish an official mission there yet.

In 1926, after four years of mission work, Ingrid Løkken briefly returned to Norway and then went to the US. It seems that her purpose for returning to the US was to try to raise funds among Scandinavian-Americans and get the necessary provisions for her mission in Mozambique. The economic support from her church *Evangeliesalen* was not enough, and it seems she considered America her best option to increase the support.[29] Her base was the Norwegian Pentecostal community surrounding *Eben-Ezer* and Tom Christensen in Brooklyn. After this stay, the Salem Gospel Tabernacle, which was first pastored by Arne Dahl, also became a regular supporter of her missions work.[30] Ingrid seems to have traveled quite a bit during her stay and visited many churches because she became well-known among the Scandinavian Pentecostals "all the way" from Brooklyn to the West Coast.[31] From 1927 there were reports on offerings to her in the Swedish-American periodical *Sanningens Vittne*, and

---

27. Upton, *Miracle of Mozambique*, 93; Chawner, *Have You Heard about Mozambique*, 13. These are Bantu-speaking peoples inhabiting the southern part of Mozambique and what was the British territory across the border.

28. "Fra portugisisk Øst-Afrika," *KS* (November 8, 1930) 5.

29. "Mocambique," *SV* (December 1931) 6. In 1931 she wrote that her church gave her ten pounds each quarter, but she needed that amount every month to have her basic needs met at the mission.

30. It seems some of her siblings also moved to Brooklyn. In 1926 Tom Christensen was still listed as her contact/friend. Ingrid and Arne Dahl even traveled on the same ship to New York in 1926, when he came to become pastor of the newly formed church in Brooklyn.

31. "Fra Afrika," *KS* (May 10, 1930) 5–6.

she was regularly in contact with its editor Andrew August Holmgren.[32] *Evangeliesalen* in Norway was still her sending church, but the economic aid from Pentecostals in the US was of great importance in her pioneer work.

EARLY MISSION WORK IN MOZAMBIQUE

By early 1928 Ingrid Løkken had established a "Pentecostal Missions Station" in Lebombo, Namahacha in Mozambique, right across the border from Swaziland.[33] She was alone as a missionary at the station. The loneliness did not bother her much since she was working "from morning to evening," but sometimes she thought it would have been "nice to see a white face."[34] From her station Ingrid used much of her time to go by foot to visit villages in the area. She had traveled on horseback in Swaziland, but she did not have horses in Mozambique because "they cannot live here."[35] Walking from village to village from her mission station, Ingrid found one man whom she considered a believer. His name was Johannes, and according to Ingrid, he was converted in the mines of Johannesburg and then testified to his family members when he came home. The family converted, but she believed that since they did not have anyone to guide them, they had gone back to their old ways. One day she decided to visit him but found that he had gone to a gathering to drink beer. She went to the place, and before the people had started drinking, she preached to them about salvation. According to Ingrid the people did not know what to do since they had never had a missionary visit them, and they offered her beer. She told them that believers did not drink beer and that preaching the gospel was for free. Several of those present said that "today God had visited them" and Johannes gave her a chicken to show his appreciation. Ingrid walked all the way home again with her feet full of blisters, but wrote that she was happy that she had been able to preach.

32. "Från Skilda Håll," *SV* (November 1927) 8; "Från Skilda Håll," *SV* (December 1927) 8; "Från Skilda Håll," *SV* (August 1928) 8; "Från Skilda Håll," *SV* (October 1928) 8; "Från Skilda Håll," *SV* (November 1929) 8; "Från Skilda Håll," *SV* (November 1929) 8. The following years she received offerings from Chicago, Montana, New Jersey, New York, New Auburn, Wisconsin, etc. Ingrid also starts sending letters to *Sanningens Vittne* in Minneapolis for publication.

33. "Namahacha, Portuguese East Africa," *SV* (August 1928) 7; "Lebombo," *SV* (November 1928) 7.

34. "Lebombo," *SV* (November 1928) 7.

35. "Lebombo," *SV* (November 1928) 7.

She claimed that alcohol was one of the great evils affecting people. When mothers became intoxicated, it sometimes led to terrible accidents that caused their babies to be injured and even die.[36] Temperance was an important part of her message to converts, and she was very disappointed if she found that they had "backslidden" and were drinking alcohol again.[37]

From her early days in Mozambique, people came to Ingrid with their sick children and sought her assistance for different types of ailments and diseases.[38] Both at her mission station and in her itinerant preaching tours Ingrid often functioned as a nurse although she had no such formal education. She described vividly what kind of health trouble people suffered from, like wounds caused by vermin, insects that had gone into an ear, sores full of worms, and different kinds of fever sicknesses like malaria.[39] Learning from experience she kept a supply of basic equipment for medical care like bandages, antiseptic liquid, and ointments in case of burns, wounds, and different kinds of injuries. When she had the opportunity Ingrid taught about hygiene and explained the necessity of treating sores with clean hands and care so as not to spread bacteria.[40] She tried to help those who came to her and found ways to relieve their pain and to pray for their healing.

One of Ingrid's major concerns was the prevalence and consequences of "superstition," fear of the spirit of the ancestors, and belief in spirit possession among the Thonga and Shangana people.[41] In her book she recounted several examples of her encounters with these phenomena. She believed it was her responsibility to "bring light into the darkness" of affected people. In her early years, she met a sick woman named Kinki, who according to Ingrid had not washed for seven years due to their custom that people should not wash when they were ill. Kinki had acted according to the instructions of the witch doctor and had put on different kinds of remedies that they thought would heal her legs and make her able to walk again. The remedies were bracelets and necklaces made of

36. "Lebombo," *SV* (November 1928) 7.
37. Chawner, *Nkosazana—Kongedatteren*, 129–44.
38. "Lebombo," *SV* (November 1928) 7.
39. Chawner, *Nkosazana—Kongedatteren*, 103–4.
40. Chawner, *Nkosazana—Kongedatteren*, 84–85.
41. Chawner, *Nkosazana—Kongedatteren*, 10–15, 39; "Lebombo," *SV* (November 1928) 7. One day she visited a place called Esibofwini, where people from the Shangana tribes lived. She explained that they were easy to recognize because of their many body tattoos and that it was especially common to have a tattoo of a snake coiled around their body. She believed this was a picture "of their spiritual condition."

grass and special types of local medicine. Around her neck, she had small containers with fat from a hippopotamus, a lion's tooth, powder made from the skin of a snake, intestines from a crocodile, crushed herbs, and roots from the forest. Around the waist, she had only some rags. According to Ingrid, the woman's hair had not been combed for years and she had vermin all over her body. When Ingrid told her to take off the magic remedies, she refused and answered that she did not dare to for fear of the witch doctor. Ingrid described how deep and paralyzing the fear of witch doctors and the power they could tap into could be.[42] Through her evangelistic efforts she wrote that Kinki was both converted and healed and that Kinki afterwards described her experience as having "been raised from the dead."[43] Ingrid clearly believed in the existence of evil spiritual forces and she also told the stories of four women characterized as spirit mediums.[44] She argued that demonic powers were torturing their victims and tried to help people and free them from the "lies of the kingdom of Satan."[45]

Ingrid's preaching was leading to some results and in February 1929 she reported that she had "prayed with 10 souls the last weeks, and more are beginning to see the difference between darkness and light."[46] She held meetings at her mission and the places she traveled to either by foot or in wagons pulled by oxen. The climate made traveling very harsh for Ingrid. It was very hot and during the rainy season also muddy. In addition, there were swarms of dangerous malaria-carrying mosquitos, large rivers to be crossed, and long distances to be walked. Travelling could also prove quite dangerous and she encountered crocodiles, elephants, lions, poisonous snakes, and hippopotamus on her journeys.[47] She was frequently sick with malaria and other diseases, and several times she was close to dying. The first report of her suffering from a serious illness came in 1929. A note published in the US read as follows: "Missionary Victor

---

42. Mbiti, *Introduction to African Religion*, 17.

43. Chawner, *Nkosazana—Kongedatteren*, 10–15.

44. Chawner, *Nkosazana—Kongedatteren*, 85.

45. Chawner, *Nkosazana—Kongedatteren*, 69, 85. Ingrid distinguished between witch doctors and herbal doctors.

46. "Namacha," *SV*, February 1929, 7. She also thanked the "friends" in West New York, New Jersey, for a check of twenty-four dollars.

47. Chawner, *Nkosazana—Kongedatteren*, 129-44; Chawner, "Mozambique," *PT* (February 1, 1941) 8; "Evangelizing in Mozambique," *PT* (April 15, 1943) 11; "Itinerating in Mozambique," *PT* (January 1943) 10; "A Miraculous Deliverance," *PT* (October 15, 1952) 9.

Svedin in South Africa writes that Ingrid Lökken has been seriously ill, and they thought she would die. For five days she lay unconscious and showed no sign of life, but the Lord gave victory and raised her up."[48] Ingrid had suffered from both malaria and Black Water Fever and was close to death. Slowly she started to recover, and she continued her work in Mozambique, though for a while with less strength.[49]

By 1930 Ingrid had relocated to the capital of the country, Lourenco Marques (now Maputo). There she established her new main mission station where she started holding meetings and established a school.[50] Ingrid organized the school day quite similar to that of her own childhood. She started with a hymn and prayer and continued with teaching the alphabet, reading, writing, and mathematics. She taught Bible stories and the children memorized Bible verses. The favorite activity was singing and school days ended with prayer. Ingrid also taught young girls to sew and do crocheting.[51] School activities were essential for the foundation and the growth of the work, and she hoped several of the students would become evangelists.[52] Though Ingrid worked primarily among the Thongan people in Lourenco Marques she also became concerned for the souls of the other people groups in the city:

> There is much to do here. There are 30,000 natives and several thousand Chinese and Indians in this place who have immigrated. But we cannot reach these Chinese and Indians because we do not know their languages and they are completely by themselves. But there are also 10,000 Portuguese here and among them there is not a single Christian.[53]

She hoped "God would send someone to start a work" among these people. From 1927 to 1930 she worked alone as a missionary, but accompanied by a few Mozambican evangelists.

---

48. "Från Skilda Håll," *SV* (October 1929) 8.

49. "Från Portuguese East Africa," *SV* (February 1930) 7. Her address was then Rua Infante de Henrique 7 A.

50. Chawner, *Nkosazana—Kongedatteren*, 105–6.

51. Chawner, *Nkosazana—Kongedatteren*, 105–6.

52. Chawner, *Nkosazana—Kongedatteren*, 109.

53. "Från Portuguese East Africa," *SV* (February 1930) 7.

REINFORCEMENTS FROM ABROAD

By early 1930, Ingrid reported that they had a good meeting hall at the mission and eight outstations along the railway. They were planning to send evangelists to new places. According to Ingrid, they had recently established outstations in Tamango and in Loes Luck, where they had built small churches solely on funds raised by the natives. In one of the places, they held revival meetings where several had been baptized in the Spirit.[54] On May 8, 1930, Ingrid welcomed the first Pentecostal missionary to join her work in Mozambique. This was Hilda Johnson (Johanson) from Värmland, Sweden, who was sent out from Grand Crossing Assembly in Chicago. She rejoiced in this but also repeatedly asked and prayed that more missionaries would soon come since they were only "two Pentecostal missionaries among Mozambique's four million people."[55] Ingrid explained that Johnson as soon as she arrived started studying Portuguese to pass the required government exam to do mission work in the country. Ingrid had passed the exam and was helping her new coworker to prepare for it.[56]

A few months later the two women sent what was the first explicit appeal for more funding for their mission in Mozambique to Scandinavian Pentecostals in America. They hoped for funding for two native evangelists and explained the special circumstances that led to this request. Across the border, in Transvaal, there were several missions that successfully evangelized among the natives from Mozambique who crossed the border to find work.[57] One of these missions was the Emmanuel Mission in Nelspruit, which was led by Mr. and Mrs. H. C. Phillips, missionaries from the Elim church in England. Ingrid Løkken had previously spent some time at this mission and had a good relationship with the missionaries and native evangelists there.[58] According to Løkken, the natives in Mozambique were allowed to stay in Transvaal to work for long periods before 1930 and several had converted and become Pentecostals during their stay. Several of these had become evangelists and received a salary

---

54. "Lourenco Marques," *SV* (April 1930) 7. She writes that it was difficult to end the meetings, but they had to comply with a law that demanded that all the natives in cities be in their homes by 10 PM.

55. "Portuguese East Africa," *SV* (July 1930) 7; "Lourenco Marques," *SV* (September 1930) 6–7; "Lourenco Marques," *SV* (November 1930) 7.

56. "Lourenco Marques," *SV* (September 1930) 6–7.

57. "Lourenco Marques," *SV* (November 1930) 7.

58. "Fra Afrika," *KS* (May 10, 1930) 5–6.

from the missions. In 1930, a new "passport law" was passed that only permitted natives from Mozambique to stay in Transvaal for six months at a time on special visas. Many were thus forced to return to Mozambique, and among these were believers and "precious, Spirit-baptized, evangelists."[59] These evangelists lacked funding and struggled in poverty, but they still felt called to evangelize.

Six such evangelists had arrived or were about to arrive in Lourenco Marques to join Løkken's mission. However, because of the Great Depression, and the difficult economic situation in the US, she wrote that she did not dare to ask for funding for all of them. They selected two older male evangelists, who had been Pentecostals for many years, and requested salaries for them so they could work with the two women at the mission.[60] One of them was Paulo Kossa, who became especially important for Ingrid and the expansion of the Assemblies of God in Mozambique. According to Ingrid, he "had been saved and baptized in a Pentecostal mission in Johannesburg" around 1910 and was later baptized in the Spirit.[61] Kossa had then worked mostly with missionaries in Transvaal who highly recommended him for his character and as an effective evangelist. It seems he had also to some extent evangelized in Mozambique during the 1920s.[62] The women wrote that they needed more help at the mission and that it would be of great aid if they could pay salaries for two evangelists, and especially for Kossa.[63] Their petition seems to have been successful because offerings for native evangelists started to be sent the very next month.[64] Ingrid later reported that she traveled with several male evangelists on her evangelistic tours in the country. The sudden return of native Pentecostals to Mozambique undoubtedly was beneficial for the growth of the Pentecostal movement in the country and for Ingrid's mission which now had welcomed six new experienced evangelists.

Ingrid's main mission station was now in Lourenco Marques but she tried to spend as much time as possible traveling with evangelists

---

59 "Lourenco Marques," *SV* (November 1930) 7.

60. "Lourenco Marques," *SV* (November 1930) 7.

61. "Lourenco Marques," *SV* (June 1931) 7.

62. "Lourenco Marques," *SV* (June 1931) 7; Upton, *Miracle of Mozambique*, 94.

63. "Lourenco Marques," *SV* (November 1930) 7. They requested fifteen dollars a month for each evangelist.

64. "Från Skilda Håll," *SV* (December 1930) 8; "Från Skilda Håll," *SV* (January 1931) 8; "Från Skilda Håll," *SV* (February 1931) 8;"Från Skilda Håll," *SV* (June 1931) 8; "Från Skilda Håll," *SV* (July 1931) 8.

to visit groups of believers in the region and to preach in new places. She was hesitant to call the places "outstations" because they only had a grass or mud hut, and a new law required them to build brick houses for the stations.[65] On one of her trips in 1930 she visited several groups where people asked her to baptize them. In one place there were nine that wanted to be baptized, and they were very disappointed when she said she could not do it. They insisted and only accepted her refusal when she said she was too exhausted to do it and promised that the next time she visited, they would be baptized. Ingrid clearly believed she could not baptize them because she was a woman, and wrote that she did not know how she would be able to get a male missionary in Transvaal to accompany her the next time and thus keep her promise. Everyone was busy with their own mission work, and it meant walking two hundred kilometers through burning hot sand.[66] It is not clear from her letter whether the natives disagreed with her view that women should not baptize or if she did not tell them that this was her real reason for refusing to do so. Her problem was solved when they started receiving funding for Paulo Kossa, who could perform the baptisms.[67]

After the arrival of more coworkers at the mission, Ingrid started to hold meetings in Portuguese in Lourenco Marques. She wrote the following about these early meetings:

> It was quite challenging in the beginning because I had never heard a sermon or a prayer in this language, but God helped me wonderfully. There are some that are interested. Pray that God will bring them to an understanding of salvation. I find it more difficult to work among the Portuguese than the natives, they are more informed, but, oh, such fanatic Catholics.[68]

Ingrid felt that her life mission was in Lourenco Marques and the surrounding region, and that this was the place God had called her to. But her coworker Hilda Johnson felt called to establish a mission further to the north. Ingrid was in one sense glad about this because she had long prayed that a missionary would go to that region, but they agreed that

---

65. "Lourenco Marques," *SV* (January 1931) 7.
66. "Lourenco Marques," *SV* (January 1931) 7.
67. "Mocambique," *SV* (December 1931) 6.
68. "Lourenco Marques," *SV* (June 1931) 7.

Hilda should wait until more missionaries came to help Ingrid at the mission.[69]

REGISTERING "THE ASSEMBLIES OF GOD"

Though Ingrid was clearly doing mission work in Mozambique from 1927, preaching and praying for people and attending to various needs, the government had still not officially given her permission to start a Pentecostal mission in the country. She continued to apply for government approval, but it was proving very difficult to obtain. Her plan was to register the mission as "Scandinavian Assemblies of God."[70] Austin Chawner and Upton state that Ingrid went once or twice a week to a government office for four years to petition an official authorization to conduct mission work in the country.[71] According to Chawner, it was very difficult to get permission to do mission work in Mozambique because:

> The officials regard Missionaries as the political agents of foreign governments and fear that under the guise of religious teaching, they will spread foreign political propaganda. Much earnest effort has been made by various Missionaries to prove that they are only messengers of the Gospel and not agents of any foreign government, but very few have gained permission to work.[72]

If this was indeed the reason for the government's restrictions, then the fact that Ingrid was a woman from Norway may have been one of the reasons she was able to stay so long in Mozambique and do mission work without official approval from the government. In 1930 she wrote:

> I have been alone here until now and it is not easy to start work in a new country, especially when one is dealing with a Catholic government. Several missions have had to give up their work here lately. It is especially Englishmen and Americans they are opposed to, so I have often been happy that I am Scandinavian.[73]

Being both Norwegian and female would have made it less likely that she was a threat and was spreading "foreign political propaganda." Austin

---

69. "Lourenco Marques," *SV* (August 1931) 7–8.
70. "Från Portuguese East Africa," *SV* (February 1930) 7.
71. Chawner, *Have You Heard about Mozambique?*, 11; Upton, *Miracle of Mozambique*, 93; "Mocambique," *SV* (December 1931) 6.
72. Chawner, *Have You Heard about Mozambique?*, 10.
73. "Lourenco Marques," *SV* (February 1930) 6–7.

Chawner wrote that Ingrid had an "undaunted determination" to receive permission to establish a mission.[74] Among other activities, she studied Portuguese intensively for six months to pass a difficult examination required by the government. She continued preaching in several places in Mozambique knowing that the government could deport her at any time.[75] In July 1931 the government officially recognized and approved Ingrid's mission.[76] She said she had worked two years to accomplish this and wrote: "We are so incredibly grateful that the Portuguese treat us so well compared to other missions, some of which had tried for more than 10 years to be approved but without success."[77] Ingrid registered the mission work as "Assemblies of God." According to Upton, this was a wise decision since it made it possible for more Pentecostal missionaries to enter the country and do mission work.[78]

With the government's approval, Ingrid could now continue her mission work and the expansion into new areas with even more confidence. She continued to visit the outstations and to plan for new places to preach. It seems around this time that she acquired a motorcycle which she called her "Steel Horse."[79] In Swaziland they had used horses, and now she had something in Mozambique that enabled her to travel much faster and farther than before. However, riding a motorcycle was not without its challenges. On one occasion she planned to go eighty-five kilometers with the motorcycle.[80] She calculated that she would spend seven hours to reach her destination, but it took her more than two days to get there. She experienced all kinds of trouble with the cycle on this trip. The engine had taken in water after sliding into a river, and she needed to carry the motorcycle over rocky stones to avoid punctures. She also ran out of petrol. In addition to this, she lacked food and drinking water, met dangerous buffaloes, and made an unscheduled stop to preach to people she encountered on her way who had run away from their village. However,

---

74. Chawner, *Have You Heard about Mozambique?*, 11; Upton, "Austin Chawner Called Home," undated manuscript, PAOC historical archive, 3.

75. Chawner, *Have You Heard about Mozambique?*, 11; Upton, "Austin Chawner Called Home," undated manuscript, PAOC historical archive, 3. Upton accredits her with first having established the Pentecostal work in Mozambique in 1926.

76. "Mocambique," *SV* (December 1931) 6.

77. "Mocambique," *SV* (December 1931) 6.

78. Upton, *Miracle of Mozambique*, 93.

79. Chawner, *Nkosazana—Kongedatteren*, 53–66.

80. Chawner, *Nkosazana—Kongedatteren*, 53–66.

when she finally reached her destination, she concluded that the joy she saw in the faces of the Christian friends in the small church was worth all her hardships.[81] Their mission work continued to grow slowly. In 1931 they opened two new outstations and according to Ingrid, many were converted there, and several were baptized in the Spirit.[82]

FINANCIAL AND HEALTH STRUGGLES

In 1931 Ingrid Løkken wrote a letter to A. A. Holmgren at *Sanningens Vittne* that was quite desperate. A lady in the US who had taken upon her to fund the evangelist Paulo Kossa, had become sick and could not do so anymore. They had not received funds to pay him, and Ingrid received so little funding for herself that she could not cover the extra expense. She said that she could live frugally but that the evangelists needed money for food, rent, clothes and taxes. Ingrid explained that "Paulus Kossa is indispensable to us because we have no white brother here on this field so the consequence is that brother Kossa has to perform baptisms and other things where a brother has to partake."[83] She further added that they had nine evangelists at their station but only one of them was receiving a salary. Ingrid and Hilda Johnsen supported him but with great difficulty. They had seven outstations and it was costly to travel to visit these.[84] Ingrid said she understood there was a worldwide financial crisis but pleaded that Holmgren and the readers would not forget about them in Mozambique. All the money she received went to food, rent, and paying for meeting halls, and even by managing their income frugally they did not have enough to help the evangelist. Holmgren recommended that someone help "sister L." with the fifteen dollars a month she was asking for.[85] Reports in the subsequent issues show that people sent offerings to help cover Kossa's salary.

Ingrid Løkken had several times suffered malaria and other debilitating deceases, but in February 1932 reports came that she was gravely ill and hospitalized in Johannesburg, South Africa. Holmgren said they had not heard from her in a while and asked the "friends" to pray for

---

81. Chawner, *Nkosazana—Kongedatteren*, 53–66.
82. "Mocambique," *SV* (December 1931) 6.
83. "Mocambique," *SV* (December 1931) 6.
84. "Mocambique," *SV* (December 1931) 6.
85. "Mocambique," *SV* (December 1931) 6.

her healing.[86] By May 1932 the periodical published a letter from Ingrid in Johannesburg where she said she was still very sick and was having financial difficulties due to her hospitalization. Even though she had been in the "section for the poor" of the hospital, which was supposed to be free of charge, she had now received a bill for 63 sterling pounds.[87] At the time of writing she was at a "convalescent home" and the doctors said she could not return to Mozambique for at least three months. The doctors had tapped fifty-six ounces of water from her lungs and said she had tuberculosis. Ingrid wrote that, "I am certain God will heal me. The doctors say there is nothing more they can do for me, but nothing is impossible for God."[88] Amid the distress, she received letters from the evangelists in Mozambique that "God was blessing the work" and that people were being Spirit baptized. Several new converts wished to be baptized, and it seems the evangelists were asking Ingrid for permission to do so. She was hesitant to give them this permission while she was away because: "We must check if the young girls are sold or not before they can be baptized, and if the young men have bought more than one girl. I long to be with them again, they are not mature enough to be left alone. Pray for my healing."[89]

A few months later, Ingrid was back at the mission in Lourenco Marques, though still weak.[90] She was then spending most of her time organizing the work to build small houses at the station. One building was a prayer room, and they built a couple of small cement houses for the missionaries. When they could afford to build something better they planned to pass the houses on to the native evangelists. Ingrid said that they were now living in shanty sheds made of corrugated tin, but that she dared not live through another rainy season in these living conditions after having been so sick.[91] She made the cement blocks to build with herself, though likely with some aid.[92]

---

86. "Från Skilda Håll," *SV* (February 1932) 8. The report came from missionary Arne Høyland in South Africa.

87. "Lourenco Marques," *SV* (May 1932) 8. This was significantly more than her annual pay of forty pounds from *Evangeliesalen*.

88. "Lourenco Marques," *SV* (May 1932) 8.

89. "Lourenco Marques," *SV* (May 1932) 8.

90. "Lourenco Marques," *SV* (October 1932) 3. She said her x-ray showed that one lung was smaller than the other and asked the readers to pray for her healing.

91. "Lourenco Marques," *SV* (October 1932) 3.

92. "Lourenco Marques," *SV* (June 1935) 7.

Reflecting on the year 1932, Ingrid said it had been "a difficult year with disease and trials, but therefore we are so much more grateful to God that he has led us through to victories."[93] People were still being converted and baptized in the Spirit at the outstations, but she wished there would have been more results of their work and said they needed a large revival in East Africa. Ingrid wrote that they had been able to open a new main station in Lourenco Marques. There they had had a large room they could use as a church and a school, and housing for "white and for the natives, all under one roof."[94] They had also been able to establish an outstation in a new place, called Kamakapa, where about eighty to ninety people attended their meetings.[95] In 1934 Ingrid's health was still weak. She reported that their work was advancing, "but not as fast as we wished it would."[96] In Lourenco Marques several young men became Christians after attending their evening school. Five women, one of which had been a witch doctor, had also converted. Ingrid wrote that the witch doctor "the Sunday after she accepted God came with all her gods, medicine and magical items and after the meeting we let the whole lot go up in flames."[97]

1934: A YEAR OF REINFORCEMENTS AND MARRIAGE

In 1934 two new missionaries from Norway joined Ingrid's missions in Lourenco Marques. The women were Martha Nielsen and Elisabeth Pedersen, and they were also sent out from the church *Evangeliesalen* in Oslo.[98] It was a great relief for Ingrid to have two new missionaries with whom to share the workload. Nielsen and Pedersen soon took over the school, the Sunday school work, and the orphanage at the main mission station. This meant that Ingrid was now free to travel much more with the evangelists than before and she could help to establish outstations further away.[99] One new outpost was about two hundred miles from Lourenco Marques, and to get there they had to cross the great Limpopo River.

93. "Lourenco Marques," *SV* (March 1933) 7–8.
94. "Lourenco Marques," *SV* (March 1933) 7–8.
95. "Lourenco Marques," *SV* (March 1933) 7–8. Ingrid also reported that a girl who was bitten by a mamba snake had been healed.
96. "Lourenco Marques," *SV* (January 1935) 6.
97. "Lourenco Marques," *SV* (January 1935) 6.
98. Nilsen, *Modne marker*, 49.
99. "Lourenco Marques," *SV* (January 1935) 6.

To get to another new outpost, they crossed the river Rio do Espiritu Santo, traveled seventy kilometers sitting on benches in a truck, and then walked the rest of the distance. They gathered around fifty people for their meetings and then stayed overnight sleeping on hard dirt floors. On their way back the riverboat ran out of gas in the middle of the river and started drifting and taking in water. People on board panicked but they were eventually rescued by another riverboat and arrived safely. That night Ingrid preached about how "dangerous it was to lose one's power halfway" and two young men were converted.[100]

The same year that Nielsen and Pedersen arrived, Ingrid decided to marry the Canadian Pentecostal missionary Austin Chawner. He was the son of the missionary couple Emma and Charles Chawner, and he was a young boy when he first came to South Africa in 1909.[101] As a young man he also felt a calling to be a missionary and specifically to Mozambique.[102] In 1927 Austin married his first wife, Carrie Slaybaugh, whom he had met at Bible school. The young couple traveled to Transvaal Province in preparation for entering Mozambique.[103] There he spent time studying Portuguese and Thonga and visiting Mozambique on a temporary visa while waiting and hoping for the government's permission to establish a mission in the country. During this period, he saw that thousands of Thongas had moved into the Northern Transvaal Province. When he was not granted a work permit in Mozambique he decided to establish a mission among the Thonga in Shingwedzi in Northern Transvaal.[104] Austin's

---

100. "Lourenco Marques," SV (January 1935) 6.

101. Andersson, *Spreading Fires*, 170; "En Route for Africa," *PT* (January 1924) 6; "A Great Man Hath Fallen in Israel," *PT* (March 15, 1949) 7, 14; "En Route for Africa," *PT* (January 1924) 6; "Sailing for Africa," *PT* (November 1925) 9; Chawner, "A Cry from the Dark Continent," *The Promise* (February 1909) 4–5; Chawner and Chawner, *Called to Zululand*, 23. Ingrid Løkken Chawner demonstrated that she greatly admired her father-in-law in her note on his passing.

102. "En Route for Africa," *PT* (January 1924) 6. He highlighted the great need in the country and that in 1924 there was no Pentecostal missionary there.

103. "Missionary Wedding," *PT* (March 1927) 2. They knew each other from studying at the Bethel Bible School in 1925; "Bethel Bible School Principal and Graduates, 1925," *Full Gospel Missionary Herald* (July 1925) 1; "Called Into His Vineyard," *PT* (April 1927) 4.

104. "News from Portuguese East Africa," *PT* (April 1927) 4; Upton, *Miracle of Mozambique*, 51–52; Austin Chawner, "A Contrast," four-page manuscript from The PAOC historical archive, undated. In 1928 Austin Chawner partnered with the English civil engineer, Hubert Phillips, to start a printing press to reach the Thongas. The following year they started printing pamphlets, songbooks, tracts, and booklets. This was the beginning of Emmanuel Press which in the coming years would provide evangelistic literature all over Africa.

wife, Carrie, became very ill from malaria and after just two years on the mission field she passed away on March 23, 1929.[105] Losing his wife after just a little more than two years of marriage was very difficult for Austin.

Sometime after the loss of his wife Austin and Ingrid met at a missionary conference in Basutoland (in present-day Lesotho).[106] After this, Ingrid invited him to come to her mission in Lourenco Marques to teach at a Bible conference. Austin Chawner accepted the invitation and left Shingwedzi on June 28, 1933. During the Bible conference four meetings were held every Sunday as well as devotional meetings every morning, a Bible class for workers later in the day and an evangelistic meeting in the evening. According to Upton, the Mozambican evangelists were delighted by Austin's teaching.[107] After the conference ended Austin (and his missionary friend Andersson) accompanied Ingrid together with Mozambican evangelists for a trip to visit outstations. They endured some of the hardships Ingrid had suffered many times before. According to Upton, the native evangelists told Ingrid that they wanted Austin Chawner to stay at Lourenco Marquez. Ingrid replied: "Very well, then I can go to another place. No, they said,—we would like you to stay too."[108] Ingrid and Austin felt God was leading them to get married and shortly after they announced their engagement. They were married on December 31, 1934, while at a missionary conference in South Africa.[109] Austin Chawner expressed that he was grateful for marrying someone who was such an experienced and skilled missionary.[110]

At the time of their marriage, Ingrid had been in Africa for seven years without a furlough and Austin for ten years.[111] Ingrid wrote that

---

105. "Mr. and Mrs. Austin Chawner," one-page manuscript without author or date at PAOC historical archive; "In Memoriam," *PT* (April 1929) 2; "Editorial," *PT* (May 1929) 14; "Events in the Life of C. Austin Chawner," unpublished manuscript of two pages, PAOC historical archive.

106. Upton, *Miracle of Mozambique*, 85.

107. Upton, *Miracle of Mozambique*, 94–96.

108. Upton, *Miracle of Mozambique*, 98–99; Upton, "Grace of God in Mozambique," *PT* (June 1, 1948) 10.

109. Upton, *Miracle of Mozambique*, 100; "Från Skilda Håll," *SV* (January 1935) 8.

110. In a letter to a friend, Rev. A.G. Ward, he underlined that she was an experienced missionary, having undergone hardships and trials. She was fluent in English, Portuguese, Zulu, and Thonga, and of course Norwegian. She knew the culture and the customs of the Thonga people and she had been on many travels to Mozambique, Swaziland, and Northern Transvaal. Upton, *Miracle of Mozambique*, 99–100.

111. "Från Skilda Håll," *SV* (January 1935) 8.

they hoped to come home soon because they were both exhausted after their long terms in the harsh climate. They now had the responsibility for both Ingrid's station in Lourenco Marques and Austin's station in Shingwedzi and a total of twenty outstations. The two Norwegian missionaries, Pedersen and Nielsen, were in charge of the Lourenco Marques station while they were abroad, but they could not leave until someone took care of the mission in Shingwedzi as well. Ingrid said it was hard for them to leave their work, but they felt they had to do so to recover their health.[112]

In the Fall of 1935, Ingrid and Austin arrived in New York, where they stayed three weeks before they continued to Canada. By then several of Ingrid's siblings as well as her mother had immigrated to the US and they stayed with Ingrid's mother in Brooklyn. She wrote in a letter from there, "It feels so good to be home again," indicating that she thought of America as her home.[113] Ingrid Løkken Chawner was by then "well known among the Scandinavian Pentecostals" in the US and Canada.[114] When she visited the Scandinavian Pentecostals in Westerose, Canada, her visit drew crowds to the meetings.[115] Ingrid had had very weak health for over a year, and she and her husband thought her weakness was due to exhaustion, the climate, and various serious attacks of disease in Mozambique.[116] In March 1936, she was so ill that she was hospitalized while in Brooklyn. There they discovered she had abdominal tumors. She was in critical condition and needed surgery to remove them. Austin said she could have passed away, but the operation was successful, and she slowly recovered.[117] A year later, they were able to leave America and return to Africa, stopping by Norway and Sweden on their way back.[118]

---

112. They tried to improve the buildings at Lourenco Marques before they left, but they did not have any money so they took up a loan to buy the basic materials. At the main mission in Lourenco Marques, they arranged Bible weeks and conferences for the evangelists before they left and were able to build a new meeting hall with a loan. Ingrid and Austin also took a tour to visit all the outstations before they left for furlough to Scandinavia and North America. "Lourenco Marques," *SV* (June 1935) 7.

113. "Brooklyn, N.Y.," *SV* (October 1935) 7.

114. "Missionärsparet C. Austin Chawner," *SV* (November 1935) 5.

115. She held three meetings there. "Från Skilda Håll," *SV* (January 1936) 7; "Opprop!," *SV* (February 1936) 6; "Från Skilda Håll" *SV* (January 1936) 7.

116. "Från Skilda Håll," (March 1937) 8.

117. "Brooklyn, N.Y.," *SV* (April 1936) 6; "Från Skilda Håll," *SV* (June 1936) 6.

118. "Lourenco Marques," *SV* (December 1937) 6.

MINISTRY WITH AUSTIN CHAWNER

In the Fall of 1937, the Chawners were back at their mission in Lourenco Marques. There they encountered increasing difficulties and restrictions from the government, even though Ingrid had received formal approval to establish her mission and "The Assemblies of God" six years earlier. Ingrid wrote: "The difficulties regarding the work is almost unbearable. The authorities will not let us have meetings or school in our present building and it seems imperative for the work's sake that we get another church in which to gather the people."[119] They were conducting meetings on their verandah, but this was too small and the rainy season was soon coming. Having meetings outdoors was a constant worry due to the "millions of malaria-carrying mosquitos swarming around us."[120] However, she said several were being saved and that they believed "God is going to give us a real revival here before the day comes that the missionaries are chased back to their home countries again. And it looks as if that day is not very far off."[121]

When the Chawners returned they soon felt overwhelmed by the responsibility of two mission stations and all the twenty outstations.[122] The mission stations in Lourenco Marques and Shingwedzi were four hundred miles apart, and they were constantly traveling back and forth. Their health made it even more difficult as Ingrid continued to be weaker than she had been in her first years in the country, and Austin had also been very ill with malaria. Therefore, their joy and relief were great when a young couple from Canada came in May 1938 to take over Austin Chawner's mission in Shingwedzi. Thus they could stay at the mission *Kampfumu* in Lourenco Marques. Ingrid praised the native evangelists connected to their mission and wrote, "I wish you could see all these great young men that God has saved and baptized with his Spirit. They go out one after the other and start to testify about God."[123]

Now that there were new Canadian missionaries in charge of Shingwedzi, and Martha Nielsen and Elisabeth Pedersen were still in Lourenco Marques, Ingrid and Austin dedicated much more time to

---

119. "Lourenco Marques," *SV* (December 1937) 6.
120. "Lourenco Marques," *SV* (June 1938) 6.
121. "Lourenco Marques," *SV* (December 1937) 6.
122. "Lourenco Marques," *SV* (June 1938) 6. Chawner, *Have You Heard about Mozambique?*, 17–19.
123. "Lourenco Marques," *SV* (June 1938) 6.

itinerant ministry. They were able to get a car, which made travelling much easier, though still challenging. Together with other evangelists, they toured large parts of Mozambique to visit the outstations, or "Gospel lighthouses," as they now called them, and to establish new communities of believers. Austin wrote that he wished they could have two missionaries for each of the one hundred and ten administrative districts in Mozambique, but since this was not possible, they took it upon themselves to travel to as many of these districts as possible.[124] Ingrid and Austin believed the native evangelists were the best at preaching the gospel and both had the training of evangelists and establishment of new outstations as their main strategy for expansion.[125] By 1943, they reported that there were seventy-seven native evangelists and pastors, 148 "native helpers," seventy-two assemblies, and seventy-one places with new believers. They counted a total of 2636 members of the churches and 1039 adhering children.[126]

As the Pentecostal mission work grew, they experienced increasing hostility from the Roman Catholic Church and the government both in Lourenco Marques and in the interior. In 1943 the authorities officially closed the mission. According to Upton, the orphanage and school were closed, the missionaries were forbidden to travel throughout the country, and the evangelists were no longer allowed to preach or sing Christian songs. Ingrid and Austin went through several interrogations, and several of the native evangelists were interrogated and imprisoned. The aim of the authorities was apparently to make the Pentecostal church disappear.[127] On one occasion, in October 1943, Ingrid was interrogated for two and a half hours.[128] She was the main target of the interrogations since she was the one who obtained the certificate of authorisation to start the Assemblies of God in Mozambique. One policeman argued she had only been given permission to run an orphanage, but she was able to demonstrate that this was not the case. Austin was also questioned in detail concerning the activities of the mission. According to Upton, this

124. Chawner, *Have You Heard about Mozambique?;* "Latest Word from Mrs. Chawner," *PT* (February 1 1941) 8; "Evangelizing in Mozambique," *PT* (April 15, 1943); "Itinerating in Mozambique," *PT* (January 1943) 10; "A Fruitful Year in Mozambique," *PT* (June 1, 1942) 10.

125. "Aggressive Evangelism and Spontaneous Expansion in Mozambique," *PT* (September 15, 1943) 10–11; Upton, *Miracle of Mozambique*, 111–12.

126. "Challenge of Mozambique," *PT* (April 15, 1945) 10–11.

127. Upton, *Miracle of Mozambique*, 129.

128. Upton, *Miracle of Mozambique*, 130.

was the beginning of a systematic opposition with lying, limitations, false accusations, and interrogations.[129]

After the mission was officially closed in 1943 Austin and Ingrid did everything possible to restore the authorization, but they did not succeed.[130] The opposition against the Pentecostal movement was strong and the missionaries were accused of spreading anti-Portuguese propaganda among the Africans. Years of uncertainty concerning their residential permits followed and the immigration authorities informed them that in case they crossed the border for any reason, their residential permits would be cancelled.[131] This made them feel like prisoners in the country and since they had missionary responsibilities in other parts of Africa they would have to leave for certain periods. The Chawners were informed that if they lost their residential permits they could apply to visit the country and stay for ninety days at a time. This became their practice and they did not encounter problems in coming and going.[132]

After Ingrid and Austin left Mozambique as their permanent basis for mission work, they welcomed the possibility of having children. They did not feel they had this opportunity in Mozambique since their demanding mission activities, and frequent traveling in the interior, had not been conducive to family life. Now the situation was different and Ingrid and Austin adopted two children who needed a home. The children were Marilyn and Stanley and they soon learned to speak both Portuguese and Thonga languages fluently. Ingrid and Austin also stepped into new ministries and new responsibilities within the Pentecostal work in South Africa.

After many years of ministry in Africa Austin Chawner passed away in a tragic accident in 1963 while they were staying in Durban. On the evening of October 20, Austin crossed the road to park his car in the hotel garage when he was run over by another car. Ingrid received the news of his passing in the morning the following day.[133] At least a thousand people attended the funeral service to express their grief and appreciation

---

129. Upton, *Miracle of Mozambique*, 130–32; Juul, *Til jordens ender*, 194–95.

130. "Challenge of Mozambique," *PT* (April 15, 1945) 10–11.

131. Upton, *Miracle of Mozambique*, 179.

132. Upton, *Miracle of Mozambique*, 179.

133. Upton, "Austin Chawner Called Home," undated manuscript, PAOC historical archive, 1; Upton, *Miracle of Mozambique*, 198.

for Austin Chawner. One person present stated, "Never before has there been such a multiracial crowd gathered in a town in South Africa."[134]

Ingrid Løkken Chawner continued her life and ministry in Africa after this and frequently visited Mozambique. In the 1970s she said there was a great revival in the country and she rejoiced in how much the movement had grown. According to Upton, she said: "Here in Mozambique we are seeing revival as never before. I remember the beginning of the work when we had seven people out to a Sunday service. Now we have well over one thousand every Sunday, in one assembly, not to speak about all the others, and I'm still here to see it!"[135] On December 8, 1976, Ingrid Løkken Chawner passed away while in South Africa. She was buried next to her husband Austin in Nelspruit.

INGRID LØKKEN CHAWNER AS AN "UNKNOWN" NORWEGIAN MISSIONARY

Even though the impact of Ingrid Løkken Chawner's pioneer work in Mozambique was significant, little has been written about her life and she has been a relatively unknown missionary.[136] There are several likely reasons for this. The first is that she was not sent out as a missionary with the Norwegian Pentecostal missions organization NFEH, established in 1915. Ingrid had support from her local church, *Evangeliesalen*, and went as a missionary "in faith" that God would provide. This may have been by choice or because she was not taken up as a missionary by the organization. By 1922 the NFEH was already struggling to provide for their missionaries and therefore accepted very few new candidates. Thus, many Norwegian Pentecostal missionaries went out supported by friends and local churches or were self-financed.[137] The early Pentecostals in Norway were divided as to whether there should exist a sending organization or whether missionaries should be "faith missionaries."[138] Ingrid seems to have had the conviction that one should go in faith and not belong to

---

134. Upton, "Austin Chawner Called Home," undated manuscript, PAOC historical archive, 1. In January 1964 Ingrid went to Mozambique for a memorial service for her husband. There was a service both in Lourenco Marques and in one of the districts in the interior.

135. Upton, *Miracle of Mozambique*, 215.

136. "Pinsevennenes ukjente heltinne," *KS* (April 23, 2017) 20–21.

137. "Fra Afrika," *KS* (May 10, 1930) 5–6.

138. See Bundy, *Visions of Apostolic Missions*.

organizations. She was happy that T. B. Barratt decided to dissolve the NFEH in 1929.[139] In her letter to Laura Barratt concerning this she writes that she and other missionaries that were not part of the organization always felt that they were "on the outside." She welcomed the change and thought everyone should be sent by local churches. All the Norwegian Pentecostal missionaries would then be on the same standing.[140] The Barratts did not know about Ingrid until they met in Brooklyn in 1927/1928.[141] After the NFEH was dissolved Ingrid regularly reported to *Korsets Seier* and her name was now listed in the regular overviews of Norwegian missionaries on the field.

Another reason Ingrid may have been "forgotten" in Norwegian missions history is that her connections and support increasingly came from Scandinavian Pentecostals in the U.S. and Canada after 1927. Most of her reports from Mozambique were sent to Minneapolis and not to Oslo. Ingrid occasionally referred to the U.S. as her "homeland," and when several family members immigrated to the U.S., she started calling Brooklyn her "home."[142] Her plan to register the mission as "Scandinavian Assemblies of God" further demonstrates how strong her connection to the Scandinavian Pentecostals in America had become.[143] However, as time passed and most Scandinavian-American descendants stopped using the Scandinavian languages, most primary sources of her life became relatively inaccessible to American scholars. Ingrid was one of many Scandinavian missionaries who were largely supported by their countrymen in the US and who did not return to Scandinavia. The consequence was that some missionaries were not considered either "Scandinavian" or "American" and were thus more likely to be left out of the historical accounts in both places. Ingrid Løkken Chawner is notably absent in overviews of Norwegian Pentecostal mission history.

Finally, Ingrid's situation also changed significantly when she married Austin Chawner. *Evangeliesalen* in Oslo had supported her financially from 1922 to 1934, but when she married a Canadian missionary, they considered it the responsibility of the Pentecostal Assemblies of Canada to provide for her.[144] However, even though *Evangeliesalen* as a

139. "Fra Afrika," *KS* (May 10, 1930) 5–6.
140. "Fra Afrika," *KS* (May 10, 1930) 5–6.
141. "Fra Afrika," *KS* (May 10, 1930) 5–6.
142. "Namacha," *SV* (February 1929) 7.
143. "Från Portuguese East Africa," *SV* (February 1930) 7.
144. Evangeliesalen, *Evangeliesalen 80 år*, 6.

church stopped their economic support for Ingrid, many of her friends continued to contribute to her ministry through the mission's treasurer Olaf Andersen.[145] The decision to stop her support may have been due to a lack of funds. The year she married Chawner, *Evangeliesalen* sent two more single female missionaries to Mozambique and it was likely difficult to provide for all of them. A solution was for the Canadians to send funds to Ingrid.[146] Significantly, Ingrid is referred to as "a Canadian missionary's Norwegian-born wife" in a book on the first fifty years of Norwegian Pentecostal foreign missions."[147] Ingrid did, however, maintain a connection to Norway by sending letters to *Korsets Seier* and by publishing two books. The Chawners also seem to have been well-received when they visited Scandinavia in 1938. They preached several places in Norway and Sweden and were also to speak of the mission work in Africa at the Filadelfia church in Stockholm.[148]

FINAL THOUGHTS

Ingrid Løkken Chawner has an important role in Pentecostal mission history but due to different circumstances her story has been largely unknown. She had connections to Pentecostals in Scandinavia, the US, and Canada, as well as on the mission field and is an example of how complex early Pentecostal mission history can be. In our opinion, Ingrid was also a woman who embodied two characteristics that were important for many early Pentecostal missionaries, namely courage and endurance. During her pioneer work in Mozambique, she endured many hardships with disease, climate, financial difficulties, and opposition from the government. Even though there were many dangers, she was committed to traveling in harsh conditions to evangelize and plant Christian communities in the country. Her "warrior mentality" might be best described in her following reflection on her hardships during World War II:

---

145. "Kvittering," *KS* (March 17, 1945) 71. "Pinsevennenes ukjente heltinne," *KS* (April 23, 2017) 20–21. Evangelina Casqueiro expressed great thanks to the Norwegian regional coordinator for Africa for donations to the work given by Ingrid's friends over many years.

146. "Letter from George Upton to Gunnerius Tollefsen." Dated August 15, 1949. Pentecostal Assemblies of Canada Historical Archive.

147. Juul, *Til jordens ender*, 195.

148. "Filadelfia, Stockholm, Sweden," *PT* (March 1938) 3.

After all, look at what our soldiers are doing for us and for their country during this terrible war. When I have seen pictures from the different fronts I marveled at what they are able to endure. So why should we grumble if we must go through a little hardship in our great fight against sin and the devil. We are soldiers for the Cross and we have a much greater reward coming to us than any earthly soldier has.[149]

BIBLIOGRAPHY

Alegre, Rakel Ystebø. "Trans-Atlantic Influence from Norway on Scandinavian-American Pentecostalism, 1906–1930." In *Revising Pentecostal History: Scandinavian-American Contributions to the Development of Pentecostalism*, edited by Rakel Ystebø Alegre et al. Eugene, OR: Pickwick: 2024.

Andersson, Allan. *Spreading Fires: The Missionary Nature of Early Pentecostalism*. Maryknoll, NY: Orbis Books, 2007.

Barratt, T. B. *Erindringer*. Oslo: Filadelfiaforlaget, 1941.

Birkeli, Fridtjov, et al. *Norsk misjonsleksikon I*. Stavanger: Nomi, 1965.

Bratlie, J. *Pinsevekkelsen gjennem 30 år 1907–1937*. Oslo: Filadelfiaforlaget, 1937.

Bundy, David. *Visions of Apostolic Mission: Scandinavian Pentecostal Mission to 1935*. Uppsala: Uppsala Universitet, 2009.

Chawner, Austin. *Have You Heard about Mozambique?* Toronto: Full Gospel, 1936.

Chawner, Charles, and Emma Chawner. *Called to Zululand: A Story of God's Leading*. Toronto: Self-published, n.d.

Chawner, Ingrid Løkken. *Nkosazana- Kongedatteren*. Oslo: Filadelfiaforlaget, 1935.

Evangeliesalen. *Menigheten i Evangeliesalen 80 år*. Oslo: Evangeliesalen, 1996.

Juul, Kåre. *Til jordens ender: Norsk pinsemisjon gjennom 50 år*. Oslo: Filadelfiaforlaget, 1960.

Mbiti, John S. *Introduction to African Religion*. Nairobi: Heinemann Educational, 1975.

Nilsen, Oddvar. *Modne marker: 90 års pinsemisjon i Sør- og Øst-Afrika*. Oslo: Rex, 2003.

———. *Og Herren virket med: Pinsebevegelsen gjennom 75 år*. Oslo: Filadelfiaforlaget, 1981.

———. *Ut i all verden: Pinsevennenes ytre misjon i 75 år*. Oslo: Filadelfiaforlaget, 1984.

Palmqvist, Efraim. *Fredrik Franson*. Oslo: Ansgar Forlag, 1948.

Ski, Martin, et al., eds. *Fram Til Urkristendommen: Pinsevekkelsen Gjennom 50 År. Volume I*. Oslo: Filadelfiaforlaget, 1956.

———. *Fram Til Urkristendommen: Pinsevekkelsen Gjennom 50 År. Volume II*. Oslo: Filadelfiaforlaget, 1957.

———. *Fram Til Urkristendommen: Pinsevekkelsen Gjennom 50 År. Volume III*. Oslo: Filadelfiaforlaget, 1959.

Tollefsen, Gunnerius, et al. *En såmann gikk ut til Swaziland*. Oslo: Filadelfiaforlaget, 1956.

Tollefsen, Gunnerius. *Men gud gav vekst: En pionermisjonær ser tilbake*. Oslo: Filadelfiaforlaget, 1963.

---

149. "Itinerating in Mozambique," *PT* (January 1943) 10.

Upton, George R. "Austin Chawner Called Home." Undated manuscript, PAOC historical archive.
———. *The Miracle of Mozambique.* Clearbrook, BC: A. Olfert & Sons, 1980.
Witzøe, Ivar M (ed.). *Norges Frie Evangeliske Hedningemisjon* (NFEH). *De aapne døre.* Oslo: N. F. E. Hedningemissions forlag, 1925.

Image #12. Alma Halse.

10

Alma Halse
Pentecostal Pioneer in Northern Norway[1]

Kristina Undheim

INTRODUCTION

Alma Hale (1907–1969) was born at the same time as the initial wave of the Pentecostal revival spread throughout Norway in 1907. Halse became one of the Pentecostal movement's foremost social reformers and evangelists in the north of Norway. Halse was a notable preacher and evangelist in the Norwegian Pentecostal movement. Although a second-generation Pentecostal, she had a personal relationship with both Laura and Thomas Ball Barratt. She was announced as one of the speakers together with T. B. Barratt at services arranged by the church in Filadelfia, Oslo, in 1938 and 1939.[2] In 1944, a part of a letter written by Halse to Laura Barrat was published in *Korsets Seier*.[3] In several services, she was coupled with renowned pastors like Sverre Orlien, Martin Ski, and Arne Dahl. Judging by the amount of newspaper notices, she spoke at services

---

1. All translations in this chapter are the author's own.

2. "Religiøse møter: Filadelfia," *Arbeiderbladet* (June 22, 1938) 13; "Religiøse møter: Filadelfia St. Olavs gt. 24," *Arbeiderbladet* (May 5, 1939) 17.

3. Halse, "Fra Barnehjemmet Betania, Alta," *KS* (1944), 58.

all over Norway, from 1933 onward. Her impact as a Pentecostal evangelist and spiritual leader cannot be overstated. Her life is particularly interesting from the viewpoint of Women's history as a minister in the Pentecostal movement. Furthermore, she received national recognition for her contributions as a social entrepreneur in Finnmark, a region in Northern Norway. To this day, the organization she established thrives. A pragmatic, bold faith characterized the life and ministry of Alma Halse. Her prominent stature within the Pentecostal movement calls for further investigation of her ministry.

This chapter aims to explore the cultural and spiritual environment in which Halse's ministry evolved. I will especially examine the influence of Pentecostal spirituality, but also the influence of other local traditions. Hence, this article is not an in-depth biography of Alma Halse. Rather, it attempts to give an account of Halse's religious context. Her conversion, her Spirit baptism, her crisis experiences, her call to ministry, her mission to the North, her cultural appropriation, and her overall ministry are events that will be considered and speak to a Pentecostal spirituality that evolved in a changing society. Some of these elements are chosen because they functioned as paradigm shifts in Halse's life and illustrate transitions from earlier religious practices. It is not within the scope of this article, therefore, to address everything that pertains to Pentecostal spirituality or even all the aspects of the decisive experiences I have chosen. Other elements combine to further illustrate how spirituality and practices mirrored cultural shifts.

METHOD

When considering the cultural and spiritual environment of Halse's ministry, I have looked at historical material of spiritual movements around the turn of the twentieth century, as well as the place of the Lutheran Church in Norwegian society. I have examined how these movements and currents influenced the life and ministry of Halse as recorded in biographies and newspaper articles. Halse was heavily influenced by Pentecostal spirituality. It has therefore been of the essence to carefully assess parts of this spirituality, especially how it views conversion, Spirit baptism, mission, and the calling experience.

In acknowledgement of the major Sami presence and culture in the areas where Halse ministered, a few considerations are appropriate.

Halse's passion for the Sami people coincided with a controversy connected to mission work directed toward the Sami population. I will take a closer look at this debate, as well as Halse's cultural appropriation of the Sami garment.

Finally, a few very short considerations will be made regarding Halse's ministry as evangelist, orphanage headmaster, and social entrepreneur. The scope of the paper does not permit a longer elaboration on the place and function of private initiatives like orphanages and nursing homes for older adults. Moreover, the article cannot address the history of abuse that occurred at Betania orphanage.[4] However, I will briefly mention it where it pertains to the ministry of Halse.

LITERATURE

For the historical portions of this article, I will utilize perspectives offered by theologians such as Steven Land, Russell P. Spittler, and Ulrik Josefsson, who have analyzed core aspects of Pentecostal spirituality. Moreover, I will interact with Jonathan Z. Smith who deliberates on a spatial understanding of religion.[5] Land argues for several distinct values and a "mutual conditioning" of accepted beliefs at the core of Pentecostal spirituality.[6] Right praise, or belief (orthodoxy), right practice (orthopraxy) and right affections (orthopathy) are of equal significance for Pentecostal spirituality.[7] Spittler, on the other hand, identifies five implicit values: "experience, orality, spontaneity, otherworldliness, and biblical authority." Spittler affirms personal experience as the place of true religion within Pentecostal and Charismatic spirituality. Hence, experiences that include emotions such as joy and sorrow are at the core of this spirituality.[8] Ulrik Josefsson, who based his research on the Swedish Pentecostal movement's initial years, offers unique insight as to how one understood the Spirit, Spirit baptism, and mission in the budding Scandinavian Pentecostal movement.[9] These three perspectives will be treated more thoroughly

---

4. Tjelle, *Omsorg og overgrep*. This book contains eyewitness accounts of abuse at the orphanage.

5. Smith, *Relating Religion*.

6. Land, *Pentecostal Spirituality*, 12; Spittler, "Spirituality, Pentecostal and Charismatic," 1097–99.

7. Land, *Pentecostal Spirituality*, 12.

8. Spittler, "Spirituality, Pentecostal and Charismatic," 1097.

9. Josefsson, *Liv och över nog*.

and considered along with the biographical material. Smith's depiction of spatial religion, or geographical locations where religion is lived and practiced, sheds light on Halse's encounter with other forms of Christian practices. His three spatial categories "here, there and anywhere" enable us to observe subtle changes in what geographical locations were recognized as acceptable when practicing religion. First, "here" includes domestic religion with a focus on the home. The second, "there," represents the public or state religious sphere with a focus on churches or temples. And finally, "anywhere," focuses on a diversity of religious practices between the two first spheres.[10] Church buildings, the domestic sphere, and "anywhere" as locations for religious practice or communication with the divine, have always had varying merit, depending on faith tradition.

A few biographical works, written for or by Pentecostals, are conferred in this article, such as John-Willy Rudolph's (1961) biography *Alma Halse—en kvinne i kamp* [Alma Halse—A Woman in Battle], and Jacob Tangstad's (1987) biography *Alma fra Alta* [Alma from Alta].[11] Both biographies were written from a Pentecostal perspective and had an evangelistic purpose. They were also meant to encourage the church. Their contribution to this article will be considered within the framework of Pentecostal spirituality. *Alma Halse—en kvinne i kamp* is not written from the first-person perspective, even though it is obvious that she was influential in the writing of the book. The second biography, "Alma fra Alta" contains more material written from a first-person perspective. It is based on interviews, speeches, letters, and conversations with Alma Halse recorded by her supporters. Though sincere, these biographies are a bit hagiographical. However, the accounts illustrate elements of Pentecostal spirituality, not only in what they emphasize but in how they are written. In addition, the eighty-year time span from when Halse experienced and retold her story, to the last biography was published, indicates an evolving spirituality. Hence, coupled with theory from the above-mentioned theologians, I will utilize these biographies to not only address parts of Halse's story but to trace changes in Pentecostal spirituality.

Relevant missiological questions will be considered when addressing Jon Todal's and Lovise Mienna Sjöberg's biography of Edvard Masoni, and Ingrid Eskilt's article *Misjonærkallet og kulturens subjektive vending* [The Missionary Call and Culture's Subjective Turn].[12] Although the in-

---

10. Smith, *Relating Religion*, 325.

11. Rudolph, *Alma Halse*; Tangstad, *Alma fra Alta*.

12. Todal and Sjöberg, *Edvard Masoni*; Eskilt, "Misjonærkallet og kulturens subjektive vending."

terviews in Eskilt's article stem from another free church tradition, there are some strong similarities in how the "veterans" (all born before the Second World War) describe their calling and how Halse's call to ministry is described in her biographies. Edvard Masoni was a Sami missionary to China who held a degree in both theology and medicine. The peak of Masoni's political engagement on behalf of the Sami people took place a couple of decades before Alma Halse moved to Finnmark. However, through Masoni, Todal provides a picture of how the missions to and among the Sami population were perceived by the non-Sami population during Halse's formative years. In the book *En samisk verdenshistorie* [A Sami world-history] written by Hugo Luritz Jenssen, Masoni is accused of cultural appropriation.[13] This provides us with a backdrop to discuss why Alma Halse wore pieces of the Sami garment.

In addition, smaller contributions have been added from newspaper notices and articles. I have also conferred with non-academic historical sources, such as *Alta boka* [The book about Alta] for less central elements of the paper.[14] In 2023, I published an article that considered the sustainability of Alma Halse's ministry and what virtues she exhibited throughout her life.[15] Hence, some of the bibliographical entries and parts that pertain to Pentecostal spirituality may seem familiar. Here, I have attempted to highlight additional perspectives on the life and ministry of Alma Halse.

A SHORT BIOGRAPHICAL INTRODUCTION

Alma Halse (1907–1969) was born and raised on a farm on the west coast of Norway. Her family belonged to a fellowship of non-affiliated believers who, according to Halse, carried the "fire of God."[16] From a young age, Halse longed to help orphans and children living in poverty. After completing elementary school, she served as a domestic servant. At the age of seventeen, she was converted, Spirit-baptized, and later baptized in water. After two or three years she ventures out as an evangelist.[17] She

13. Jenssen, *En samisk verdenshistorie*.
14. Alta historielag, *Altaboka*.
15. Undheim, "Sustainability in the Ministry of Alma Halse." Historical sources from the first half of the twentieth century bear witness to several prominent women ministers who spread the gospel all over Norway. Alma Halse (1907–1969).
16. Halse, "Med Gud i storm og stille," *KS* (1945) 440.
17. Halse, "Med Gud i storm og stille," *KS* (1945), 440–41.

first received a short mentorship, as she traveled with Bertha Sætre, a seasoned evangelist. Soon she ventured on her own as a traveling evangelist. Halse built friendships and sought out relationships within the adolescent Pentecostal movement. In Oslo, she met with several women, including Laura Barratt, who received her with lovingkindness.[18] In 1933 she left for Alta, Finmark. There she continued to travel as an evangelist. In 1936 she adopted an orphaned Sami boy. He was the first of four children she started to care for. Nurse Thea Veen, who had introduced the first boy to Halse, joined Halse and the children as they traveled across Norway raising money for the ministry in Finnmark.[19] Halse ministered as an evangelist in several of the places they visited. Based on volunteer work, and financial support from supporters, she established the Betania orphanage. Right before Norway was pulled into the Second World War, Halse opened an orphanage for children in the fall of 1939. Halse intended the orphanage to serve both as a social home for the children and a platform for evangelistic advances in the area.[20] During the war, Halse obtained and ran one of Finnmark's biggest farms. At the end of the war, everything in Alta, except the Lutheran state church, was burned to the ground by the Nazis. Halse was the first to raise a building in Alta after the war. While continuing to travel as an evangelist, she established a nursing home, a new orphanage, a private elementary school, a brick manufacturing facility (*Alta Vibrostein*, established in 1950), and even a seafood factory (*AS Fiskemat* established in 1947).[21] She also was the vision bearer and initiator of a school for young adults that was completed after her death. Today this school is called *Helgeland Folkehøyskole* [Helgeland Folk High School]. Alma Halse succumbed to an illness in 1969.

The foundation that carries the name "Betania Alta" remains an influential health and welfare provider in Alta, Finnmark. In 2021, the municipality of Alta took over the running of nursing homes and built a new nursing home to cover the needs of the town and surrounding areas. Thus, approximately seventy-six years of running nursing home facilities ended for Betania. Currently, Betania Alta manages two kindergartens, various initiatives (including housing) for substance addicts, and mental healthcare patients in addition to senior housing. The Betania Foundation has recently also signed an agreement with the foster

---

18. Rudolph, *Alma Halse*, 50.
19. Hykkerud, *Betania Alta 50 år*, 13.
20. Halse, "Med Gud i storm og stille," *KS* (1945), 448.
21. Emaus, "Altaboka," 127–29.

care system to provide two sites for institutional housing for teenagers in Alta and Kirkenes.

This concludes a short bibliographic presentation of Alma Halse. In the following discussion, I will point to significant experiences in Halse's life, such as conversion, Spirit baptism, and her call to ministry. These experiences are highlighted in Tangstad's and Rudolph's books and are central to understanding Pentecostal spirituality. In the following section, I will attempt to show how the practices that accompanied these experiences often pointed to developments in society or changes in the general understanding of religion.

HALSE'S RELIGIOUS CONTEXT

In this section, I will look closer at the religious situation in Norway before and after the turn of the twentieth century. The Lutheran state church had virtually a religious monopoly before 1845. The law that restricted Christian assembly, without the approval or presence of a state-approved priest was then abolished, and as a result, several denominations and non-affiliated fellowships were established towards the end of the century.[22] Lutheran mission societies and organizations established local chapels or prayer houses. This also promoted a larger lay engagement and fora for women's ministry. G. A. Lammers (1802–1878), a former Lutheran priest in the state church, founded the first free Lutheran church in 1856. His congregations soon accepted believers' baptism and came to influence the theological understanding and practice of several budding fellowships that eventually joined other denominations, such as the Baptists or the Pentecostal movement. Laura Barratt, the wife of Thomas Ball Barrat who founded the Pentecostal movement in Norway, grew up in a congregation founded by Lammers in Bergen.[23]

Between 1865 and 1938, about 840,000 Norwegians emigrated to the US.[24] Some returned with new spiritual impulses. In 1905, Norway regained its sovereignty and national pride, and protectiveness characterized cultural and political life. Infant baptism, followed by confirmation, had for a long time been the prerequisite for full partition in the state church. Membership in the state church affected marriage, burial and in

---

22. Hegdal and Bauge, "Nordmennenes møte med Amerika," 49.
23. Barratt, *Minner*, 11.
24. Hegdal and Bauge, "Nordmennenes møte med Amerika," 49.

some instances employment. It was for instance, still a prerequisite for teachers to belong to the state church. Elementary education was still considered the main place of baptismal instruction, leading up to confirmation.[25] The un-baptized were addressed as heathen.

On Halse's farm, they were often frequented by preachers who brought revivals to the area in and around the village and along the West Coast.[26] Evangelists connected to Erik Andersen Nordquelle (1858–1958), later to be associated with Barratt, were among the visitors. From 1895 Nordquelle propagated believer's baptism.[27] In 1902, before Alma was born, her father Peder Halse received believer's baptism. They became the first family in the area to leave the Lutheran church.[28] Their unbaptized state put Alma and her sibling in a peculiar state, and they became targets of ridicule. In this position, Alma struggled to confess her faith and with spiritual questions to the point of not being able to pay attention in school.[29]

Society was moving away from collective religious adherence towards a culture in which more individualistic or subjective religious practices were appreciated. This can be seen in the ministry of Sven Foldøen (1878–1953). He emigrated to the US in 1899, where he had a radical conversion experience. Upon his return in 1903, he claimed all true Christians should have a subjective, immediate, and decisive experience of salvation, preferably connected to some kind of incident in that individual's life. This experience had to result in an assurance of salvation.[30] This practice was quite unheard of in Norwegian Christianity. The idea of receiving a personal experience of God's presence was not unheard of. The famous entrepreneur and revivalist Hans Nilsen Hauge had a radical conversion experience in 1796. However, until 1903, it had not been part of common religious practice or this close to being a prerequisite for salvation. Foldøen also instigated prayer in the after-service, with intersession for people to receive an encounter with God.[31] These practices spread quickly across the south-west of Norway until they became a

---

25. Sødal et al., *Religioner og livssyn i skolehverdagen*, 303–4.
26. Rudolph, *Alma Halse*, 10.
27. Froholt, *Erik Andersen Nordquelle*, 28.
28. Parr, "Det du har gjort mot ein av mine minste små. . ..," 8.
29. Tangstad, *Alma fra Alta*, 13.
30. Todal and Sjöberg, *Edvard Masoni*, 187.
31. Todal and Sjöberg, *Edvard Masoni*, 193.

natural part of the free church practice across the country, including the Pentecostal movement.[32]

CONVERSION

According to Rudolph's and Tangstad's biographies adolescent Alma Halse sought a salvation experience since she had not given her life fully to God. In 1925, a time of awakening came to her village, Sunndalen, with divine healings and fillings of the Spirit. Halse would have none of this and decided it was time to leave. She took a position as a domestic servant in another village far away. However, according to Tangstad, Jesus spoke to Halse and made it clear to her, as soon as she stepped off the boat, that he was with her, and it would not be easy to resist his pulling on her heart.[33] Rudolph pointed out that Halse asked Jesus to leave her alone, without any result. According to Rudolph, Halse struggled for a long time with a longing to be a Christian, at the same time as she was unwilling to follow God's call to conversion and ministry. Halse tried to pray in hiding. If she was discovered kneeling, it would signify a public confession. From home, she heard of miracles, conversions, and Spirit baptisms among her former classmates.[34] One night she decided she needed help. After work in the evening, she walked in cold, rainy weather, kilometer after kilometer. Halse wanted to reach the house of a Christian woman. When she arrived, she woke the woman up. Halse desperately asked for a word of God or something that might give her peace. Her host read a word from the Bible and said Halse had to come to the church service on Sunday morning and bow her knees there. When Sunday arrived, she finished work and ran to the church in desperation. When the congregation bowed their knees in prayer, Halse hesitated, holding on to the bench with both hands. According to Rudolph, Halse is unsure of what happened next, as she suddenly found herself bowing her knees with the others. Her whole body started to shake, and she prayed out loud for Jesus to save her.[35] Halse had her individual encounter with God.

When considering this conversion narrative, it is noteworthy that the woman Halse requested help from, indicated Halse's need to partake

32. Todal and Sjöberg, *Edvard Masoni*, 183.
33. Tangstad, *Alma fra Alta*, 15.
34. Rudolph, *Alma Halse*, 17–18.
35. Rudolph, *Alma Halse*, 21–22.

in the fellowship of believers, to obtain that personal experience of salvation. Hence, it was a subjective or individual experience closely knit to or born out of the fellowship of other believers. Though this does not prove whether this was how salvation was perceived in general by free churches, it is plausible that the fellowship of believers was the main arena for salvation experiences, also because of its role as a place of public confession.

When Smith depicts how one might perceive religion, he claims that we may point to spaces of religion.[36] His "here" category is perceived as a religion practiced in the home—a domestic religion. Halse did not pray on her knees in the home where she stayed, because she knew she would easily be detected, and the implications that entailed. At the same time, the woman she sought out, did not intercede for Halse to receive her individual experience in her home. From this, we might conclude that "home" was by some not perceived as the right 'space' for conversion/salvation. Church buildings fit into Smith's second category "there." Halse came from an environment of religious practice, where the "here" or the domestic environment had a more dominant role in religious practice. For Halse, the practice of religion and its experiences may take many forms both in the home and in the spaces between home and church. This is Smith's third category, "everywhere."[37] According to Halse, her home was a place where the many came to be filled with the Holy Spirit and the power of God often was revealed.[38]

In line with this understanding, Rudolph's rendering did not restrict the individual experience to the fellowship of believers. In the barn the next morning, Halse had a vision of Jesus standing before her. She felt unburdened, set free with an extreme joy.[39] Joy was one of the emotions Spittler noticed often accompanied the Pentecostal experiences. It is also an emotion that Halse returned to when describing the baptism of the Holy Spirit and much later the ability to work relentlessly for the Kingdom of God without financial compensation.[40]

In the following discussion, I will expound further on what might be identified as Spirit baptism and how Halse's experience of this is portrayed. Her conversion, her calling to ministry, and her Spirit baptism are experiences that are profound experiences and paradigm shifts in Halse's

36. Smith, *Relating Religion*, 325.
37. Tangstad, *Alma fra Alta*, 13.
38. Tangstad, *Alma fra Alta*, 13.
39. Rudolph, *Alma Halse*, 21–22.
40. *Et liv i tjeneste*, Norwegian Broadcasting Corporation (October 16, 1969).

spiritual life and influence her ministry. I have opted to treat "calling" after her Spirit Baptism, because her calling ties her experiences of her childhood longings, conversion, Spirit baptism, and following ministry, together.

ALMA HALSE AND EARLY PENTECOSTAL THEOLOGY OF SPIRIT BAPTISM

Espinosa states that there are two beliefs and experiences that most Pentecostals, Charismatics and Neo-Charismatics tend to unite over. The first is a personal experience of conversion, often referred to as being born-again.[41] Every believer must have a personal experience with Jesus, resulting in an assurance of salvation. In addition, they tend to unite over the "desire to be baptized and filled with the Holy Spirit."[42] The baptism of the Holy Spirit most commonly denotes a separate experience to both salvation and water baptism. Testimonies of Spirit baptisms, accompanied by Biblical text from Acts, often encouraged the believers to seek after this experience. Testimonies also functioned as patterns worth following.[43]

There are different views within Pentecostalism as to whether tongues are the initial evidence of Spirit baptism. However, historically the mainstream Pentecostal movement in Norway affirmed tongues as the initial physical evidence of the baptism in the Holy Spirit. A longing or need for consecration, holiness, and sanctification often preceded the baptism of the Holy Spirit. In the biographies about Halse, her conversion is described as a powerful, personal experience, accompanied by a vision of Christ. Rudolph also describes several instances, where the power of God makes both her and the chair she is kneeling at shake, including the hut she was in.[44] Coinciding with Pentecostal praxis, this is not labeled a baptism of the Holy Spirit. As can be seen from her biographies, Halse, herself did not see the need for what others called the baptism of the Holy Spirit. If one looks at this through the Pentecostal "pattern," one might wonder if this testimony was a nod to Christians who did not see the necessity of Spirit baptism. There are two accounts of Halse's Spirit baptism. I will later return to point out a couple of differences between

---

41. Espinosa, *William J. Seymour*, 1.
42. Espinosa, *William J. Seymour*, 1.
43. Josefsson, *Liv och över nog*, 118.
44. Rudolph, *Alma Halse*, 22.

the accounts. In the following section, I offer a brief summary of how this experience from 1925 is rendered in Rudolph's biography of Halse.

The news of her salvation brought much joy to her parents. However, Alma Halse felt an uneasiness as soon as she arrived in Sunndalen that fall. She had decided she did not want to become "a tongue speaker," yet everyone spoke of divine healings and the baptism of the Holy Spirit. To her surprise, they displayed a greater liberty and joy than she experienced. The very night she arrived home, she was invited to join a prayer meeting with her sisters. She joined them hesitantly. According to the biographies, she felt God's call to holiness, and consecration that evening. Again, she experienced the power of God, and again she felt compelled to surrender to God's will. At this point, Rudolph notes that Halse, experienced God's call to surrender, as a call for a life of surrender. In addition, he describes what Halse perceived as a need for cleansing. At this point, according to Rudolph, Halse calls out to God for help and freedom, and Halse has another vision of Jesus where he sets her completely free. Furthermore, God fills her with his power. As a result, Halse started to praise God in both comprehensible and incomprehensible languages. According to Rudolph, this experience is termed the baptism of the Holy Spirit.[45]

This rendering from 1961, shows how traditional Pentecostal Spirituality, understood Spirit baptism as a distinguishable experience. A believer might have experienced the power of God in many powerful ways; however, it was not recognized as the Baptism of the Holy Spirit, unless it was accompanied by tongues. The need for sanctification was also a strong motive in Rudolph's rendering. In the earlier stages of Pentecostal history, sanctification was identified as a part of the preparation prior to, or closely connected to Spirit baptism. Barratt's testimony of Spirit baptism, the primal "pattern" of this experience, consisted of a separate experience of sanctification, prior to the Spirit baptism.[46] This understanding of sanctification changed gradually within the Pentecostal movement. Rudolph's rendering is, even though it is written in 1961, based on Halse's own description of her experience of what happened in 1925—a time when Barrat's testimony still was the primal pattern of this experience. Though the common understanding of sanctification within the Pentecostal changed, it seems the testimonial narratives still reflected Barratt's understanding of sanctification. By 1982, sanctification

---

45. Rudolph, *Alma Halse*, 23–27.
46. Josefsson, *Liv och över nog*, 119.

had become closely associated with conversion, as an immediate result of being born-again, coupled with the notion that sanctification was a lifelong growth process.[47]

When Halse's Spirit baptism narrative is retold in 1987, the emphasis on the need for consecration and sanctification is toned down. It is a shorter account, yet the need for surrender is still present. Halse's spiritual experiences between conversion and baptism of the Holy Spirit are also omitted in the 1987 version. These discrepancies between the 1961 and 1987 versions may reflect how Pentecostal theology and spirituality gradually changed.

Spirit baptism had a purpose. The missional aspect of the baptism of the Spirit was to equip the believer with power, love, and courage, and to be a part of ushering in the Kingdom of God by bringing the gospel to every nation, essential to hasten the second coming. Hence, Spirit baptism endowed the believer with the power to share the gospel or one's testimony of the effect of the gospel. Rudolph describes the outcome of Halse's Spirit baptism as follows:

> God had given her something lasting. Her experience of the Spirit baptism was not a shallow experience, it went deep, and caused a change in her character because God had taken hold of her will. During this time, she was baptized as a believer. She was freed from her love of self and was able to give him her love. Alma had said yes to the call of God.[48]

Hence, Spirit baptism, for Halse was also the beginning of God's call on her life. This is even more evident in Tangstad's biography where he describes Spirit baptism. The chapter is entitled: *The beginning of my life-calling*.[49] Both Halse's call and her missionary advances relate to Spirit baptism, which they also did for the Pentecostal movement. The mission theme and what the call entailed will be discussed in the following section.

HALSE'S CALL TO MINISTRY

When Lucy Leatherman laid her hands on T. B. Barratt on November 15, 1906 bystanders reported that tongues of fire appeared above his head. Barratt later noted that "the devil taunted him by pointing out the

---

47. Nysæter, "Helliggjørelsen og kristen etikk," 43.
48. Rudolph, *Alma Halse*, 27.
49. Tangstad, *Alma fra Alta*, 17.

irregularity of asking a woman for prayer."[50] Traditional social barriers fell apart in the heat of the early Pentecostal revival.[51] Though egalitarian values have suffered several setbacks throughout Pentecostal history, women enjoyed relative freedom of ministry in its initial stage. They shared their testimonies, preached, evangelized, and in some instances served as leaders and founders of impactful ministries, movements, and churches.[52] In 1933, Barratt wrote a book where he insisted that spirit-filled women could fill any ministry of the church.[53] Missionaries became role models of a surrendered life, and the testimonies of their calling and experience became a prototype or pattern to follow. Their willingness to follow the will of God was considered admirable.[54]

The mission field often provided a place of spiritual leadership for women from different traditions.[55] Women connected to the Holiness Movement often had more freedom in terms of evangelizing and preaching compared to women in other church traditions. These were often women who, like Halse, had to raise their own support.[56]

After her Spirit baptism, Halse felt drawn to share the Gospel with the unsaved, the lonely, and the elderly.[57] Halse's pragmatic take on the situation is recorded by Rudolph.[58] He notes that Halse was invited to house churches and prayer meetings that lasted until midnight. As the call to evangelize became clearer to Halse, she realized she would need more equipment to travel further. Rudolph describes how Halse turned to God and asked for his provision. Would God provide her with the necessary bedclothes? Most of the places Halse visited were quite poor and did not have bedding for her to stay the night. In Norway at that time, it was still possible to obtain what you needed in a store without paying for it if the shopkeeper trusted that you paid your debt as soon as you could. According to Rudolph, this was Halse's plan. She, therefore, shared her need with her friends. They were skeptical at first and said that

---

50. Wacker, *Heaven Below*, 38.
51. Wacker, *Heaven Below*, 103.
52. Agnes and Dagmar Engstrøm are known for bringing the Pentecostal movement to Germany.
53. Barratt, *Kvinnens stilling*, 33.
54. Josefsson, *Liv och över nog*, 256.
55. Skeie, "Kjønn og åndelig lederskap," 31.
56. Skeie, "Kjønn og åndelig lederskap," 32.
57. Rudolph, *Alma Halse*, 27.
58. Rudolph, *Alma Halse*, 27–28.

she should save up her money and wait to travel until she had the money she needed. Rudolph notes Halse replied that her "heavenly Father knew what she needed," and she went out to obtain the bedclothes. It cost a lot of money. Two weeks went by, and an envelope arrived through the mail with the money she needed. Halse had no clue who sent the money but was grateful to God for His provision.[59]

This example from Halse's life illustrates her pragmatic faith and her approach to provision, a position she would come to hold throughout her ministry. In short, God had called her, she was his responsibility, and he had promised that if she followed that calling and took care his interests, he would take care of her needs.[60] Also, the supernatural element of her experience is a returning theme in Pentecostal spirituality and "calling-testimonies."[61] Josefsson explains how the supernatural element had several purposes. First, it verified and determined God as the Lord of the missional effort. Secondly, it confirmed and legitimized the call, and assured the person of their mission.[62]

In both descriptions of Halse's call, the authors include a childhood narrative. God's call on Halse's life to help orphans and homeless children burdened her as a child. According to the biographies, she would steal away from others when they were playing, pray for the children, cry over them, and think about them deeply.[63] "I want a house full of children but no husband," Halse told her mother as a young child.[64]

Ingrid Eskilt describes what it meant to be called by God throughout the twentieth century.[65] In her research, the generation born before the Second World War, like Halse, is labeled veterans. The shift from living life in light of the external expectations from society, to a life where individual authenticity and self-realization, not only caused a cultural shift but a shift within the religious landscape.[66] This coincides with what the theologian Paul O. Brunstad notes is a shift from a society marked by commitment and duty to one another, to a society where individual

---

59. Rudolph, *Alma Halse*, 28.

60. Tangstad, *Alma fra Alta*, 7, 29, 52. Rudolph, *Alma Halse*, 45. Rudolph ties this promise to Halse's call to travel to Finnmark.

61. Josefsson, *Liv och över nog*, 257.

62. Josefsson, *Liv och över nog*, 257.

63. Rudolph, *Alma Halse*, 13; Tangstad, *Alma fra Alta*, 14.

64. Parr, "Det du har gjort mot ein av mine minste små...," 1.

65. Eskilt, "Misjonærkallet og kulturens subjektive vending."

66. Eskilt, "Misjonærkallet og kulturens subjektive vending," 5.

rights are emphasized.[67] The culture that fostered Alma Halse set duty before individual rights, and service through volunteering and working together before any thought of personal compensation. Alma Halse asserted, "I travelled up here to meet a need. I met many who were needy. Was it not my duty to do something?"[68] In Halse's mindset, it would be wrong not to act upon the needs of society. However, Halse's call far exceeded the answer to a need. It entailed a personal experience.

When considering "calling experiences" in the early twentieth century, Eskilt notes that there is little mention of personal or academic qualifications. All the applicants accentuate their individual conversion experiences and their personal conviction of a call to the mission field.[69] Tangstad describes Halse's struggle during her primary education, but he does not mention any further formal education.[70] It is not her formal education that is of the essence, but it is her personal experiences of the Spirit and visions of Christ, urging her to go, that are emphasized. According to Eskilt, the experience of an individual calling was often described as a one-time, soul-wrenching paradigm shift, where God spoke to the individual.[71] However, God's calling might also come through the means of bible verses, sermons, information about a need, other people, or extraordinary experiences.[72] Josefsson also points to similar calling experiences occurring in the Swedish Pentecostal movement.[73] Halse's calling experience seems to have consisted of a series of experiences of God's voice and visions.[74]

In Eskilt's veteran missionary statements, a personal struggle with the calling was in some instances part of these testimonies.[75] The crisis-development narrative has a central place in Halse's call to ministry.[76] Halse doubted and struggled with her call to Finnmark for a period. Rudolph explains how Halse built relationships with people who encouraged

67. Brunstad, *Klokt lederskap*, 109–10.
68. Tangstad, *Alma fra Alta*, 69.
69. Eskilt, "Misjonærkallet og kulturens subjektive vending," 6–7.
70. Tangstad, *Alma fra Alta*, 14.
71. Eskilt, "Misjonærkallet og kulturens subjektive vending," 16.
72. Eskilt, "Misjonærkallet og kulturens subjektive vending," 7–8.
73. Josefsson, *Liv och över nog*, 257–58.
74. Tangstad, *Alma fra Alta*, 17–20.
75. Eskilt, "Misjonærkallet og kulturens subjektive vending," 7.
76. I will elaborate further on Steven Land's crisis-development narrative in the next section of the article.

her, interceded with her, and offered her advice and wisdom for the choices she was about to make. In this way, she involved and engaged new and old acquaintances, friends, and family in the call God had put on her life. Halse recognized the cost and responsibility of the task God granted her. This caused her to seek God until he gave her a vision that provided her with the reassurance she needed.[77] Here the crisis experience caused a longing for a spiritual resolution until God intervened supernaturally and made it possible up until that point. Halse sought out other believers during her crisis, and this formed a fellowship with people who later supported her ministry.

Those who followed their calling to mission described that they went as an act of obedience to God.[78] Calling for the generation born before World War II was a lifelong commitment.[79] Eskilt's research also reveals something interesting pertaining to the gifts of the Spirit. The veterans expressed no awareness of their gifts prior to going to the mission field. They simply expected God to provide the gifts they needed to enable them to fulfill the call God had given them.[80] This is similar to Halse's promise from Jesus that he would take care of her needs if she looked out for his interests. Furthermore, in describing her calling, she does not seem to be limited by ministry gifts, or labels. Her calling was simply to meet the needs of the people God sent her way.

Halse believed that our very existence hinges on our ability to meet the needs of others, as best as we can. In essence, "we are put here on earth to fulfill an assignment." According to Halse, every single person carried more worth than the entire world. Hence, she saw herself as a steward over an immense wealth—a wealth that consisted of every soul that she encountered at Betania. No cost was too high, no effort too great when it came to helping the orphaned, the widowed, the old or the frail.[81]

To further enhance the meta-perspective on the nature of testimonies within the Pentecostal movement, and the biographical accounts of Halse's ministry, the crisis-development narrative of Land offers valuable insight.

---

77. Rudolph, *Alma Halse*, 44–49.
78. Eskilt, "Misjonærkallet og kulturens subjektive vending," 13.
79. Eskilt, "Misjonærkallet og kulturens subjektive vending," 11.
80. Eskilt, "Misjonærkallet og kulturens subjektive vending," 9.
81. Tangstad, *Alma fra Alta*, 69.

THE ROLE OF "CRISIS" EXPERIENCES IN HALSE'S LIFE AND PENTECOSTAL SPIRITUALITY

"A period full of battles and struggles lay ahead of her when she went ashore in Alta, September 27th, 1933. However, she knew now, God would grant her victory, and success."[82] This quote and the title of Rudolph's biography of Halse from 1961, "A Woman of Battle" indicates Halse was someone who had struggled, fought, and who was willing to go through whatever life brought. Here I will show how this struggle or moments of crisis was an important part of the Pentecostal testimony.

For Land, the crisis-development narrative is part of a narrative praxis connected to the apocalyptic vision that characterizes Pentecostals. There is an "already-not yet" tension within the eschatological vision of God's presence. It is evident in the immanent Kingdom of God, and at the same time, undisclosed in the yet-to-be consummated Kingdom of God.[83]

According to Josefsson, all parts of Christian life were supernatural for Pentecostals, and experiencing the Spirit could bring about that which before had not been possible. The Spirit provided the strength to overcome weaknesses and experience freedom from sin. Acknowledging one's own weaknesses made the believer long for and seek after more of the Spirit.[84] According to Land, "crisis points were times when God did something decisive which made possible a personal or corporate development that, before that time, was not possible."[85] This fostered an environment of orality and testimonies. Spittler pointed to orality as a "fundamental quality of Pentecostal piety."[86] Conversion, sanctification, divine healing, and Spirit baptism were experiences that radically changed a person's life and were considered crisis events, but also everyday occurrences, such as daily support, divine revelation, and surprises were all considered part of the walk with God.[87] Tangstad records a testimony of God's provision that holds an element of surprise.

> We're out of tea, Alma," Alf Hansen said. "Did you check the pantry?" "Yes, I checked the pantry behind the kitchen and every

---

82. Rudolph, *Alma Halse*, 8.
83. Land, *Pentecostal Spirituality*, 56.
84. Josefsson, *Liv och över nog*, 116.
85. Land, *Pentecostal Spirituality*, 117.
86. Spittler, "Spirituality, Pentecostal and Charismatic," 1097.
87. Land, *Pentecostal Spirituality*, 79.

grocery store in this area. There is no tea, and to get tea from Tromsø will take several days." World War II had ended, but there was still a shortage of tea and coffee. "No" Alma responded, "I did not mean that pantry,—I meant our Father's pantry." They got on their knees and prayed to God. Alma thanked God for the promise in His word to answer them before they cried out to Him. When they stood, Alma requested that the kettle be set on the stove to boil. Before the water boiled, the mail arrived with a box of tea. It had been sent three weeks earlier.[88]

According to Land, points of crisis represent "present manifestations of the life of the coming kingdom."[89] Testimonies were a familiar expression of faith to edify the believer and call non-believers to faith. Hence, it was a natural part of the evangelistic advancements and regular services. Living in the end-times signifies God is active and causes the believer to act.[90] The points of crisis were then the main content of the testimonies. Points of crisis also denote a highly pragmatic faith, expected to have a real-life expression.[91] They also indicated a level of struggle, facing opposition or strife, affirming one's identity in God, and holding the potential of strengthening the fellowship of believers. According to Brunstad, there is nothing like a bit of strife and passing through hard times that strengthens common identity and fellowship.[92]

The most valued expression pragmatic faith could take was to spread the gospel, either through mission or evangelization.[93] The only distinguishable difference between being a missionary and an evangelist depended on location. Usually, missions indicated that you left the country, and an evangelist stayed within the country's borders.[94] As I will show in the next section, this distinction was a bit obscure when it came to the northern areas of Norway. However, Alma Halse was first and foremost a renowned evangelist, but also often addressed as a missionary.

---

88. Tangstad, *Alma fra Alta*, 62.
89. Land, *Pentecostal Spirituality*, 79.
90. Land, *Pentecostal Spirituality*, 117.
91. Josefsson, *Liv och över nog*, 27.
92. Brunstad, *Klokt lederskap*, 69.
93. Josefsson, *Liv och över nog*, 251.
94. Josefsson, *Liv och över nog*, 252.

HALSE'S MISSION TO THE NORTH

The Spirit equipped the believer with the power to spread the Gospel through testimonies and mission work. Mission work was an important part of Pentecostal self-awareness and identity.[95] Alma Halse felt God's call to Finnmark, and in her eyes, a place neglected not only by the Norwegian state but also by the witnesses of God. It was full of desolate places where no witnesses of God would visit.[96] Looking back after thirty years in Alta, she described Finnmark as a dire place during the 1930s, where people received no benefits, where the welfare of people was grim, where living conditions were hard, and where unemployment rates were high.[97] How one perceived Finnmark, and especially the Sami population, during the 1930s depended largely on whom one asked.

Edvard Masoni (1870–1930) was of Sami ancestry and spoke out against the predominantly negative opinion of the Sami people in Norway, an opinion that was also propagated by contemporary academics at the time.[98] Sami history, as it was retold by the non-Sami population, clashed with the history as retold by generations of Samis. This dispute not only regarded territorial entitlement, but also Christianity's expansion in Northern Norway, and how one was to perceive the Sami population living there.

At the beginning of the twentieth century, people could read about the deprived state of the Sami people in newspapers, and mission organizations urged people to support advances to reach the Sami population with the gospel. Masoni argued that the Sami were a diligent, hardworking, well-informed, and Christian people group, with no need for mission.[99] The northern parts of Norway had a long history of missional advances, both Orthodox, Catholic, and Lutheran.[100] The Sami population could, according to Masoni, take care of their own mission, since there were many Sami preachers, especially in the Laestadian movement. The Laestadian revival spread throughout the northern areas from the middle of the nineteenth century and had a huge influence on the

---

95. Josefsson, *Liv och över nog*, 251.
96. Rudolph, *Alma Halse*, 47.
97. Tangstad, *Alma fra Alta*, 67.
98. Todal and Sjöberg, *Edvard Masoni*, 153.
99. Todal and Sjöberg, *Edvard Masoni*, 169.
100. Jernsletten, "Varangersamenes kristne praksis i møte med misjon og kolonialisering."

Sami population. From Masoni's perspective, mission among the Sami population did more harm than good. Mission organizations with a Sami mission were often based in the south, and they portrayed Sami people as deprived, poor, dirty, heathen, alcoholics with horrible material living conditions, just to awaken empathy and collect money for their organizations.[101]

Outreaches to the Sami areas in the north were largely considered as foreign mission. Halse likely grew up with the notion that the Sami people, and the north in general was an area in dire need of evangelization. Moreover, adhering strongly to the belief that all believers need a personal and decisive experience of conversion, Pentecostals perceived members of other denominations also in need of salvation. As a missionary to a place that most Norwegians associated with its Sami population, Halse wore items from the Sami garment.

CULTURAL APPROPRIATION AND HALSE'S MINISTRY

In 1963, at the award ceremony arranged by a popular women's magazine for her outstanding social service, Halse posed for the photographer in a full Sami garment.[102] Moreover, in 1965, when Alma Halse received *the Medal for Outstanding Civic Service* [*Kongens fortjenestemedalje i gull*], the highest medal of honor for humanitarian work in Norway, she expressed that she felt most at home in her Sami hat and garment during the ceremony.[103] Unfortunately, Rudolph or Tangstad, do not describe any other instances or reflection on why Halse wore Sami clothes. Several short notices in local newspapers from 1936, 1938 and 1939 inform the readers that Alma Halse will pose in Sami garments during several services.[104] According to her son Josef Halse, it was not often she wore this garment, but she often wore a Sami hat. Halse recalls that "No one seemed to care that she wore the hat."[105]

When Masoni considered Christian mission to the north, he criticized the way the Sami people were portrayed, which at its best

---

101. Todal and Sjöberg, *Edvard Masoni*, 160–62.
102. "Alma fra Alta hedres," 8.
103. Tangstad, *Alma fra Alta*, 63, 81.
104. "Finnmarksevangelist Alma Halse," *Dagen* (December 19, 1936); "Filadelfia Askim." *Folkets Røst* (February 2, 1939); "Evangeliehuset," *Dalane Tidene* (January 7, 1938).
105. Josef Halse, personal telephone conversation, November 6, 2023.

was negative and relegating. He noted that the Sami's were no better or worse than other Norwegians; they were just as Christian. Masoni argued against what he perceived as colonialism from the Norwegian state. He found the same mindset and attitudes in various Christian missionary organizations. Masoni saw the same thing happening in China when he was a missionary there. The Chinese were oppressed by the British. Hence, Masoni did not want Christian mission to be influenced by colonialism or an expression of cultural imperialism. On the contrary, the gospel message needed to be spread across national and cultural borders to bring all people into the Christian communion. Thus, the message was meant to be international, transnational, and universal.[106] For Pentecostals, the baptism of the Holy Spirit underlined the universal need for mission. Accompanied by tongues, Spirit baptism was at first perceived as God's provision of languages to urge the evangelization of the world, before the second coming of Christ.[107]

Though he was outspoken against colonialism, Masoni utilized a method that could be described today as cultural appropriation. When he spoke of China and his mission efforts there, Masoni wore a Chinese garment from the Qing dynasty.[108] He consciously used the Chinese garment to arouse attention and interest in his mission among the Sami and other Norwegians. His silk garment must have been perceived as quite exotic.[109] Differences attracted attention and had been used by the entertainment industry to arouse attention and earn money. Putting people with various handicaps or nationalities on display was also practiced. In addition, race-hygienists utilized "differences" to propagate their distorted racist "science." Samis had been put on display, for decades.[110] It is therefore quite interesting that Masoni used a Chinese garment.

Definitions of cultural appropriation often carry some notion of disrespect and lack of understanding in the acquisition of something from a culture that is not your own.[111] There is always a question of interpretation of the situation at hand. Who defines when something is disrespectful? A summary of Masoni's visit to a church in Polmak portrays how he used

---

106. Dunch, "Beyond Cultural Imperialism," 320.
107. McGee, *People of the Spirit*, 26, 34.
108. Jenssen, *En samisk verdenshistorie*, 284.
109. Jenssen, *En samisk verdenshistorie*, 284.
110. Jenssen, *En samisk verdenshistorie*, 192–96.
111. *Cambridge Dictionary*, "Cultural Appropriation."

the Chinese garment.[112] While wearing Chinese clothes, he informed the congregation about Chinese culture in positive words. He even stated that their worship of idols was more praiseworthy than the Western worship of God. He drew the comparison of how the Sami people consist of several groups to how the Chinese also consist of different groups. Furthermore, in a letter recounting this service, Masoni described how the Sami drew comparisons between their own Sami garments to Masoni's Chinese clothes and were proud and excited for their "big brother" in the east.[113] In Masoni's eyes, he was not partaking in something disrespectful but rather highlighted something transnational.

Likewise, Halse may not have perceived what she did when she wore Sami garments as disrespectful. Rather she might have signaled where her heart and mission belonged, namely with the Sami population. Halse loved the people she ministered to and was renowned for the interest she showed the Sami population.[114]

HALSE IS ADMIRED WHILE THE ORPHANAGE IS ACCUSED OF ABUSE

Halse filled many ministry positions. Her efforts for young and old were admired both within and outside the Pentecostal movement. A search through newspaper articles that mention Alma Halse, and her labor at Betania reveals praise from the local government, local and national newspapers, the television station, and national awards committees.

Halse traveled a lot, sharing the Word of God and reports of her ministry. She built relationships and encouraged people all over the country to join her mission, either as volunteers, intercessors, or financial supporters. When she traveled, she was often joined by other women. Evangelist and nurse Augusta Schiørn from Filadelfia, Oslo, often joined her. Several newspaper notices announce the two preaching together. Another coworker from Betania was Pauline Fauskanger, she often helped Halse, drove her around and assisted her in the ministry.[115]

---

112. Todal and Sjöberg, *Edvard Masoni*, 171–72.
113. Todal and Sjöberg, *Edvard Masoni*, 173.
114. Tjelle, *Omsorg og overgrep*, 81.
115. Thoresen, "Betania barne- og pleiehjem—et eksempel på hva Gud kan gjøre med villige hender," *KS* (1967) 4.

As mentioned above, Halse and Betania received praise from many. However, when people and media became more aware of the abuse that occurred at orphanages run by different mission organizations, Betania did not receive a clean bill. Heartbreaking renderings of abuse were reported at the orphanage. Halse traveled a lot and does not seem to have been aware of all that went on during her absence. Ingjerd Tjelle has interviewed several people who lived at Betania orphanage during their childhood.[116] Some testify to a wonderful time, while others report incidents, that we today would label, as spiritual, physical, and sexual abuse. In the following section, I have included a few of their statements.

A boy who lived at the orphanage during the 1950s reported "Alma Halse [. . .] was a good-hearted person, but she had so much to do, that we almost never saw her. She sometimes visited or she was called on when there was trouble at the orphanage. The other employees were like strict military officers that held us in line and commanded our actions."[117]

Corporal punishment was first prohibited by law in foster care institutions in 1953. This was not a general prohibition, and orphanage staff likely continued to use corporal punishment for disciplinary purposes after 1953. Another man who lived at the orphanage during the 1950s testified to regular corporal punishment. Attending the movie theater was one of the offences that often resulted in corporal punishment. He also testified to ten years of sexual abuse from one of the staff members who was connected to the farm at Betania.[118] A woman who lived at the orphanage during the 1940s recalled how they were "terrorized psychologically with hell and judgment day," and "we were hit and beaten by Christian people who told us we would go to hell and that they themselves would go to heaven."[119] During one incident she was locked in a dark basement for a week. Her only access to light was during mealtimes.[120]

In the complaints, Halse is described as a loving and caring, yet absent head of the orphanage who employed people who never should have been anywhere in the vicinity of children.[121]

---

116. Tjelle, *Omsorg og overgrep*.
117. Tjelle, *Omsorg og overgrep*, 81.
118. Tjelle, *Omsorg og overgrep*, 101.
119. Tjelle, *Omsorg og overgrep*, 104.
120. Tjelle, *Omsorg og overgrep*, 110.
121. Tjelle, *Omsorg og overgrep*, 104.

CONCLUSION

The article has aimed to explore literature and records of Halse's ministry that shed light on the cultural and spiritual environment in which Halse ministered. The biographies brought forth an important description of the cultural and spiritual environment. What they emphasized enables us to go back and track the cultural changes, and changes in spirituality.

Culturally, this article has pointed to the turn from a collective perspective to a more individualistic viewpoint, where the subjective experience is valued. It demonstrated how society's view of religious adherence and religious praxis changed over time and became an object of personal choice. This meant that the collective awareness of the duty to serve and uphold the rights of others, despite one's own abilities, gave way to a focus on individual resources and self-realism.

Culturally, the Sami people were diminished, through discriminating descriptions, posed as either in dire need of help or exotic examples of something different. In the shade of a nationalistic wave, they were objects of assimilation. Sensitivity towards cultural appropriation was not present as today. Masoni used cultural appropriation to highlight the transnational nature of the gospel. Likewise, for Pentecostal Alma Halse, baptism in the Holy Spirit emphasized the transnational urgency of missions. She crossed into what was considered foreign areas to spread the gospel and answer the needs of the orphaned and poor. Wearing her Sami hat Halse signaled that her heart and mission belonged with the Sami population and to the North.

The spiritual environment mirrored the cultural changes in many ways. Individual and decisive conversion experiences became important ingredients in most parts of protestant Christian praxis and spirituality. Some religious praxis that formerly had been bound to church buildings were just as naturally performed at home or anywhere else. For Pentecostal spirituality, individual praxis also included a time of sanctification, Spirit baptism, water baptism, and calling. The move away from emphasis on sanctification is notable in the biographies. The first account posts a clear illustration of the notion that a person might have powerful personal encounters with the Holy Spirit, without being Spirit baptized. In this narrative sanctification and surrender precede Spirit baptism. In the second biography the intermediate fillings of the Spirit and the reference to sanctification are omitted. The need for surrender is still present. However, in both accounts, one needed the initial evidence of tongues to identify the experience as Spirit baptism. In both accounts, the lasting effects of joy and freedom followed Spirit baptism.

A testimonial praxis that included a crisis narrative is especially notable in Rudolph's biography, but also in the number of miracles recorded in both biographies. God acted and made that which had been impossible up until that time possible.

The call was individual, yet in Halse's account still held a collective perspective. Halse responded to the needs of others. The emphasis on the supernatural elements of her calling narrative also legitimized the call, giving both Halse and the reader an assurance that this was a mission instigated by God. As a woman authorized and called by God, she was often invited to speak at conventions and church services, together with others or alone. The Pentecostal spirituality is missional, making evangelism and mission its ideal expression, and its propagators role models.

This article has also pointed to a society that was less equipped to disclose and prevent child abuse. Working with children does not seem to have required any personal abilities. Leadership was by Halse, not delegated, though it needed assistance.

Through this article, Halse has formed an example of what it meant to adhere to Pentecostal spirituality, from its beginning in 1907 to the middle of the twentieth century. Her pragmatic faith, spiritual experiences, and crisis-narrative, display an evolving spirituality, and a changing society.

BIBLIOGRAPHY

"Alma fra Alta hedres." *Samhold: Vestopland og Gjøviks blad* (October 28, 1963) 8.
Alta historielag. *Altaboka*. 2022. Norper. Alta: Alta historielag, 2022.
Barratt, Laura. *Minner*. Oslo, Norway: Filadelfiaforlaget, 1946.
Barratt, Thomas Ball. *Kvinnens stilling i menigheten*. Oslo, Norway: Korsets Seiers Forlag, 1933.
Brunstad, Paul Otto. *Klokt lederskap mellom dyder og dødssynder*. Oslo, Norway: Gyldendal Akademisk, 2009.
Cambridge Dictionary. "Cultural Appropriation." https://dictionary.cambridge.org/dictionary/english/cultural-appropriation.
Dunch, Ryan. "Beyond Cultural Imperialism: Cultural Theory, Christian Missions, and Global Modernity." *History and Theory* 41 (2002) 301–25.
Emaus, Randi. "En imponerende kvinne i Alta." In *Altaboka 2022.*, 127–29. Alta, Norway: Alta historielag, 2022.
Eskilt, Ingrid. "Misjonærkallet og kulturens subjektive vending." *Norsk tidsskrift for misjonsvitenskap* (2012) 4–22.

Espinosa, Gastón, ed. *William J. Seymour and the Origins of Global Pentecostalism: A Biography and Documentary History*. Durham and London: Duke University Press, 2014.

Froholt, Asbjørn. *Erik Andersen Nordquelle: En Biografi*. Moss, Norway, 1981. https://janchristensen.net/NORDQUELLE.pdf.

Hegdal, Else Matilde, and Henriette Rosvold Bauge. "Nordmennenes møte med Amerika—med utgangspunkt i Rølvaags 'Giansts in the Earth.'" In *Pionerliv i Amerika og bygdeutvikling på Sletta*, 49–55. Bergen, Norway: Vestnorsk Utvandringssenter, 2011.

Hykkerud, Karl. *Betania Alta 50 år: 1937–1987*. Alta, Norway: Betania Alta, 1988.

Jenssen, Hugo Lauritz. *En samisk verdenshistorie: hvordan et arktisk urfolk erobret verden, kolliderte med rasismen og blandet blod med kapitalismen*. Oslo, Norway: Cappelen Damm, 2019.

Jernsletten, Jorunn. "Varangersamenes kristne praksis i møte med misjon og kolonialisering." *Scandia* 88 (2022) 290–316.

Josefsson, Ulrik. *Liv och över nog: Den tidiga pingströrelsens spiritualitet*. Skellefteå: Artos, 2005.

Land, Steven J. *Pentecostal Spirituality: A Passion for the Kingdom*. Sheffield: Sheffield Academic Press Ltd, 2003.

McGee, Gary B. *People of the Spirit: The Assemblies of God*. Springfield, Missouri: Gospel, 2004.

Nysæter, Bjarne. "Helliggjørelsen og kristen etikk." In *Pinsebevegelsen i Norge 75 år, 1907–1982*, edited by Terje Hegertun, 35–44. Oslo, Norway: Filadelfiaforlaget, 1982.

Parr, Maria. "Det du har gjort mot ein av mine minste små. . .." *Synste Møre*, March 8, 2001.

Rudolph, John-Willy. *Alma Halse—En kvinne i kamp*. Oslo: Filadelfiaforlaget, 1961.

Skeie, Karina Hestad. "Kjønn og åndelig lederskap." *DIN—Tidsskrift for religion og kultur* (2015). https://ojs.novus.no/index.php/DIN/article/view/1215.

Smith, Jonathan Z. *Relating Religion: Essays in the Study of Religion*. Chicago: University of Chicago Press, 2004.

Sødal, Helje Kringlebotn, et al. *Religioner og livssyn i skolehverdagen*. 2nd ed. Oslo, Norway: Cappelen Damm, 2020.

Spittler, Russell P. "Spirituality, Pentecostal and Charismatic." In *The New International Dictionary of Pentecostal and Charismatic Movements*, edited by Stanley M. Burgess and Eduard M. Vand Der Maas, 1096–1102. Grand Rapids: Zondervan, 2002.

Tangstad, Jakob. *Alma fra Alta*. Oslo: Filadelfiaforlaget, 1987.

Tjelle, Ingjerd. *Omsorg og overgrep: møter med barnehjemsbarn*. Alta, Norway: Nordnorsk, 2005.

Todal, Jon, and Lovisa Mienna Sjöberg. *Edvard Masoni—Ein Samisk misjonær i kolonialismens tidsalder*. Oslo: Pax, 2023.

Undheim, Kristina. "Sustainability in the Ministry of Alma Halse: An Exploratory Literary Study Featuring a Pioneer within the Norwegian Pentecostal Church." *Scandinavian Journal for Leadership and Theology* 10 (2023) 200–219.

Wacker, Grant. *Heaven Below*. Cambridge, MA: Harvard University Press, 2001.

www.ingramcontent.com/pod-product-compliance
Lightning Source LLC
Chambersburg PA
CBHW070239230426
43664CB00014B/2356